Public Heroes private felons

Public Heroes

private felons

*Athletes
and Crimes
against
Women*

Jeff Benedict

Northeastern University Press
Boston

Northeastern University Press

Copyright 1997 by Jeff Benedict

Library of Congress Cataloging-in-Publication Data

Benedict, Jeff.
    Public heroes, private felons : athletes and crimes against
women / Jeff Benedict.
        p.   cm.
    Includes bibliographical references and index.
    ISBN 1-55553-316-7 (alk. paper)
    1. Women—Crimes against.   2. Athletes—Psychology.
    3. College athletes—Psychology.   I. Title.
HV6250.4.W65B46   1997
364.15′3—dc21   97-6528

Designed by Peter M. Blaiwas

Composed in Times Roman by Coghill Composition, Richmond, Virginia.
Printed and bound by Quebecor Printing/Book Press, Brattleboro, Vermont.
The paper is Quebecor Liberty, an acid-free stock.

MANUFACTURED IN THE UNITED STATES OF AMERICA
01 00 99 98 97   5 4 3 2 1

11/98

Contents

Acknowledgments

In writing this book, I benefited greatly from the help of many individuals who advised and guided me through the process, but none more so than my wife, Lydia. For three years she put up with my eighteen-hour days and solo nights and weekends. She was my biggest supporter, and never once doubted my ability to publish this book.

After my family, I am most indebted to the three individuals who were mentors to me throughout this project: Bob Lipsyte, Alan Klein, and Todd Crosset. Bob provided a much needed critical voice, prompting me to reexamine my arguments and positions. His honesty with me was priceless. Both Alan and Todd patiently tutored me, sharing their wealth of knowledge and experience. They continually exposed me to research and literature that strengthened the final manuscript.

Armen Keteyian and Basil Kane believed in the importance of the project and guided it at crucial stages.

Bill Frohlich and Scott Brassart proved exceptional to work with in bringing the book into print. I am particularly grateful to Bill, who showed trust in a first-time author.

I owe a great deal to Michael Dukakis, who was behind this project from the start, and was instrumental in helping me find a publisher.

I am particularly indebted to my editor, Steve Richards, and to my research assistant, Craig Ball. Steve spent hours reading the chapters; his skills and speedy responses were crucial. Craig spent three years helping me to track down articles and statistics and placed countless phone calls on my behalf.

I am appreciative of the technical support provided by JLM Technologies, particularly the president, Justin Lindsey, who on more than one occasion provided relief in a time of crisis; also to Rick Scranton, who graciously gave me the use of his office; and to Eileen McDonagh and Michael Tolley, for sound advice and counsel in the early stages of the project.

Finally, I am indebted to the countless individuals who go unnamed in this book but who graciously provided me with critical insight and knowledge about the cases discussed.

Author's Note

Between 1986 and 1996 over 425 professional and college athletes were publicly reported for violent crimes against women.[1] In 1995 and 1996 alone, 199 athletes were charged with physical or sexual attacks on women.[2] Few were successfully prosecuted, much less incarcerated. The fact that popular athletes, society's most recognized male role models, routinely escape accountability for domestic violence, rape, gang rape, and other crimes has dulled public consciousness of their increasing levels of deviance.

In the interest of full disclosure, I want the reader to know that from 1992 through 1996 I worked for the nation's leading organization for characterizing and using athletes as role models, the Center for the Study of Sport in Society. Recognized as an institution committed to maintaining the integrity of organized athletics, the center nonetheless relies on the NBA, the NFL, and many NCAA athletic departments for its financial and political support. As the director of research for the center, one of my responsibilities was to collect data to counter the growing perception that athletes are disproportionately involved in violence against women. Specifically, I was asked to monitor metropolitan newspapers from around the nation for reports of athletes being charged with rape and domestic violence.

Emphasizing the many thousands of rapes and domestic assaults that occur annually in the United States, the center pointed to the handful of press clippings implicating athletes as evidence that exceptional media coverage had fostered a distorted perception of athletes. This position was consistent with the sports industry's position and, in the absence of research into the matter, was a convenient response to critics who challenged the center's promotion of athletes as society's best example for youth.

Nonetheless, in the face of mounting speculation following each new arrest of a famous athlete, the center commissioned a first-of-its-kind study to examine the prevalence of sexual assault and domestic abuse among athletes at NCAA schools with basketball and football teams perennially ranked among the top twenty in the nation. The center's trusted relationship with athletic departments brought unprecedented cooperation from ten schools. Promising them anonymity, we were permitted to examine their records of internal judicial affairs. The documents revealed that of the sixty-nine sexual assaults reported internally on their campuses between 1991 and 1993, male athletes were responsible for nearly 20 percent, despite the fact that they constituted just 3 percent of the student population.[3] These findings were particularly compelling because they represented incidents that were largely unreported to the police or the media.

Sure that these results would offend the center's most loyal supporters—namely, athletic directors, coaches, and players—the center decided not to publish the findings. Instead, my fellow researcher Dr. Todd Crosset and I published the results independently in the form of two journal articles. Moreover, I initiated a much more comprehensive inquiry into athletes' crimes against women, taking advantage of my unique position to probe into questions that scholars and critical journalists had not been able to answer.

After researching hundreds of reported incidents of sexual assault and domestic abuse involving athletes, I selected approximately twenty-five for in-depth study. Wanting a diverse collection, I included cases representing varying relationships between perpetrator and victim, degrees of severity in the alleged violence, and final disposition by the courts. By chronicling these cases, I set out to discover those factors that give rise to the frequent complaints against athletes for violating women; the way in which those complaints are treated by the courts; and the manner in which the sports industry responds to such incidents.

I relied most heavily on interviews with the individuals involved. In all, I conducted over three hundred interviews with professional and college athletes (primarily the defendants and their teammates), victims of sexual assault and domestic violence, criminal prosecutors, defense attorneys, plaintiff attorneys, judges, jurors, witnesses, police officers, victim witness advocates, medical personnel, rape crisis counselors, coaches, sports agents, and team and league officials. Many of the interviews were tape recorded. I also conversed or corresponded with countless individuals who chose not to be formally interviewed. Finally, I reviewed thousands of pages from criminal and civil case files, public records, and press reports.

In November 1995, before completing this book, I appeared on the CBS news program *48 Hours* to discuss a rash of criminal complaints against football players at the University of Nebraska. I stated that sports figures' role-model status hampers victims who attempt to bring charges of acquaintance rape against them. The center's director, Richard Lapchick, immediately demanded that I either resign as research coordinator or enter into a formal agreement to refrain from publicly criticizing athletes for the duration of my employment. Besides undermining the center's mission, Lapchick worried, my critique of the University of Nebraska threatened to strain the center's relationship with football coach Tom Osborne, a prominent name on the center's advisory board.

Lapchick told Osborne that my conclusions were based on unreliable research, and furnished him with statistics which Osborne used to defend his program's rogue image. In his 1996 book, *On Solid Ground,* Osborne wrote, "Richard Lapchick, the Director of 'The Center for the Study of Sport in Society,' disagrees with the 'research' cited by Benedict. Lapchick said Benedict's conclusions were based on a study including a small sample of only 69 cases and did not control for key factors such as alcohol use."[4] This was a clever statement by Lapchick. As my employer at the time, he was well aware that my comments on *48 Hours* were based not on a single study, but on a combination of studies—one of which was a case-by-case analysis of allegations of acquaintance rape against athletes, including three police complaints brought against Nebraska's Christian Peter.

With regard to the role of alcohol in cases of violence against women by athletes, I categorize it, along with drugs and steroids, as a companion to violence in some cases. But men in the sports industry are much more comfortable than I in blaming substance abuse for athletes' violence against women. The purpose of this book is not to emphasize the commonly accepted knowledge that substance abuse can aggravate abuse and violence. Rather, I have focused my attention on the seldom-explored environmental contributions of life as a sports celebrity to the frequent abuse of women.

Smothered beneath the futile debate over whether athletes are more likely to abuse women than others is a point of more lasting significance: Far too many of the younger generation's male role models possess a fundamental disrespect for women. Athletes' commonly held notion of women as sexual prey lies at the core of a growing number of crimes, from sexual harassment to battery and rape. Sadly, too few men in leadership roles are willing to condemn such violence against women. The risk of offending athletes or losing the status that an association provides has encouraged otherwise well-meaning men to shrink from standing up to America's most popular batterers and rapists.

Introduction

Decades before sports icon O. J. Simpson stood accused of two vicious murders resembling the random, senseless crimes frequently attributed to gang violence, he risked becoming a youthful offender. A fatherless juvenile who resorted to thuggery and intimidation while growing up in a San Francisco housing project, Simpson received a life-altering visit from baseball legend Willie Mays. The San Francisco Giants centerfielder was the biggest sports star in the Bay Area. His personal interest in Simpson persuaded the high school football phenomenon that his juvenile delinquency and gang affiliation threatened to abort his only viable escape from the dead end that awaits many urban youths. Simpson's rare athletic gifts could prove a ticket to a better life.

Impressed by Mays, Simpson pursued the glory of athletic achievement. After attending the University of Southern California on a football scholarship, he went on to achieve Mays-like fame as a professional football legend. Simpson's public persona underwent a similar transformation. Despite his adolescent tendencies, he became arguably the most recognizable athlete-endorser for commercial products from the 1970s to the 1980s and 1990s.[1]

During the 1980s, Simpson repeatedly abused his wife, provoking numerous interventions from police. In 1989 he was finally arrested and convicted of brutally beating his wife at their Los Angeles home. Using his trademark smile and charm, Simpson publicly dismissed the incident as an overblown, one-time domestic quarrel. But five years later, when his then ex-wife and a male associate were found slashed to death in a pool of blood, Simpson was again arrested and became a symbol for those who suggest that violent, combative sports were contributing to an increasing number of popular athletes abusing women.

Rarely does a sport convert a man into a violent criminal, however, nor can athletic training be blamed for off-the-field violence by athletes. Football per se did not make Simpson violent, or train him to beat his wife or transgress the law. On the other hand, professional sports teams have little reservation in extending contracts to athletically gifted young men whose developmental years were rife with socially derelict behavior, including violent crime. And as long as the perpetrator can contribute to on-field success, the sports industry turns a blind eye to the black eyes and bruised bodies of women.

Less than three months after Simpson's acquittal for double murder, just days before the 1996 Super Bowl, the United States Congress called on the National Football League to address "repeated tragic examples [of violence against women] involving professional football players." In a letter dated January 24, 1996, Representative Bernard Sanders of Vermont informed NFL commissioner Paul Tagliabue, "We are writing to ask in the strongest terms that the NFL join with us and commit to work together to fashion a multi-faceted strategy to deter domestic violence, including counseling, strong disciplinary action when warranted, and a high-profile education and advertising campaign against domestic violence." The following passage is excerpted from that letter:

We believe the time has come for the NFL to step forward . . . and assume a leading role in deterring domestic violence among current and future NFL personnel. . . .

For far too long a pointless, circular debate has raged over whether the high incidence of domestic violence among professional and collegiate football players is a sports problem or a societal problem. Clearly, it is both. Regardless of how thoroughly we can quantify that athletes commit violence against women at a rate greater than the average population, common sense and repeated tragic examples involving professional football players cry out for coordinated non-governmental and legislative action.

Surely you recognize the enormous influence that big-time football players at the professional and collegiate levels, as role models, have upon our society. Many men identify with NFL players and look on them as both heroes and role models to be emulated off the field. Undoubtedly when instances of domestic violence receive little more than a slap on the wrist in courts and go unpunished by the NFL . . . that sends an insidious and harmful message to many Americans. Unfortunately, the current message being sent seems to be that domestic violence is not to be taken too seriously and that it is not the indefensible and serious crime that it is.

Finally, we are also troubled by public comments of the NFL's Communications Director, Greg Aiello, to the effect that unless domestic violence affects the business of football, then the NFL should be reticent about taking disciplinary action against professional football players who are charged with domestic violence for fear of possible legal action. That sounds like a short-sighted rationalization to justify the NFL continuing to ignore domestic violence in its own ranks.

We are appealing to you to make it a top priority to see to it that the men who are privileged to play professional football, as role models, help to publicly condemn domestic violence as a serious crime and do not sluff it off.[2]

Subsequently, in a letter dated April 19, 1996, Joe Browne, the NFL's senior vice president of communications and government affairs, denied the existence of a problem among NFL players with regard to abuse of women, and successfully put Representative Sanders at bay by insisting that statements to the contrary were inherently racist. "To single out athletes will unfavorably serve to perpetuate stereotypes—including as to ethnic and racial groups—that impair efforts to deal with these issues," wrote Browne:

It will also unfairly stigmatize athletes by inevitably suggesting that they have a particular propensity to engage in such behavior when there is no basis for such an implication. . . . We believe that any resolution on this subject selectively directed at athletes (or any other groups selectively defined without a clear-cut basis for doing so) is highly inappropriate and necessarily open to criticism as discriminatory.[3]

Amidst a proliferation of arrests for abuse among celebrated athletes, race has become the most serious obstacle to understanding and correcting the problem. Revenue-producing sports are played predominantly by black athletes. In 1994, 82 percent of the members of the National Basketball Association and 70 percent of the members of the National Football League were blacks.[4] Not surprisingly, corresponding majorities of the basketball and football players charged with crimes against women are also black—as are most of the law-abiding players. Nevertheless, the high-profile nature of college and professional sports, and the disproportionate number of black athletes, combine to foster a warped perception linking race to crime, resulting in an undue emphasis on race whenever an athlete is charged with a crime.

The fact that so many athlete-offenders are black is not a function of race, but rather a result of the rising recruitment of poorly prepared young men, the majority of whom are black, whose social backgrounds are rife with problems. "A lot of the people who are criticizing [athletes] don't understand the circumstances in the first place," said Roger Headrick, head of NFL Properties and president of the Minnesota Vikings:

For many of these people [professional athletes], you cannot believe the lack of discipline, good fatherly advice, counsel and guidance they have missed throughout their life. For many of them, there are no fathers in their life. The mother or grandmother has been trying to keep them together. They have a very different perception of what their individual responsibilities are because they've never had anyone to set an example for them. I hate to bring up family values as a solution to all this—that is sort of a political buzzword these days—but [they have] never had a father who said, "Son, you don't do that," or "Get your act together." The mother is out working two jobs a day to keep the family together financially. For many of these young men, their whole goal in life is to try to make it in professional sports so they can buy their mother a home so she won't have to continue working sixteen hours a day.

It is unrealistic to expect that poorly prepared young men from urban areas will suddenly abandon their ways after receiving an athletic scholarship and arriving at an elite college campus. On the contrary, the enticements that accompany big-time athletics can be acutely problematic for young men from deprived backgrounds. There should be little hesitation in addressing squarely the glaring problem of ill-prepared young black men being brought to college campuses to play sports, only to find themselves arrested for rape, battery, and other crimes.

Nonetheless, a racially charged political climate, with its accompanying threat that critics will be labeled racist, has perplexed both the popular press and scholars in their attempt to address the growing level of female abuse within society's male hero culture. As a result, the predominant explanation that is offered for athletes' recurring abuse of women is that it is an extension of the violent contact sports they play, with their rewards for aggression and domination, their sexist jargon, and their gender-exclusive membership. But this cursory explanation skirts the more fundamental underpinnings of athletes' crimes against women: (1) the sports industry's indifference to incorrigibles and (2) the rampantly permissive lifestyle of many athletes.

There is no foolproof set of predictors for male athletes prone to criminally violate women. The two most common traits found among athletes who have been charged with violating women are a previous history of criminal behavior (particularly crimes against women) and indulgence in deviant but legally permissible sexual behavior. This volatile combination frequently leads to the abuse or continued abuse of women, as well as to sexually transmitted disease, illegitimacy, family violence, and divorce. And a unique social climate reinforces the athlete's perception of women as sexually compliant.

The insular-minded sports industry has been slow to confront both the presence of players who are predisposed toward violence and the sexually deviant lifestyle that has become the calling card for a growing number of successful athletes. Instead, there has been an altruistic tendency to project college and professional sports as an opportunity for young men who would otherwise be destined for crime and despair. Yet these are the players who are disproportionately responsible for the litany of sexual assault and domestic abuse charges filed against athletes.

Public Heroes private felons

1

weak men
in wide bodies

IN 1989, THE NATION WAS REPULSED BY REPORTS FROM GLEN RIDGE, New Jersey, that a group of high school athletes had sexually assaulted a mentally handicapped girl who lived in their affluent neighborhood. Details of the victim being forced to perform acts of oral sex, as well as being violated with a baseball bat and a bottle, were met with profound disbelief by those who had envisioned promising futures for these college-bound young men. Particularly handsome and popular in school, the defendants did not fit the image of a sexual deviant who preys on a vulnerable girl possessing the IQ of a six-year-old.

Though the depravity of the boys' actions cannot be attributed to their athletic prowess, their status in their small community made their crimes all the more disturbing, because athletes are seen as a symbol of what so many boys aspire to become. But men whose identity derives solely from athletic achievement can be particularly vulnerable to fears that their manhood is being challenged. A number of the Glen Ridge boys were quite uncomfortable with the actions of the group's leaders, and chose to watch rather than join in directly. Nonetheless, they were unwilling to stop the incident. "I didn't feel comfortable being part of some sort of group sex," said one of the boys. "Something wrong was going on . . . [like] a group of guys watching one of their friends feeding a tank of piranhas."[1]

Despite typically being very popular and esteemed, athletes are not immune to the kind of peer pressure that can lead to gang rape. On the contrary; because their social standing is a direct result of their physical prowess, some athletes are particularly sensitive to challenges to their manhood and sexuality. Thirty-three percent of the alleged sexual assaults involving college and professional athletes that were reported between 1986 and 1996 involved multiple perpetrators.[2]

That gang rapes are rooted more in an athlete's need to sustain his standing among his peers than in his need to satisfy sexual urges is apparent in the circumstances that frequently surround such incidents, and in the common characteristic the victims share. Most often, in addition to being outnumbered and severely overmatched physically, the victims tend to be especially vulnerable because of either instability resulting from mental impairment (typically associated with alcohol or drug consumption) or their employment in the male entertainment industry (as prostitutes, exotic dancers, and the like).

The counter clerk at Kinko's copy center held four crumpled dollar bills in his outstretched hand as Victoria Alexander searched through her purse for the final dollar she owed for use of the store's fax machine. Stuffing the receipt into her jeans, she moved to the end of the counter and nervously glanced from the fax machine to the clock and back again. Finally, the green light began blinking, and the machine began spewing the first page of paper, headed by the bold letters RELEASE OF ALL CLAIMS.

As the paper spilled out in scroll fashion, she spotted her name in the first paragraph. "Whereas, Victoria Alexander of Seattle, Washington, has alleged that on Thursday, October 4, 1990, certain persons had contact with her in Seattle, Washington, which contact was offensive to her and which contact was without her consent . . ." Hovering over the fax paper, she read further, "the certain persons against whom Victoria Alexander's allegations have been made have jointly and severally determined to settle all claims . . . [and] wish to remain anonymous and further desire that the terms of the settlement receive no public disclosure."[3]

As she scanned down to the fourth paragraph, Alexander saw what she had been promised: $30,000. She paid less attention to the words that followed, which indicated that the names of those paying the money would be secretly preserved by the lawyer who wrote up the agreement, James E. Perry.

Alexander was so eager to sign her name on the document that she rushed out of Kinko's without bothering to make a photocopy. She raced to her apartment and immediately placed a phone call to James Perry's law office in Cincinnati.

A criminal defense lawyer with twenty years' experience, and a former member of the Board of Commissioners on Grievance and Discipline for the Supreme Court of Ohio, Perry had been retained after fourteen professional football players accused of gang raping Alexander in a Seattle hotel room. He drafted an agreement releasing them from liability and barring her from publicly disclosing information about the incident. The players offered $30,000 in exchange for her signature on the release.

Having assisted numerous Cincinnati Bengals players in criminal matters in recent years, Perry came immediately to the mind of the team's general manager, Mike Brown, after his office learned of allegations involving a rape in star player Ickey Woods's hotel room a year earlier. Brown, himself a lawyer, called a private meeting in his office with Woods and another player singled out by Alexander. He began by reading Alexander's allegations from a note that had been passed to him by the team's public relations director. The two players were told, "This may or may not be true or this may be some type of prank joke. I don't know."

As Brown relayed Alexander's version of events, the expression on Woods's face made clear that it was no joke. Never directly asking Woods whether the woman's claim was true, Brown reached across his desk and handed him a small piece of paper. "There's a lawyer named James Perry that you may want to contact," Brown said. Woods also wrote down Alexander's home telephone number.

After leaving Brown's office, Woods returned to practice and told some of his teammates why he was late. By the end of practice a group of players had gathered at Woods's locker. Many who had bragged following the incident a year earlier were now scrambling to silence it.

Woods, married and one of the players with the most at stake should the allegations have become public, pulled from his pocket the crumpled piece of paper with Alexander's telephone number. Players began scribbling it down on anything they could find to write on. While several players placed calls to Alexander, Woods negotiated the financial settlement, and eventually contacted Perry. Although Alexander had not requested money when she first contacted the Bengals' front office, Woods persuaded nine of his teammates to help him pay for a promise from her that she would never make her charges public. Woods turned the $30,000 over to Perry in cash, leaving him to formalize the deal and complete the transaction.

With the faxed agreement in her hand, Alexander reached Perry at his office and was instructed to have her signature notarized before returning the document. After hanging up the phone, Alexander walked to the nearest used car lot and had her signature notarized before dashing off to the Spokane airport to dispatch the agreement via Federal Express to Cincinnati before the weekend.

On Monday morning a courier arrived at Perry's law office with the package from Spokane. One of Perry's assistants promptly wired $30,000 directly to Alexander's newly established account at Washington Trust Bank. The flurry of transactions had seemingly brought closure to a one-year ordeal that began when Alexander entered the Doubletree Inn lobby in Seattle hoping to meet a famous athlete, and emerged hours later insisting she had fallen victim to a group sexual assault.

When the Bengals arrived in Seattle on September 30, 1990, to play the Seahawks, the National Football League was under scrutiny for alleged mistreatment of women in the locker rooms. Two weeks earlier, *Boston Herald* beat writer Lisa Olson had complained she was the victim of sexually explicit gestures and jeering comments while conducting an interview in the New England Patriots' locker room. After instructing all twenty-eight teams to uphold the league's equal access rule, NFL commissioner Paul Tagliabue had announced the appointment of Harvard Law professor Philip Heymann to oversee an investigation into Olson's charges.[4]

During the Bengals' week-long stay in the Northwest, their head coach, Sam Wyche, managed to shift the national spotlight from the Patriots to his own team. Following a loss to the Seahawks on *Monday Night Football,* he barred *USA Today* reporter Denise Tom from entering the locker room for postgame interviews. Declaring, "I will not allow women to walk in on 50 naked men," Wyche insisted that Tom's interview with quarterback Boomer Esiason be conducted in a hallway beneath the Kingdome.[5]

Tagliabue responded by fining Wyche $25,000—the largest penalty ever imposed on a head coach in league history. Remaining in Seattle until the team's weekend trip to Los Angeles to play the Rams, Wyche began a week-long crusade on behalf of "human decency." He started on Wednesday morning, October 4, by appearing on ABC's *Good Morning America.* Following the program, Wyche called a closed-door meeting with the team, in part to discuss the presence of women in the locker room. At the conclusion of the meeting, a brief practice was held before players were given the rest of the day off.

The Doubletree Suites, in addition to housing the Bengals and the large press corps that was following the Wyche incident, was sponsoring its weekly Ladies' Night in the Infinity Lounge, a nightspot that was popular with Seattle-area athletes. While some players chose to go into the city to get away from the commotion at the hotel, most remained in their rooms.

Unaware of the controversy swirling around the team, thirty-four-year-old Alexander, a two-time divorcée and mother of four children, entered the lobby dressed in leggings, pumps, and a shirt that exposed her stomach. Hoping to meet one of the visiting Cincinnati Bengals, she hung around for over an hour before two large men carrying Bengals jackets stepped off the elevator and headed toward the exit. Positioning herself in their path, she confronted rookie Lynn James and veteran player Solomon Wilcots.

"Hey, do you live around here?" James asked.

"Why?" responded Alexander.

"Well, we need to know where a liquor store is," said James.

Indicating that there was one just around the corner, Alexander offered to drive James and Wilcots there in her car, and the players accepted. Wilcots had seen Alexander's type before—she had attended Monday night's game, knew the players' names and numbers, and now was hanging around the hotel lobby. Later, arriving back at the hotel parking lot, Wilcots placed his brown paper bag inside his coat and quietly climbed out of the back seat, leaving James and Alexander behind. Shortly after, James invited Alexander to his room for a drink. She turned the ignition off and followed him back into the hotel.

On entering James's suite, they found the bedroom occupied by teammate Reggie Rembert and his date, Connie Hepworth, a very attractive cruise ship attendant whom Rembert had met in a Seattle restaurant. After James had made eye contact with him, Rembert asked Hepworth if she would mind taking their Chinese food and video to another room.

Less than thirty minutes later, Alexander, still adjusting her clothing and fixing her hair, exited the bedroom with James. He escorted her past Rembert and Hepworth and into the adjoining suite, which belonged to Ickey Woods. Although Alexander was the only woman present, she chose to remain in the room. A party was under way, and she was the center of attention.

After watching his teammates pass in and out of Woods's room, Rembert went to see what was going on. During his brief absence, James returned to his room and found Hepworth alone.

"Come here, come here," he pleaded as he put his hands on her waist.

"What do you want?" she asked.

"Come here," he repeated, moving her toward the bed.

"What are you doing?" she demanded, as she pushed him away.

"I thought—" he began.

"Well, you thought wrong," she interrupted.

Hepworth resented Lynn's advances. "He was just assuming that since I was up in the room, I was up there for sex," she said. "Some people are thrilled with meeting athletes, but it is not that big of a deal to me."

Hepworth had been acquainted with Rembert for only three days, having been introduced to him by a girlfriend who had attended college with one of Rembert's teammates. She felt no particular attraction to Rembert, other than the opportunity to be escorted around Seattle for a few days by a wealthy man. So she did not hesitate to leave the hotel after Rembert returned to the room and reported what was taking place next door.

"You wouldn't believe what's going on over there," Rembert said.

"What?" Hepworth asked.

"She's over there having sex with everybody," he said.

Rembert's shameless portrayal of the events taking place in the adjoining room convinced Hepworth it was time to go. "He didn't come off as though something's wrong over there," Hepworth said. "It was just kind of a matter-of-fact statement that she was having sex with them. Not only did it surprise me, it really upset me." She later learned that following her departure, Rembert joined his teammates in sexually exploiting Alexander. "When I found out he did that, I was like, 'Well, that just figures.'"

The ease with which Rembert joined in the affair was shared by many of his teammates. One of the defendants in the case explained how the incident spiraled out of control. "The peer pressure to perform in front of the guys, like the peer pressure to drink in front of the guys, was the overlapping problem that occurred," he said. "A married man normally would have just slid on out of that room, but all of the 'Hey, hey,' you get caught up in it. There was a lot of noise, music. It was like, 'Hey [name deleted], your turn, buddy.' Well, it was hard to say,

'Nah, no,' because you're gonna be ragged about it. You're gonna be teased about it.

"That's peer pressure. It may be peer pressure for thirty-year-old kids, but it's pretty much in the same line with a teenager who's been asked to drink a shot of vodka. Do you want the ramifications that come with saying no? Do you want that label?

"I think the best way to sum it up is peer pressure to meet the challenge around the guys. If I walk away, they know my personality. It's like, 'He never drinks with us.' I think there is a parallel here."

After agreeing to have sex with James, Alexander found herself in a situation that quickly got out of hand. "One bad thing about us," the player-defendant continued, "is we've learned to accept challenges. We've grown to accept the challenge of an opponent, so to speak. We, as athletes, we've always accepted challenges, 'I can beat you. I can physically beat you. I can mentally beat you.' If we feel for one split-second that we cannot achieve or we cannot beat the opponent, mentally we have failed. The challenge here was not even with the young lady. It's the pressure to meet this challenge around the . . . guys."

Just five months after receiving the $30,000 payoff from the players, Alexander had spent the money. She decided to seek legal help in obtaining an additional settlement. Remembering the name of a lawyer who had handled some well-publicized sexual assault cases in the Spokane area, Alexander called attorney Dick Eymann. After failing to convince the Bengals organization to pay a more equitable settlement, Eymann filed suit against the franchise in April 1992.

Although no players were named in the suit, the sensational nature of the allegations evoked great interest from the press. Mike Brown responded, "If it develops that players of ours were involved in some kind of consensual sexual orgy, their behavior as far as I'm concerned would be reprehensible. They would not have crossed over a line that would automatically lead to their suspension, but it would be a mark against them."[6]

After filing the suit, Eymann enlisted the help of Seattle lawyer Victoria Vreeland, the former president of King County Rape Relief, an organization that later became a national model for responding to and treating sexual abuse. Vreeland also had assisted in drafting the Victim's Rights Bill for the State of Washington.

As part of an effort to amend the lawsuit and include the individuals who were involved, Vreeland and Eymann worked with Alexander on identifying the players. "We asked for photographs, videos, the list of names [in Perry's agreement]," Vreeland said. "They [the Bengals] would only provide us the game program. We wanted pictures, not programs."

The task of accurately naming over a dozen players involved in an incident that had occurred two years earlier presented great risks for Alexander and for those Bengals who were not involved. Any errors on Alexander's part would stigmatize innocent people as rapists, and provide defense lawyers with ammunition to question her credibility when the case went to trial.

Many team members who were at risk of being falsely accused were well aware of the details of the incident. One player admitted, "Actually, we found out the next day that something had happened. Well, the guys was just talkin' about . . . they had this girl. . . . That ain't something that's common, but you don't sit there and look all shocked and surprised. But we didn't find out the details 'til [we] got back here [Cincinnati]. Then the guys were talking about it a little bit more and more."

Although many players knew who was involved and much of what went on, they were loyal to their teammates and remained silent. "Nobody wanted . . . to tell on each other," admitted one of the players.

Like his teammates, James had no interest in naming names, but he did want to be sure that he was not included in the lawsuit. In a telephone conversation with Alexander, he attempted to persuade her of his innocence. "I thought you were leaving. You know. . . . And that's when all the other guys bombarded the room and I didn't know what was going on. I . . . I can't control those other guys' actions. And I did not, um . . . in no form or fashion . . . uh . . . try to bring that upon you . . . no form or fashion," said James.[7]

When Alexander completed her list of twenty names to be added to the lawsuit, James's name was left off. The federal judge presiding over the case ordered the names sealed until days before the Bengals' first game in Seattle following the incident. After the Bengals organization had been informed of the identities of the accused players, head coach David Shula held a team meeting just before the squad was scheduled to fly west. Players were warned that subpoenas would be issued by federal marshals while the team was in Seattle.

Sitting at their lockers after hearing the announcement, defensive player Barney Bussey and star wide receiver Tim McGee snickered to themselves. Neither player had been involved, but both were familiar with the allegations.

"I feel bad for those guys," said McGee.

"Man, that's going to be kind of messed up," said Bussey.

"Man, you know, they got themselves into it, if they got themselves into it. . . . It's going to be a big mess around here. I'd hate to be in some of their houses," McGee said.

Later that afternoon, Shula called McGee into his office. One of the most respected of the Bengals players, both on the team and in the community of Cincinnati, McGee sat down anticipating that he would be asked to testify on behalf of his teammates.

With the door shut, Shula told McGee, "You've been accused as one of the rapists."

In stunned silence, McGee wondered, "What will my wife's family think? What would my family think? Our friends?"

Arriving at his suburban home, he walked through the front door and said to his wife, "You're not going to believe this."

Aware that some of her husband's teammates were facing legal action over an incident with a woman, McGee's wife responded, "What?"

"She named me," he said.

"Wait a minute," she protested.

"Well, it's like she got everybody that wasn't there," he complained as his kids ran into the room to greet him. The following morning, McGee's name appeared alongside those of nineteen of his teammates on the front page of Cincinnati's newspapers. He was now identified as a rapist. In addition to McGee, Bernard Bussey, David Dixon, Eric Ball, Leo Barker, David Fulcher, and Lewis Billups all claimed to have been nowhere near the hotel at the time the incident took place.

Furthermore, a number of players who had sexual contact with Alexander, and had even contributed to the original payoff, had not been named in the lawsuit. Elated to be in the clear, they showed no sympathy for the seven who had been falsely accused.

Enduring great public humiliation, the innocent players wanted their teammates to clear their names. "Our pictures were right on the front page of the paper, color photos," McGee said. "Here it is, I'm married and Bussey's married and Barker's married.

"We wanted somebody to come out and say, 'I was there and I

deny the rape charges, but she has named several guys, including McGee, Bussey, Ball, and Barker, who were not there.'

"But some guys who were there, [but were] unnamed, kind of just sat back and said, 'Well, she didn't name me. Ha ha ha. Let them deal with it.'

"We all talked with them . . . and it was like, 'What are you guys doing going home and laughing about it? Why are you guys letting us take the blame for it?' What made me angry was that nobody defended us. They let us take the fall when they knew we were not there.'"

Although their reputations were being tarnished in the press and their families subjected to tremendous shame, the innocent players refrained from speaking out against their teammates. "I would never have protected them because my main concern was protecting my family," McGee said. "But the ultimate question was, 'Was she raped?' I did not know what happened in the room, and it was advised to us to say nothing."

The legal advice given to McGee and the others in his situation was to remain silent in order to avoid potential liability. Although this approach benefited those actually involved in the incident more than those who were falsely accused, it did not satisfy those who had joined in the affair and were trying to avoid culpability. One married player approached McGee and the other misidentified players in hopes of convincing them to endorse his version of what had transpired in the hotel on the night in question. "He was basically saying, 'Help us,'" McGee recalled. But McGee's response was, "We can't help you because if we do, that puts us at the scene of the alleged crime."

McGee's sense of betrayal was deepened by the fact that Rembert, whom he considered his friend, was directly responsible for his name being falsely associated with the affair. While having sexual contact with Alexander, Rembert had identified himself as Tim McGee. Nevertheless, McGee remained reluctant to criticize Rembert. "You don't want to say something that's going to get someone else in trouble," explained McGee. "You don't want to make a statement that turns around and works against your friend."

Vreeland insisted that the bond formed through being a member of a team strengthened the players' resistance to coming forward and implicating their teammates. "The team concept is driven into them," said Vreeland. "The team is more important than the individual and you never rat on your friend. This code of silence from the street—if somebody is injured or somebody's shot, don't tell who did it or you're dead—carries over to the team."

Of the seven players claiming they had not been present, McGee was not the only one whom Alexander insisted had taken a direct role in the gang rape. Alexander maintained that Lewis Billups, a defensive star, had initiated the entire incident by dragging her from the bathroom, forcing her down on the bed, and holding her there against her will.

This was not the first time Billups had been accused of violent crimes against women since joining the Bengals. In addition to a litany of arrests in Cincinnati, Billups, along with a male friend, had been arrested in Florida and charged with rape and extortion less than three months after Alexander amended her civil complaint in Seattle. The victim in the Florida case claimed to have been drugged by Billups before he and his friend raped her. Billups and his partner had videotaped the assault.

Although Billups managed to avoid prison as part of a plea bargain agreement, in spring 1993 a federal judge in Georgia sentenced him to a year in jail in connection with a separate incident. An FBI wiretap on the victim's phone had recorded Billups making threatening phone calls to her home from across state lines.

Because of Billups's incarceration in Georgia, Alexander's attorneys were unable to take his deposition in preparation for the civil trial in Seattle. Yet they became increasingly convinced that his behavior supported Alexander's allegations. Vreeland said, "After his arrest down in Florida and then this MO of his with the drug, we started thinking, 'My God! Was that going on up here? Was she set up by the first guy [Lynn James]?'"

The extreme nature of the incident, as well as the number of the accused, resulted in the assembly of a powerful legal defense. Numbers of prestigious Seattle law firms were flown to Cincinnati for interviews. Accompanied by their agents and personal attorneys, players put the prospective defense lawyers through a battery of questions. Attorneys accustomed to dealing with corporate executives involved in business litigation found themselves meeting with millionaires in sweat suits who had been accused of gang rape. Finally, two Seattle firms were chosen to represent the players.

Byrnes & Keller, the city's most respected and experienced trial lawyers, were hired to defend those players who claimed they had not been in the room on the night of the incident. It was the partners' first experience representing professional athletes in a highly publicized case. Their burden was to prove that their clients were not present, and thereby had no responsibility for anything that may have occurred.

Another team of lawyers, led by Spencer Hall, who specialized in commercial and civil litigation, was hired to represent those players who admitted to having sexual contact with Alexander, but insisted it was with her consent. It was not Hall's first experience representing athletes.

After being apprised of his clients' claim of consensual group sex, Hall appreciated the extent of his task. Sitting in his downtown Seattle office overlooking the majestic Puget Sound, Hall recounted how he questioned "the ability of . . . anyone else to conceive of this kind of sexual activity occurring. 'Would the average juror believe that a woman, or anyone, is capable of going into a room with a bunch of strangers and voluntarily engaging in this kind of sexual activity?' "

Having accepted the offer to represent clients whose admitted behavior was sure to be judged outrageous by the public, he reasoned, "I think it is real easy to bring your own moral standards to these kinds of situations and make judgments that are different than the judgments that need to be made in the case to decide it one way or the other.

"This was not a case about whether it was good judgment for a football player to have sex with a strange woman whom he didn't know, even one-on-one. It wasn't a case about whether it is good judgment or good morals to have group sex. It was a case about whether this woman had been raped.

"It made the case much easier for me personally when I became familiar with the evidence. It appeared what this woman claimed had not occurred. It would have been a difficult case for me if this *had* occurred because it would have been a terrible thing."

Defense lawyers were challenged not only with convincing a jury that a woman had willingly asked a dozen total strangers nearly twice her size to engage in sex with her. They also had to deal with the fact that ten of the players had paid her off in an attempt to silence her. The payoff, and the secrecy associated with it, gave a strong impression that those players had something to cover up.

The defense lawyers argued that financial disputes and liability claims are quietly resolved in settlements all the time. "You have legal disputes that are settled every day with confidentiality agreements—and it works," Hall maintained.

This was not a matter of a faceless corporation being accused of producing a defective product, however. Rather, men of role-model status were being charged with a sadistic gang rape. If the charges were groundless, paying a liar would have made little sense. But Ickey Woods didn't see it that way. He said, "[She was] a woman out trying to get some money from some ballplayers. She was in dire need of some money . . . so she came up with, 'Hey, I'll go with these professional football players and blackmail them into giving me some money, because most professional football athletes don't want to go through the whole bit of trying to prove that they're innocent.' "[8]

Hall insisted, "It was a reasonable business decision for a professional entertainer—professional football player—to say, 'Here is a woman making a false claim, but it is a situation where at least some people on the team did something with her that we don't really want shouted from the rooftops.' "

He continued, "You had some [players] that were there and were single men and didn't have to account to a spouse. You had some who had spouses, or some that had girlfriends or fiancées. So even if it was entirely consensual, it was not something that they would want made public."

Nonetheless, one of the players who contributed money to the original settlement had no interest in having his case tried in court, and decided to contact Alexander's lawyers. All-pro tight end Rodney Holman suddenly broke ranks. He said he didn't know why he was in Ickey's room that night, or what motivated him to get involved in something that was so wrong. After reaching a settlement with Alexander's lawyers, Holman was dropped from the suit.

With lawyers from both sides gearing up for what was sure to be a highly publicized trial, Judge Walter T. McGovern was assigned by the Federal Court to preside over the case after the judge initially assigned to the case recused himself. When McGovern came to the bench in the 1970s, he had selected his lifetime friend Phil Lucid, a Jesuit priest, to be his law clerk. Over the years McGovern, with the assistance of Lucid, had presided over countless high-profile political corruption cases and corporate liability suits. But he had never presided over a rape case, much less one involving twenty NFL players.

Lucid was assigned the task of reviewing the thirty-six hours of videotaped statements by Alexander, including six hours of detailed descriptions of how she was repeatedly raped and sodomized. Lucid grimaced with anguish as she listened to Alexander respond to defense attorneys' explicit questions about a most ugly and barbaric set of events.

"Her head would be down on the table and she'd be sobbing and sobbing for minutes and minutes and minutes and minutes," Lucid said. "They got into the details of what she alleged were the assaults," he continued, "multiple people involved, cheering. . . . She was just reduced to almost groveling, sobbing, weeping. It was almost too much to watch."

With shiny new copies of John Grisham and Scott Turow novels occupying the otherwise empty shelf behind his desk, McGovern discussed his discomfort with his clerk's rendition of the contents of Alexander's videotaped deposition. A former college athlete, the star of a nationally ranked basketball team in the 1950s, McGovern was nauseated by the conduct he heard described. He wondered aloud, "How do they get caught up in it? Do they get caught up in it only because they happened to be in an atmosphere at the particular time which is conducive to 'Let's let everything go?'

"But there are people who are smart enough, morally correct enough to get up and walk out. Some, less so, are maybe talked into it by their fellow peers, their football friends."

Recalling a time when competitive sports seldom included criminal allegations, he conceded, "I don't think there was such physical violence [in sports] then. I had friends who played college football and played professional football. Perfect gentlemen. Saints. Magnificent people. Anything like this would be the last thing that would ever enter their minds."

Even the players' version of events left McGovern bewildered over what is deemed acceptable by men of high social standing. "Maybe I'm naive, but I don't know how anybody can engage in group sex," McGovern said. Yet that was the defense argument—this was not a gang rape, but a simple case of group sex. "I'm not sure I ever heard them say that they were doing it in front of each other," said McGovern. "Maybe the implication was there, and I was trying to hide my eyes, ears, and nose to it because it's not very pleasant. But it wouldn't surprise me if that's what they were saying. Without even having heard the sordid details, I'm sure that [the players' conduct] would really turn off 99 percent of the people in this country."

Not only did the players' admitted behavior cast them in a bad light before prospective jurors; their insistence that Alexander was the aggressor, and therefore largely to blame for what occurred, further undermined their credibility. "These are very large males," said Vreeland. "She's about five feet tall and weighs about a hundred pounds. These guys are all huge. When I met them and took their depositions, they were scary. They're scary because they're big, they're physical, and there's a sense of meanness. I know some NFL players, including a former brother-in-law, who don't project that sense of meanness in their eyes."

The defense attorneys' greatest challenge was going to be convincing jurors that Alexander welcomed what transpired in the Seattle hotel room. "The biggest obstacle for the defense was getting people to accept that a woman would engage in multiple, serial sexual encounters," said Keller.

The contending versions of the incident were contradictory, and

McGovern had no appetite for enduring weeks of degrading testimony on whether or not a rape had taken place. Thus on February 19, 1993, he issued a stunning announcement that suspended the rape trial, and ordered a preliminary trial to determine the validity of the confidentiality agreement entered into by Alexander and numerous Bengals players.

"If the release was valid, then I didn't have to get into the sordid claims or counterclaims . . . whatever they may be," McGovern said. "I did not want to get into what I heard were the sordid details."

McGovern reminded the jury, "The issue in this trial is the validity of the agreement entitled, Release of All Claims. Although this agreement arises from disputed alleged conduct of the Plaintiff and the individual Defendants at the Doubletree Suites in October 1990, determination of the facts on that occasion is not the issue before you now. The only issue before you in this trial is the validity of the release agreement."[9]

With the release now the central focus of the case, Woods became a more important witness than most of his teammates, since he had orchestrated the idea in the first place. As a result, he was one of the only players who was scheduled to testify at the trial. At the time the incident occurred, Woods was the most celebrated person in the city of Cincinnati, having led his team to the Super Bowl in 1988. He was earning over a million dollars a year. By the time the trial started three years later, he had left football as the result of an injury, and was forced to defend himself in court because he could not afford a lawyer—a daunting challenge for a man who had left the University of Nevada, Las Vegas, as the nation's top rusher, unable to read.

Nonetheless, after hearing two weeks of testimony on Alexander's state of mind, the jury determined that she had understood the contract when she accepted the $30,000 settlement. Juror Cindi Curtright conceded that the majority of the jurors believed that Alexander had been raped, but that her state of mind had not been impaired when she agreed to settle.[10]

Woods bolted from the courtroom and performed his famous touchdown dance—the Ickey Shuffle—on the federal courthouse steps, declaring to reporters, "There was no rape, period, no mixed signals at all. I don't know why she called it a rape. She was out for the money."[11]

Lucid had witnessed many events over his two decades of federal court work, but Woods's actions were a first. "There's a spectrum of violence, and that kind of insensitivity is somewhere in that same spectrum," said Lucid. "Maybe it's on the far end or lesser, but abuse comes in many shapes and forms. Not that I expect Ickey Woods to be a paragon of sensitivity. He's hardly anything like that."

While Woods insisted to reporters that Alexander "was enjoying herself," another defendant made similar remarks. "It wasn't brutality or something that could be classified as criminal," the player contended. "It was in fun, a human act."

Looking back on the incident, the player mused, "When are we allowed to drop the role model? You can't say that athletes don't pick up *Playboy* magazines. What I mean by that is that a single guy doesn't have the pleasure . . . or the same ability . . . a married guy has. A married guy can go in the privacy of his home and whatever happens happens. But a single guy's gotta get it from somewhere."

In the aftermath of the trial, those involved in the case tried to go on with their lives, with varying degrees of success. The Bengals organization eventually traded or released all but two of the players originally named in connection with the incident.

Tim McGee completed a ten-year career with the Bengals in 1995, retiring as one of just two of the twenty accused players still on the team. "I wish there would have been criminal charges against the guys because there would have been an investigation, which would have led to the right people being named," McGee said. "It cost me $22,000. Them lawyers probably made about $800,000. There isn't anyone who's gonna pat me on the back and say 'sorry.' And in the end, you got guys that was involved who didn't even get named."

After a failed attempt to reenter the NFL, Ickey Woods began selling packaged meat door to door. He was arrested in Cincinnati in 1995 for carrying a concealed weapon and possession of drugs.

Reggie Rembert was released by the Bengals in 1993 and later sentenced to a year in jail following a series of violations of the law.

Lewis Billups completed his one-year jail term in federal prison. Six days later, on April 9, 1994, he drove his car into a cement barrier at a speed exceeding one hundred miles per hour. Both he and his passenger were killed instantly.

Victoria Alexander suffered prolonged depression and other medical problems. Her children had to be removed from her home and raised by their grandparents. She remained unemployed, and divorced again. Even her own lawyers eventually grew frustrated with her psychological instability.

2

when women
are the opponent

DESPITE THE EVER-INCREASING NUMBER OF SEXUAL ASSAULTS AND DO-
mestic beatings reported to police annually, the mainstream press af-
fords little attention to such crimes. One exception occurs when a
prominent individual, particularly an athlete, a unique blend of role
model and celebrity, is linked to such an incident. The increasing frequency of accusations of abuse against sports figures has stirred unprecedented interest in a pervasive social problem that for decades has
stirred little. Although the widespread mistreatment of women clearly
transcends the playing field, the attention and popularity enjoyed by
sports figures has brought the sports culture under intense scrutiny by
researchers looking for links between competitive team sports and the
violence that occurs away from the field. As a result, a perception is
growing that the aggressive nature and competitive atmosphere of male
athletics can lead to criminal aggression toward women.[1]

Although the attitudes associated with male sports can reinforce
sexist attitudes toward women, the suggestion that sexism is the domi-

nant influence behind the rash of violence by athletes against women both overstates and oversimplifies the relationship. Participation in athletics does not cause men to abuse women, but it can help to incite such transgressions in those athletes who are predisposed toward such acts. And certainly the culture of male athletics (using sexist locker room dialogue, rewarding aggressiveness, legitimizing violence) helps to sustain negative attitudes toward women.[2]

A stronger link between male athletes and the criminal abuse of women is the socialization process that takes place away from the playing field, and is connected with celebrity status. The elevated status of successful athletes exposes them to exceptional amounts of illicit behavior, particularly in the form of sexual activity. Operating under an increased sense of power and the mantle of public trust, athletes inclined to sexual and physical violence have ample opportunity to exploit women who often misperceive them as respectable citizens.

Among men who harbor violent tendencies toward women, athletic success may accelerate the exhibition of abusive attitudes, increasing the frequency of violent incidents. Nonetheless, that is less a function of athletics per se than a reflection of the modern athlete's status as an icon of pop culture.

But an occupation that thrives on a unique capacity for aggression among participants runs the risk of becoming a home for troubled men who cannot contain their rage against the opposite sex. Because of the physical nature of athletics; the aggressive, confrontational, supermacho attitudes surrounding them; and the social approval afforded to celebrity-athletes, the sports industry has in effect embraced those men who demonstrate a disdain for women through repeated acts of criminal violence.

Just after midnight on April 9, 1994, former professional football player Lewis Billups got behind the wheel of his 1987 Corvette convertible and began racing down Florida's Interstate 4. Released from prison six days earlier after serving a one-year sentence for threatening the life of a woman, Billups and a companion were driving over one hundred miles per hour when another car unexpectedly changed lanes. Billups jerked his steering wheel to avoid the car, sending his Corvette into a vicious spin. Suddenly out of control, the car slammed into fifty feet of metal guardrail. When police arrived at 1 A.M., Billups's body was on the ground after having been thrown from the vehicle. His passenger was pronounced dead on the scene; Billups was rushed to the Orlando Regional Medical Center, where he died hours later.[3]

Billups left behind a trail of abused women who found solace in his violent death. "Even though he's dead, I'm still scared of him," said Jenny Chapman, whose complaints of stalking had led to Billups's imprisonment. "I think about the prospect of him being alive and it's too much. I'm scared of the memories. I'm scared of what could have happened if he were alive. I don't think I could have had peace in my mind had it ended any other way."[4]

Early in his first year in the National Football League, Billups unleashed his brutal capacity for inflicting violence against women. Shortly after signing with the Cincinnati Bengals in 1986, Billups met Tracy Fair, a Cincinnati woman who soon became his girlfriend and the target of his violence. "I was inches away from dying," Fair said. "He beat me for three and a half hours and probably three of it was to my head. I had six plastic surgeries, six on my nose and one on my ear, just that I suffered from blows to my face. Then he cut my hair off."[5]

The beating that almost resulted in Fair's death came after she told Billups she was leaving him because of his repeated abuse. "He kept saying, 'I'll make you ugly,' " Fair recalled. " 'You will be with nobody but me 'cause nobody will want you. You're mine.' "

"He really messed up Tracy's mind," said one of Billups's teammates, who was familiar with the violence Fair endured. "She's a sweet girl, but he really messed her mind."

As a result of the extended hospital stay and multiple surgeries, Fair reported Billups to the police, and he was charged with assault. But before the case was prosecuted, she dropped the charges. "I knew if I went through with it, he would kill me," Fair said. "He also told me that he would pay somebody to finish my face off. People don't understand the fear that battered women live in and they think, 'Well, she dropped the charges. She's a liar. It didn't happen. He's a big football player and she's slandering his name.' I was a nobody out of Cincinnati coming after this big professional football player."[6]

Over the course of his seven-year career in the NFL, Billups raped, beat, and terrorized many women besides Fair. Despite arrests, lawsuits, and graphic evidence of his violent tendencies toward women, neither the league nor the Bengals organization saw fit to formally reprimand him. Furthermore, none of Billups's teammates ever confronted him, in part because his fury was never directed at them. "We got along fine," said one former teammate. "I knew he had problems off the field, but he never had a problem with other players."

Another teammate and friend of Billups conceded, "When I was around him he was quiet, he treated you to dinner and was fun to go hang out with. The thing about it was that Lewis was the sweetest person in the world to my wife. He was the sweetest person in the world to other players' wives. But he was an asshole to the women he dated. When he got girls behind doors, for some reason he either hit 'em or he wanted his way [sexually]. He was a spoiled brat."

Despite his history of vicious cruelty toward women, Billups displayed an appealing demeanor around unsuspecting women with whom he came into contact at clubs and in other social settings. A stylish dresser and extravagant spender, he used his impressive image to attract vulnerable women. Allured by his presence, fascinated women readily accompanied him to his home or some other isolated location, only to be mistreated.

Jenny Chapman, the sister of NBA star Rex Chapman, fell into his trap. Like Fair, Chapman quickly became the subject of frequent beatings. "He hit me close-fisted," Chapman said. "He slapped me. He choked me . . . to the point where I'd just pass out and wake up the next morning and have to deal with it all over again."[7]

Chapman saw the lifestyle that accompanies athletic success as a volatile ingredient in Billups's frequent violence. "I think it was his transition coming into football, coming into money, so quickly," she said. "Never having that great amount [of money] just to do whatever you wanted to do and then all of a sudden it brings you power and it brings you all this fame just to do whatever you want whenever you want. He was used to getting what he wanted. If I was not going to give that to him, then he would become violent."[8]

A close friend and teammate of Billups explained his penchant for controlling women. "Being an athlete you get notoriety, wealth, *and power*," the teammate said. "Lewis was a person who used his. He used his to the fullest. I mean he had wealth. He drove a Lamborghini. He drove a Corvette. He had this very plush, gorgeous home in Orlando.

"But that wasn't enough for him. He had to use the power of controlling . . . to get somebody. 'Hey, I'm Lewis Billups and you know I have all this stuff.' And then once he got 'em over to his house, he wanted to control them. And that's what he wanted to do with Jenny. He wanted to just control her mind, her body, everything."

Although he took advantage of his exceptional access to women,

Billups's desire to control them had little to do with his athleticism. Rather, a much more complex set of factors was contributing to his routine violence. "It has to do with power and control and hate . . . a disdain for women," said Victoria Vreeland, cocounsel for Victoria Alexander, who sued Billups for rape. As the former president of King County Rape Relief in Seattle, and an assistant to Washington's Attorney General in drafting the state's Victim's Rights Bill, Vreeland was quite familiar with the mentality of men who acted like Billups. "This person [the victim of abuse] isn't a person anymore, they're an object. To that extent, if you have some societal sense or you grew up with a sense of lack of power or control, or that you weren't as good, this offers power and control. 'I wanna be in charge.' It is similar to children who lack a sense of power. Their feeling of powerlessness somehow gets twisted around in their minds and so the way to be powerful is to pick on somebody else. If you grow up with crime and objectification, making people objects, then killing them or harming them doesn't matter. They are not human."

Despite his prominence within the confines of professional football, Billups's on-field accomplishments failed to compensate for the void in his self-esteem that pervaded all other aspects of his life. In a despondent attempt to replicate his sense of power and control on the field in the world beyond the gridiron, Billups resorted to violence. When Chapman informed him that she planned to end their relationship, Billups threatened to inflict bodily harm on her to make her stay. Insulted and enraged by Chapman's refusal to cave in to his threats, Billups threatened members of her family, particularly her brother Rex.

After Chapman reported Billups's violence to the authorities, the FBI installed a wiretap on her telephone and recorded numerous threats to her and her family. The following transcript of one of those calls highlights Billups's insecurity about his own manhood and his attempts to earn respect through violence and intimidation:

J.C.:   *You gonna have somebody else do your dirty work or you gonna do it yourself?*

L.B.:   *I don't ever get my hands dirty, Jenny.*

J.C.:   *Yeah, I know, because, see, a real man would.*

L.B.:   *No. A real man who got power wouldn't.*

J.C.:   *How can you sit here and think that I would want to be with you when you threaten people that I love? How can you think that I would even want to even be associated with someone like you?*

L.B.:   *Because I'm a hard mother [expletive] and I'm gonna prove it to you. I promise you that on my mother's life.*[9]

"He [Billups] had a certain dominance," confirmed one of Billups's teammates. "He felt a certain dominance over white women. He felt he had power over them. He had them in control. I think that had a lot to do with confidence. It was probably an ego thing. He felt he could control them."

While federal authorities were completing their investigation into Billups's threatening phone calls, his career came to a premature end. After six seasons with the Cincinnati Bengals, the team let him go in favor of younger talent. After being picked up briefly by the Green Bay Packers, he was released again after being outperformed by younger, more athletic players. Although Billups had earned millions of dollars during his career, his extravagant lifestyle left him penniless. His desperation on suddenly losing his only source of wealth and power is reflected in this letter, written to American Express just weeks after the Packers released him:

I, Lewis Billups, cannot pay American Express Centurion Bank. The reason is, that on or about the day of Oct. 7, 1992, I was fired from the Green Bay Packers. I am now in the process of trying to get on with another team. I have no other means of employment or cash flow. At this point in time, I have no money in the bank. I am trying to sell my house and car to get some cash, but until that happens, I have no money. Thank you and please understand.[10]

Meanwhile, lawyers in Seattle who were defending Billups against the civil suit filed by Alexander, withdrew their representation because of his failure to pay attorneys' fees. His ego destroyed, Billups's habitual abuse of women became his only means of exercising control. While trying to convince other teams that he was still capable of performing at the professional level, Billups continued to play the part of a rich, famous athlete. On November 30, 1992, the wife of a prominent Orlando resident got caught up with Billups, and was raped in Billups's home.

Experiencing marital problems, Wendy Williams* had begun to frequent a posh Orlando club. There she became acquainted with Greg Calloway, a close friend of Billups. Eventually, Calloway introduced Williams to Billups and invited her to Billups's home for lunch. "It was something interesting," said Stewart Stone, a Seminole County attorney who would later prosecute Billups and Calloway because of the incident. "She was intrigued and excited about the opportunity to go with two young, wealthy men, one of whom was a professional football player. She got in over her head."

*Wendy Williams is a fictitious name used to protect the victim's privacy.

Once Billups had Williams inside his $800,000 mansion, he secretly slipped a depressant into her beverage, then proceeded to rape her while Calloway videotaped the attack. Unaware that the assault had been filmed, Williams chose not to report the incident to police, for fear that it would attract significant attention in the local press. But days later, Billups and Calloway presented her with a videocassette showing the entire ordeal, and threatened to deliver it to her husband unless she came up with $20,000. When she resisted, Calloway threatened, "I'm going to be your worst nightmare."[11] Increasingly weary of the pair's harassing phone calls and unexpected daytime visits to her home, Williams finally called the police.

When police apprehended Billups and Calloway in Williams's neighborhood just moments after she reported their threats, they discovered a copy of the videotape in the back of Billups's car. "The tape depicted sexual contact," said prosecuting attorney Stone. "It appeared that she was under the influence, but not obviously. There was no sign of overt force, but it was not necessary to prove overt force because Billups was charged as raping someone who was mentally impaired."

The day following the announcement of Billups's arrest, six more women from the Orlando area came forward and reported being seduced, raped, and videotaped. "There was no question in my mind that Billups was guilty," Stone said. "Billups and Calloway definitely had a thing going."

In preparing to bring formal charges against Billups and Calloway, criminal investigators turned up a pile of evidence linking Billups to violence.

• Just weeks earlier, on December 3, 1992, Billups had been arrested for drunken driving. Police had been called to respond to a dispute outside an Orlando-area bar, where Billups was berating and spitting on Patty Abdelmessih. Abdelmessih had provoked Billups's wrath when she tried to prevent him from forcing another woman into his car. She had discovered the woman in the women's bathroom, moaning and sweating profusely after Billups had been buying her drinks all evening. Referring to the sick woman, Billups's male companion had said, "We didn't mean to dose her."[12] Police arrested Billups after he refused to respond to their questions and attempted to drive away.

• In November, a woman had contacted police and alleged Billups had assaulted her during a tour of his mansion. In her complaint, the woman reported being stripped, raped, robbed of the $50 in her purse, and kicked out of the house, her clothes thrown after her. No arrest had been made because she declined to press charges.[13]

• In July, an Orlando woman had obtained a restraining order against Billups after reporting that he had been hostile and abusive toward her, and had threatened to physically harm her.[14]

• In a neighboring county, sheriffs' officials confirmed that Billups had been involved in at least three additional incidents at several nightclubs, all of which required a police response.[15]

Despite a mountain of information pointing to Billups's hostility toward women, prosecutors in the Williams case accepted a plea bargain that carried no jail time. Williams, the crucial witness, was unwilling to testify, a decision that substantially reduced any chance of a conviction. "It was extremely difficult. She feared Billups," said Stone. "Second, there was the publicity and how it would affect her husband's career. He was a prominent physician."

By the time Billups pled guilty in the Williams case, he was already serving a one-year jail term in Georgia, having been convicted there for his threatening calls to Chapman. Though Billups's menacing behavior begged for stiffer penalties from the courts, he had repeatedly avoided incarceration—a fact that might suggest complicity on the part of law enforcement officials. In reality, Billups had managed to elude the law despite exceptional attempts to rein him in. "If anything, his status influenced a more aggressive prosecution," said Stone.

Professional sports leagues and individual teams are in a more influential position to discipline and deter players from this type of behavior, yet they often decline to do so. Off-the-field criminal violence is repeatedly tolerated as long as players perform on the field. Clearly Billups's conduct was exceptional. Countless male athletes live and work in a similar environment without ever engaging in criminal mistreatment of women. Nonetheless, the fact that predators like Billups are playing professional sports demonstrates the degree of indifference exhibited by owners, managers, and coaches.

As in most cases of abuse against women, the majority of women who are assaulted by athletes are their acquaintances.[16] Those few players who are inclined to violate women enjoy almost limitless opportunity to meet, and ultimately victimize, women. Using tactics similar to those employed by Billups, Mike Tyson exploited eighteen-year-old Desiree Washington's naiveté and lured her into his hotel en route to a night of dancing.

Greg Garrison, the special prosecutor who successfully prosecuted Mike Tyson for raping Washington, concluded that Tyson's violent tendencies toward women, like those of many other abusive athletes, were exacerbated by his sports career. "Professional athletics has become such a megagod that it is sometimes unresponsive to the morals of a community," said Garrison. "Sometimes it just doesn't matter what a superstar does, it's OK." This is a particularly dangerous scenario when men who are prone to violently abuse women get involved and are thrust into an environment where their contact with women increases.

"Athletes use their celebrity as their billyclub to gain the superior position [with women]," Garrison said. "Tyson knows he forced Desiree, but he doesn't care because that's what he does."

One NFL player who has seen the way Tyson interacts with women supported Garrison's position. "You can't imagine," said the player, on condition of anonymity. "I've been to social functions with him. He walks in there and goes, 'I've got to get some pussy, got to get some pussy.'

"Now, I've been around a lot of people, but nobody comes in there with the proudness that they're that macho that they can just . . . It's like a drink, an item, there's no feeling behind it. It's just something that he's got to physically conquer. He's a product of his environment."

Tyson developed a proclivity toward the abuse of women at a young age—a habit that mushroomed with his rise as a boxer. As a child he witnessed numerous incidents of violent abuse inflicted on his mother by boyfriends. As a young teen, Tyson demonstrated a disdain for young girls who repeatedly made fun of his high voice and chubby frame. After the renowned boxing trainer Cus D'Amato rescued Tyson from a life of violent street crime, handlers honed Tyson's exceptional strength and fury into a relentless fighting machine. They used his distrust and anger toward others to motivate him and elicit his aggression in the ring.

D'Amato once presented Tyson with a baseball bat, prompting Tyson to ask, "What's this for?"

"For the women," the trainer explained. "When you're the champion, you're going to need something to beat them off you."[17] Although tactics such as this were designed to strengthen Tyson's damaged ego, the message they conveyed bolstered an already dangerous attitude toward women.

A champion before his twentieth birthday, Tyson indulged in

countless sexual liaisons with women. Yet, his contempt for them only increased. He confessed to fellow fighter José Torres, "You know something, I like to hurt women when I make love, I like to hear them scream with pain, to see them bleed. It gives me pleasure."[18]

"Well, did it ever occur to you that men who behave that way probably hate women, that deep down they simply don't like them?" responded Torres.

"You may be right," said Tyson. "You're the first person to tell me that. You know, you may be [expletive] right."

Bitterly aware that women's interest in him was based solely on his high profile, Tyson nevertheless used that profile to his advantage in his quest to obtain sexual gratification and domination over women. Through repeated encounters with multiple women, often prostitutes or so-called groupies, Tyson developed an insatiable appetite for sex. In the twenty-four-hour period preceding his rape of Washington, Tyson participated in two separate sexual encounters in his hotel room.[19]

Garrison saw Tyson's training as a boxer as a lethal trigger mechanism that unleashed his disdain for women. When his sexual advances met with resistance, Tyson approached the unwilling woman much as he would an opponent in the ring. "The wife of every lawyer says, 'Don't get in an argument with them [their husbands] because they do it for a living. You may be right, but you'll never win,'" Garrison said. "When I debate with my wife or my kids, can I not listen with an inquisitive ear to everything that they say to find the logical flaw in their position and then seize it? Of course I can.

"What about a boxer? Boxers are masters of physical deception; at moving in one direction, but actually moving in another; at feigning left and going right; at appearing to be at a disadvantage when in fact they are poised to strike when somebody sees and is sucked into the apparent deception. Boxing is lying for a living. You don't not be a boxer when you leave the ring. What I wanted to do was show the jury that this guy will deceive because he's good at it."

Prior to being assaulted by Tyson, Washington saw nothing in her brief encounter with him that would alert her to his sexually violent tendencies. Not a boxing enthusiast, Washington's only familiarity with the fighter was that her father idolized him, and that he was a prominent role model in the black community. As an eighteen-year-old high school graduate who had been raised in a devoutly Christian home, Washington was impressed with Tyson when she met him at the Indianapolis Black Expo, where she was a contestant in a beauty pageant. Tyson was wearing a Together in Christ pin, and participated later alongside the Reverend Jesse Jackson in a public prayer. Although she was flattered when Tyson showed interest in her at the Expo, Desiree did not expect him to follow through with his invitation to take her and a roommate dancing later that evening. She was surprised when she was awakened at 1:30 A.M. by a phone call from Tyson, who was parked in his limousine outside her hotel. She testified that he said, "'Can you come out? We'll just go around. I just want to talk to you. Can you come out?'"[20]

In preparing to prosecute Tyson, Garrison and his associates interviewed numerous women from other parts of the county who claimed to be victims of Tyson's assaults. They had no knowledge of Washington's story, as her grand jury testimony had been sealed. Garrison's talks with them revealed a pattern to the boxer's tactics. "Our intelligence that we got in terms of how he had handled other women . . . was a recurring theme verbatim," said Garrison. "'I want to talk to you' and 'Come sit down beside me' and locking the door and the whole MO."

Voicing no objection to Tyson's request to stop by his hotel to pick up some things on the way to the nightclub, Washington accompanied him to his opulent suite. Onlookers expressed awe as the two walked through the hotel lobby. Elated to be accompanying a celebrity of such high regard, Washington's ebullience waned once inside Tyson's suite, where he displayed little interest in leaving the room. The cordial small talk he had made at the Expo and in the limousine soon turned to sexually suggestive dialogue. The abrupt change in Tyson's manner left Washington totally unprepared for what was to follow. "Desiree struggled real hard with, 'How could he be like that? He's Mike Tyson. My dad idolizes him,'" said Garrison.

When Washington showed no interest in his sexual advances and tried to flee, Tyson quickly moved to snatch off her clothes and overpowered her with brute force. Despite her pleas that he stop, Washington became the object of Tyson's unchecked sexual desires. "[Tyson's training as an athlete] certainly plays a role when you realize that any [professional] athlete is possessed of such incredible physical gifts," said Garrison. "Guys that get cut from [pro teams] are physical geniuses by comparison to the man on the street. And the players at the top of their profession? Could O. J. Simpson kill two people with the same knife? Of course he could, and neither one ever even know what hit them. You watched him run. How many guys did you see tackling air? Laundry all over the field. And these are men as good as him. He was quick as smoke. Tyson's the same way. He looks like he's going someplace else and bam! You're gone."

A subtle but important distinction is that athletics did not train Tyson to be a rapist; rather, his athletic training became a dangerous weapon in his misguided conception of what qualified as appropriate treatment of women.

"'If I want it, I get it' is the mentality that they've trained him to believe," said Garrison. "'If I want to knock you out, then you're going to be knocked out.' Unfortunately, it's persuasive in many of the wrong directions. The reason that Mike Tyson won't admit rape is not because he didn't do it or because he didn't think he did it, but because he didn't think there was anything wrong with it."

The disparaging attitudes toward women held by Billups and Tyson are consistent with those of the small number of athletes who are repeatedly associated with allegations of rape and battery. While there is no short-age of men who commit crimes of violence against women, few rapists and batterers combine exceptional physical superiority with an aura of public trust, as deviant athletes do. Within the confines of revenue-producing sports, men who are inclined to abuse women are left to inflict their abuse without punishment or the stigma usually attached to sex crimes and domestic battery.

3

easy prey

WHILE DENYING THAT ATHLETES ARE MORE LIKELY TO COMMIT SEX crimes, lawyers who defend players charged with sexual assault agree that athletes possess a distorted perception of women as a result of their repeated opportunities for consensual sex. "Women chase them [athletes]," said Brad Keller, the Seattle attorney who represented numerous members of the Cincinnati Bengals accused of rape. "If you are a healthy, red-blooded American male, you don't have the access that professionals do. It impacts their views of the sexes."

Heavyweight boxer Mike Tyson's defense attorney, Alan Dershowitz, concurred that the volume of consensual sex and multiple partners available to celebrity athletes not only twists their perceptions of women, but can increase their potential to assume that they have gained a woman's consent. Because of the number of sexual engagements some athletes enter into, Dershowitz suggested, there is an increased burden on women to express their intentions explicitly when alone with high-profile athletes. Referring to Desiree Washington, Dershowitz said, "In some respects she should have known that when you go to the room of an athlete at three o'clock in the morning, who is used to groupies, you better make it *very, very* clear that you are not a groupie."

There is little question that some men, including many celebrity athletes, expect little more from women than sexual gratification. Furthermore, it defies reason to deny that men whose experiences have conditioned them to view women merely as sexual prey are increasingly susceptible to violating sexual assault statutes that require restraint when sexual advances are met with rejection. That said, there is a tendency to examine only the athletes' behavior in cases of sexual violence.

On their way to developing a perception of all women as sexually compliant and indulgent, athletes encounter sexually compliant female partners on a recurring basis. "Women who indulge athletes have got to start participating in some of the blame," said Laurie Peterson, an attorney who has represented numerous victims who have been sexually abused by professional athletes—including one whose story is presented later in this chapter. "They know athletes disrespect them and have no interest beyond sexual gratification. By acting like it is an honor to be bedded by an athlete, these women are perpetuating the stereotype and endangering other women."

Critics and scholars alike are reluctant to point out the aggravating behavior of some women, which can exacerbate the derogatory attitudes held by athletes and increase the potential for assaults. The hesitancy to confront some women's contributions to the problem rests largely in a noble effort to avoid the all-too-common trend of blaming the victim. Yet by leaving unmentioned the exceptional amount of consensual sex afforded athletes by a unique group of women, these writers overlook one of the most powerful reinforcements of athletes' attitudes toward women.

Furthermore, a notable number of the women who enter random sexual relations with athletes later become victims of their criminal abuse. Assuming that their right to grant consent is protected by law, and should thus be respected without question, they typically become victims after first consenting to a degree of sexual activity. Take, for instance, Victoria Alexander's consent to sex with Lynn James, but not the other Bengals, discussed in Chapter 1. In theory, the law recognizes consent as a continuum. But in practice, when women pursue athletes for sexual purposes, they leave themselves little recourse in the event that they are violated. Perhaps more important, their willingness to oblige athletes feeds an animal-like mind-set that contributes to other women falling victim to unwanted sexually aggressive behavior. Furthermore, their actions furnish accused athletes and their lawyers with evidence that can be used to depict virtually all accusing women as groupies.

Addressing the questionable behavior of some women does not absolve the perpetrators of responsibility for violent crimes. But it does emphasize the problems associated with indiscriminate sex stemming solely from the male's celebrity status. Such behavior has a direct impact on the significant number of complaints brought by those rape victims who possess no sexual interest in an athlete, but unknowingly traverse the consent boundaries athletes have come to recognize.

On April 21, 1991, Linda Frenzel,* thirty-three years old, finished working the dinner shift at a downtown Minneapolis restaurant and headed home to prepare for a morning flight to Miami. With frost still on the ground in Minnesota, Frenzel and her best friend, Susan Lundquist, packed bathing suits, sun screen, beach towels, and nightclub

*For this chapter I relied heavily on interviews with a woman who spent more than a decade traveling and partying with athletes. Her true identity has been protected. Because of the risks associated with speaking candidly about the subject of this chapter, I have also protected the identities of the woman's daughter, her girlfriend, and an officer on the Miami police force.

attire in anticipation of three days on the Florida coast. "Me and my girlfriend do that probably twice a year, head down to Miami and just hang out at the beaches," said Frenzel. "We just love it down there. That's our vacation spot, so we go down there every year."

Frenzel's four-year-old daughter Marcie was too young to find Florida on a map, and she was content with the idea of staying with her grandmother for the weekend. In the car on the way to the airport, Frenzel said to Marcie, "I'm going to the ocean on a big airplane."

"Don't jump in the ocean 'cause there's sharks," Marcie responded.

It was not the first time that Marcie had accompanied her grandmother to the airport to wave good-bye to Mom. "She always knew that I was going on a plane because we would always take her with us and she got to say 'good-bye,'" said Frenzel. "She would watch when I came in, and she would always be there waiting for me when I got off the plane."

Frenzel's husband left her when Marcie was a baby. As a waitress, Frenzel could hardly afford to make semiannual trips to Florida, but her close friendship with Miami Dolphins player Kerry Glenn provided her a nearly expense-free weekend, as well as a place to stay. Frenzel had met Glenn while he was on a football scholarship at the University of Minnesota in the early 1980s. While dating one of Frenzel's girlfriends, Glenn had established a friendship with Frenzel that continued throughout his eight-year career in professional football. Like Frenzel, he had experienced a difficult divorce shortly after the birth of his first child. Glenn and Frenzel's similar experiences and interests fostered a lasting association that came to resemble a brother-sister relationship.

After arriving in Miami, Frenzel, Lundquist, and Glenn spent the day on the beach. That evening Glenn was scheduled to participate in a charity basketball game in Orlando. Planning to spend the night there and return to Miami the next morning, Glenn had arranged for the women to be entertained in his brief absence. "I don't want you girls to be alone in Miami," he said. "I have a good friend. I'm going to have you hang out with him for the day and night. He'll take you to the right places."

Glenn's good friend was Michael Barber, a detective on the Miami police force. After picking the women up at Glenn's house, Barber drove them back to his condominium. Inside the beach-front home, Frenzel immediately noticed that the walls and tabletops were decorated with photographs of star Dolphins receiver Mark Duper. One door bore a life-size poster of him wearing a cape, with a caption reading, "Super Duper."

"What are you doing with all of these pictures of Mark Duper?" Frenzel asked.

"Well, this is his place," Barber responded. "He rents it out to me. This is one of his many places."

"Really?" said Frenzel.

"Yes," Barber confirmed.

"Wow," said Frenzel. "Well, that's great. I'd like to meet him sometime."

Having followed the Dolphins since Glenn joined the team, Frenzel knew Duper was one of the most highly regarded wide receivers in football. But with her knowledge of Duper limited to the commentary of play-by-play announcers, she was unaware that he had been accused of rape in 1989, and that the National Football League had suspended him in 1988 for violating its substance-abuse policy. Furthermore, she was unfamiliar with a subsequent investigation by *Sports Illustrated*, which revealed that Miami police had linked Duper to notorious drug dealers as early as 1986.[1] A police search of the car of convicted drug dealer Timothy Taylor had turned up photographs of Duper with Nelson

Aguilar, a convicted cocaine trafficker serving thirteen and a half years in federal prison. Aguilar's driver, Robert Tipton, also imprisoned for drug trafficking, claimed to have transported briefcases of cocaine to one of Duper's condominiums in North Miami. Moreover, Ricky Arroyo, a driver for a limousine service owned by Duper—Super Duper Limo—had been arrested for cocaine trafficking. Following his arrest, Arroyo provided the Florida state attorney's office with an affidavit claiming that he had frequently supplied cocaine to Duper, beginning in 1987. Although Duper had not been charged with any crimes, his close friend Herman Williams had been arrested under suspicion of agreeing to buy more than $100,000 of cocaine from an undercover cop. And Duper's business partner, Eddie Purefoye, had been found guilty of carrying a concealed weapon.

As Frenzel and her friend sat in lawn chairs, sipping cocktails on the sun deck, Barber emerged through the sliding glass doors, cellular phone in hand. "Someone wants to say hello to you," said Barber, as he handed the phone to Frenzel.

Somewhat surprised, Frenzel took the phone and said hello. The voice on the other end was Mark Duper's. Based on Frenzel's off-the-cuff remark that she would like one day to meet Duper, Barber had paged him and notified him that there was an available woman at his condo. "Because of the mentality [of professional athletes]," Frenzel said later, " 'wants to meet you' meant 'she wants to go to bed with you.' " It was evident from Duper's telephone demeanor that he perceived Linda to be a party girl available for the night.

Before hanging up, Duper arranged for Frenzel, Lundquist, and Barber to go with him later that evening to one of his favorite Miami clubs. When Duper arrived to meet Frenzel, he boldly asked her to go to the club without underwear beneath her skirt. "It kind of blew me away when he started talking like that because he asked me to do that in our first meeting," said Frenzel. While denying his request, Frenzel nonetheless was not dissuaded from becoming Duper's date for the evening. "The allure is there," admitted Frenzel. "Athletes make a lot of money. There are little perks and you get all the good treatment." Besides, she reasoned, he couldn't be too crazy if he was a friend of Glenn's friend Barber, who was a cop. "That was just Duper's lifestyle: 'Let's go crazy,' extreme wildness, kinky stuff," Frenzel said.

Frenzel rode to the club with Duper in his shiny white Porsche while Lundquist and Barber followed in a separate car. When they arrived at the Facade, a glitzy Miami nightclub, a well-dressed parking attendant greeted Duper, opening the door for him, and parked the Porsche in a specially reserved spot. Once they were inside, the owner quickly spotted Duper, shouting, "Hey, Mark," as he motioned for them to approach.

"He treated us like kings," Frenzel said. The group was promptly escorted to the Champagne Room, a special VIP suite overlooking the club. They received Don Pérignon champagne and strawberries, along with all the hors d'oeuvres they wanted. Everything was on the house. "They treated him like a king wherever he went," Frenzel said. "We might as well have been walking with the president, total king treatment. You get off on that a little. It's funny, you go to places with an athlete and you get treated like you are gold because they are looked upon so highly."

Frenzel was quite familiar with the preferential treatment accorded to famous athletes. After graduating from high school, her first full-time job had been as a waitress and bartender at a Minneapolis hotel located near the airport. Visiting opponents of the Minnesota Twins, Vikings, and North Stars often stayed there. Her carefree attitude, combined with the fact that she was perfectly content sitting around a sports bar watching a ballgame with the guys, put her on a first-name basis with many

of the athletes. Over a fifteen-year period, Frenzel formed casual friend-
ships with many players, and even some coaches, whose teams passed
annually through Minnesota and stayed at the hotel. "Because of the
environment I was in, I met and knew a lot of them," Frenzel said. "It
was interesting. You see them on TV. You're interested in meeting the
person as well. I worked right next to the stadium, so it was fun. They'd
come back into town and they would remember me. They'd tip me well
and say, 'Hey, here's a couple tickets. Come to the game tonight.'"

As a result, Frenzel attended countless baseball, football, and
hockey games free of charge, a luxury that fed her interest in sports,
which she had acquired as a child vying for attention from her father.

Frenzel's father was an outdoorsman who spent a lot of time fish-
ing and hunting. Although not an avid team sports enthusiast, he would
spend his Sundays watching the Vikings games on television. Because
he spent so much time away from home on account of his job, Frenzel
took to watching football games as an avenue to her father. "I became
a sports fan back in the days when the Vikings were real good—Fran
Tarkenton, Chuck Foreman, Sammy White, Ahmad Rashad—their
glory years," said Frenzel. "I was watching the Super Bowl. The first
question I asked my dad was, 'What is a first down?' And then, 'What
does a down mean?'"

Mingling with athletes who frequented the hotel restaurant and
bar came naturally to Frenzel. "I was never what you would call a
groupie, going searching all around the hotels trying to meet athletes,"
she said. "I hate the word *groupie*. Because you have a social life with
a certain circle of people, you get labeled a groupie. I married someone
who is not an athlete, had a daughter by someone who is not an athlete,
and I know a ton of people who are not athletes. But because of where
I worked and who I met, I am considered a groupie.

"You hear people say, 'I'm attracted to people in uniform, or officers, or doctors.' Everyone's got their own attraction. From meeting the players, nice players that have always treated me very nice, I got into a situation where I knew and felt comfortable with athletes. *Groupie* is just a stupid word."

As Frenzel and Duper sat at a small private bar in the VIP suite, a cocktail waitress approached with drinks. While the waitress stood there holding a small tray, Duper ran his eyes from Frenzel to the waitress and then back to Frenzel. "He insinuated, 'What do you think? How about her and me and you in a threesome together?' " recalled Frenzel. "I looked at him and gave him a dirty look, saying, 'Don't even think about it.' When he started insinuating stuff like that, I would give him a dirty look and then he would know that I'm not going for that."

Over the years, Frenzel had met a wide range of athletes and had seen all forms of excessive behavior, including heavy drinking, exorbitant drug use, and out-of-control gambling. Group sex was just another notch on the continuum of self-indulgence. "Because they have everything, the money and fame and girls, it's almost like they need a little more," explained Frenzel. "They're not really ever satisfied. They need more excitement, some group sex or the craziness that goes along with other things they want to do."

Although she realized that Duper's actions toward her would shock and outrage most women, Frenzel had grown virtually immune to such gestures. With celebrity athletes, it just came with the territory. "The mentality is so unbelievable," conceded Frenzel. "Players put on a big facade for the public, but in their private lives they are totally different people. I keep saying there have to be athletes out there who don't mess around, but there aren't any." She had reached that conclusion years earlier after meeting a famous baseball player whom the public generally regards as the perfect gentleman. His team, the California Angels, was in town to play the Twins, and was staying at the Marriott. A no-name rookie on the Angels had become quite friendly with one of Frenzel's friends, whom he had met at the hotel bar. As Frenzel walked with her girlfriend and the rookie through the Marriott lobby, the team's star player happened to follow them onto the elevator. Both Frenzel and her friend were immediately introduced to him. Flashing his trademark smile, he quipped to his teammate, "If you need any help with that situation, call me."

As the elevator doors opened, Frenzel paused momentarily. "I kind of knew what that meant," she said, "but I thought maybe he was just being funny with his teammate." Minutes later, when she and her friend were inside the rookie's room, the telephone rang. It was the star they had just met, calling from his room down the hall.

"Well, which one are you with?" he asked his teammate. "Then send the other one down to my room."

Though the experience lowered Frenzel's expectation of athletes as models of propriety, it did little to discourage her from hanging around them. "A lot of men are like that, whether athletes or nonathletes," she said. "I guess you get conditioned to being around certain types of men." While there was a demeaning element to being the object of men's sexist notions, derogatory barbs from athletes were offset by unique rewards. "For everything that was bad [about athletes], there were many more things that were good," insisted Frenzel. "Being able to go to the Super Bowl because of being friends with a player, or being able to get into exclusive clubs where you wouldn't be able to get in if you weren't with these guys. Being flown somewhere, which is kind of exciting—if there's no strings attached, why not? If you love sports, being able to go to games and getting the best seats." These perks, combined with a genuine feeling of acceptance in the presence of players, solidified a comfort zone for Frenzel. Players came to be more than distant television figures. Rather, they were part of a nationwide network of acquaintances.

Suddenly the owner of the nightclub entered the private suite where Frenzel and Duper were hanging out. He brought a small group of elite-looking tourists who were visiting from Canada. The owner wanted them to meet Duper, hoping that he would honor them with some autographs and pose for a few pictures. As the small group shook Duper's hand, he put his other arm around Frenzel and said, "I want you to meet my wife."

Unaware that Duper was married, Frenzel suddenly felt very cheap. Reluctantly, she posed for some photographs with the visitors. "It didn't phase him," said Frenzel. "He didn't even think that it might bother me." As the visiting party left the suite, she imagined herself being described as Duper's lovely wife by tourists proudly displaying their photographs of an encounter with a famous American athlete.

The drinking and partying continued until early morning. Duper finally decided that it was time to head out. Although both he and Barber had been belting down booze all night, neither showed any hesitation in driving home. There were very few cars on the road, so once he got on the freeway Duper quickly pushed his Porsche up to ninety miles per hour. Slightly nervous, and having had a few too many drinks herself, Frenzel said little as the warm wind sailed in through the side window, blowing her hair into her eyes. "The outside person would think it's really wild or risky or even exciting," Frenzel said. But the next day, while she and Lundquist were lying on the beach, she looked back on the ride home with relief. Considering the impact a motor vehicle death would have had on her family, she said to Lundquist, "Oh great. That's all I need. Here I am going on a little vacation and my mom picks up the headlines and reads, 'Mark Duper and woman from

Minnesota killed on highway going 90 miles per hour.' Wow. That was really wild of me to do that."

After Glenn's return from Orlando that afternoon, Frenzel did not see Duper again that weekend. But he proceeded to call her off and on for months thereafter. She saw him two more times, including once in Chicago when he flew her there for the weekend when the Dolphins played the Bears. Then in 1994, having neither seen nor talked to Duper in two years, Frenzel read in a Minneapolis newspaper that he had been arrested in connection with an alleged scheme to buy cocaine in Miami, convert it to crack, and sell it in his home state of Louisiana.[2]

Reading about Duper's arrest, Frenzel thought back to the day she first met him and their trip to the Facade. "It seemed like everybody in that whole place, in that little area we were at, was doing drugs," said Frenzel. "It was a wild, fast-type pace, but I never actually saw him use drugs. He never displayed any drugs in my presence."

Although aware of the risks of hanging around with celebrated entertainers who have deviant lifestyles, Frenzel had developed a high tolerance level for such situations. Relying largely on her sense of judgment, Frenzel fully trusted her ability to determine which athletes were safe to go off alone with. Having managed to mingle with Duper and emerge unscathed, she decided to refrain from any further contact with him.

Duper faced a potential ten-year prison term and a $4 million fine, but his attorneys argued successfully that he had been entrapped, and was suffering from a serious cocaine addiction. On March 15, 1995, a federal jury acquitted him.

"I know it's a disease and a disease that can take on and destroy your life," Duper said as he emerged triumphantly from the federal courthouse in Miami. When a reporter asked him what he was going to do next, Duper grinned and replied, "Disney World."[3]

With her daughter Marcie approaching her seventh birthday, Frenzel was growing dissatisfied with her income as a waitress. Hoping to increase what she could provide for Marcie, she began to pursue a career change. "I live in a nice apartment. I'm not rich or poor. I drive a nice car," Frenzel said. "I was able to give my daughter a nice situation, but I wanted to raise my income. I wanted to think about getting a town house. I thought, there is no way to up my income in order to do something like that."

With fifteen years of waitressing experience and no college education, Frenzel thought her options were limited to exotic dancing. "I thought I would try dancing," she said. "A couple of friends had done it and said there was nothing wrong with it. You can go dance and make in a night what the average person can make in a week. On a weekend night you can walk out of there with five, six, seven hundred bucks."

Shifts at the adult nightclub were long and arduous, often starting at 4:00 in the afternoon and running until 11:00, with a second shift continuing until 3:00 in the morning. "Every now and then you get the ones who are into drugs and prostitution on the side, but generally speaking, most of them have husbands or boyfriends," said Frenzel. "They do it, go home, and it's a job."

For the first eight months of 1995, Frenzel danced a few nights a week while continuing to wait on tables. Accustomed to looking at faceless men in the smoky room, she ignored the jeers and gestures while clinging to a strand of dignity. "Maybe it's not the best profession," conceded Frenzel, "but it is legal. My goal was to be able to put the money away and buy a town house."

When the summer of 1995 drew to a close, Frenzel had managed to put away nearly $8,000. The NFL training camps were due to open, and Linda looked forward to taking a break from her work to renew what had become a ritual—a road trip to Wisconsin, where the New Orleans Saints held their annual summer practice. From previous summer camps, Linda was on a first-name basis with some veteran Saints players. She had slept with one player numerous times, and had gone drinking and dancing with many of them after practice sessions. "When they [the Saints] came into town, players would call me up," said Frenzel. " 'We're in town,' they would say. 'We want to give you tickets.' Maybe in their minds it was a sex-for-tickets swap, but it was never brought up to me that way. If it happened, it happened. If it didn't, it didn't. They were friends and they're still gonna give you tickets. They're in a visiting town and they want people they know to come and see them play."

The Saints were housed in Sanford Hall on the University of Wisconsin campus in La Crosse, a college town that was virtually deserted in August. On Saturday, August 5, following the team's thirteenth consecutive practice day, players were given Sunday off. Frenzel and a friend arrived in La Crosse at 5:00 in the afternoon, checked into a motel, and went to grab a quick bite to eat. Although many of the players whom Frenzel had come to know over the years had been traded during the off season, Tyrone Hughes was still on the team. Frenzel and her friend met up with Hughes at a bar where many Saints players congregated. While they were there, Saints rookie Willie Lee Williams asked Frenzel to dance, and invited her to a party at the dormitory after the bar closed at 2 A.M.

Frenzel's friend declined to go to the dorm, opting to return to the motel. Frenzel rode from the bar to the dorm with three players, two of whom she had known for less than three hours. "I knew the dorm," she said. "I knew the outline. I knew it was guarded and we had to be quiet. I'd been there with one player many times before. I knew my friends from previous years would be around [although not in the same room].

Even if the worst guy on the team was to be a real jerk and say, 'I don't care. I'm going to get some because she's easy,' the other guys would intervene and say, 'No.'"

Although Frenzel and Williams had not discussed sex openly, she was no stranger to the routine expectations of professional athletes. "I'm not saying that I wasn't thinking in my mind that I was going to be with him," said Frenzel. "I'm saying that if sex happened with him, that's my choice. If the other players thought they were going to get in on the action, I wouldn't be surprised, but it would just be a matter of me saying, 'No way, José. I'm not down for that. No.'"

After spending some time in the dorm, Frenzel and Williams retired to his room. "I'm not protected," said Frenzel. "I'm not on the pill."

"Ahh," said Williams, as he paused and grinned uncomfortably at her.

"Birth control," Frenzel added, in an attempt to drive the point home.

Williams pulled out a condom and reluctantly agreed to wear it. "He wasn't thrilled about it, but he wore one," Frenzel said.

Although there had been occasions when Frenzel had chosen to engage in sex with an athlete who wasn't wearing a condom, she generally insisted on one. "I'm not going to say that I have never had sex without a condom, but my general thing is 'yes,' especially because I know how much they do get around," said Frenzel. "And most athletes do not use condoms. If I meet a guy and I date him for quite a while and it's totally just him and me, then I could slack on that [condom usage]."

Following her encounter with Williams, Frenzel was startled by the sudden approach from behind by another player, who was completely undressed. "It was bad judgment on my part to think that these guys were going to be as cool as the guys on the team whom I already knew," said Frenzel. "I let my guard down."

The second player who had climbed into bed with her was the same one who had driven from the bar with her and Williams. "What the hell do you think you're doing?" demanded Frenzel.

"Oh, c'mon, what's the problem?" asked the second player. "Go with it."[4]

Williams was laughing as Frenzel reached for her clothes and tried to dress. Suddenly, a third player entered the room fully nude. He pushed Frenzel back down on the bed and started jabbing his penis into her anus. She began screaming as he straddled her from behind.

"Shut up, bitch," said the third player.

Standing by watching, Williams said, "Oh, don't worry about him [the third player], he's just my 'cuz.'"[5]

According to Frenzel, before she managed to escape the dorm, numerous players, some of them quite intoxicated, had sexually assaulted her. One player blocked her attempt to exit the room, and when she insisted on using the bathroom in the hallway, the players demanded that she use a wastebasket, for fear of someone seeing her in the building. After urinating in the room, Frenzel desperately threw a beer can, then a chair, against the window, which awakened the others in the dorm. Worried that security personnel might enter the room, the players allowed her to leave. As she ran frantically out of the first-floor stairwell entrance, Frenzel ran into a young woman who had exited the dorm moments earlier, after spending the evening on another floor.

"Can I help you? Can I help you? What happened?" the woman asked her.

Suddenly, a patrol car pulled up, and the blond-haired woman motioned for it to stop. Officer Robert Lawrence got out of the vehicle and approached the two women. Noticing that Frenzel was quite upset and crying, he said, "Settle down, settle down. Give me a little bit of an idea of what happened. Give me an idea of what we're dealing with here."

Frenzel said she had been raped by some Saints players in the dorm. "I don't know what to do. I don't know what to do," she repeated. She wanted to get up from the curb and walk away, but the officer persisted.

The other woman stated that she had heard screaming coming from the second floor, and had seen Frenzel pounding against one of the windows.

Asking Frenzel if she wanted to press charges, Lawrence sensed some hesitancy on her part. "You probably should do the right thing," he said.

Although she wanted no part of a police investigation, Frenzel was somehow encouraged by his gentle persuasion. "He was like a person of authority," she said. "If I hadn't run into him, I would have chalked it up as just a really horrible experience. I didn't want people finding out and going through the whole mess with the law."

After being driven to the St. Francis Medical Center for an examination, Frenzel was questioned by a detective. She was asked, "Are you a prostitute? Have you ever been arrested for prostitution? Did you ask for money for sex from these guys? What kind of education do you have?" Suddenly, she was having to answer for a lifetime of decisions that in her mind had no relation to what she had just experienced.

Meanwhile, police arrived at the dorm and began to question the players. They began with the player with whom Linda admitted having had consensual sex. Police searched his room and spotted, among other things, a pair of women's panties. Before police confiscated them for evidence, the player rummaged around where they had been lying and then asked for permission to step out in the hall and use the bathroom.

Noticing that the underwear was missing, police confronted the player and found he had hid the underwear in his pants pocket.

The prosecutor's office joined the investigation, and ultimately interviewed thirty players. District Attorney Ron Kind, a former quarterback at Harvard University, was given the responsibility of sorting out the facts. "As in most cases involving sexual assault allegations, the respective credibility of the alleged victim and her assailant is always carefully weighed," said Kind. "Given the information we have collected during the course of the investigation, I believe that the credibility of the woman who reported the assaults would be insufficient to convince a jury beyond a reasonable doubt that the sexual contact she had with numerous Saints players was not consensual."[6]

The prosecutor's decision did not surprise Frenzel, nor did it upset her greatly. But the public defamation of her character in the press while the criminal case was under consideration bruised her deeply. "I've been a dancer for eight months out of my life," said Frenzel. "I'm thirty-eight years old. I worked in a hotel for fifteen years. I have a little girl. I've never been in any trouble with the law. I don't do drugs. I don't have a criminal record and I'm pretty much a straight-and-narrow type person. I happen to know some famous people and socialize with them."

The incident in La Crosse made Frenzel reassess her attitude toward athletes. In its aftermath, she withdrew from any social involvement with them. "I always used to tell people, 'I feel safe with athletes,'" said Frenzel. "'Even though some of them could be rude or crazy, and some are into things that I'm not [such as drugs], I'll never get raped or attacked or killed.'" Because she considered anything short of rape or murder "safe," and because she had been a nude dancer for eight months of her thirty-eight years, when a group of professional football players forced themselves on Frenzel, the prosecutor felt he could not bring them to justice.

Because of the complicity of women like Frenzel, athletes' distorted perceptions of women are reinforced, and the concept of consent has been trivialized. As a result, legitimate rape claims are difficult to prosecute—a fact that athletes understand and use to their advantage. Frenzel and other women who pursue social relations with athletes are seen as easy prey by players and as poor prosecution witnesses by lawyers.

4

out of bounds

Let's face it, athletes are whores. We're paid to use our bodies. So sex becomes the same thing after the game. We become like dogs sometimes.[1]

— Eddie Johnson, NBA player

ON MARCH 4, 1996, DALLAS POLICE RESPONDED TO A PHONE CALL FROM a Residence Inn manager who suspected prostitution was taking place in one of the rooms at the hotel. Arriving at the scene, police officers knocked on the door of the room in question and were greeted by twenty-one-year-old topless dancer Angela Beck and the strong odor of marijuana. On entering the room, police discovered twenty-two-year-old Nasmine Nabwangu, also a topless dancer, and two members of the famed Dallas Cowboys, including the flamboyant superstar Michael Irvin. In searching the room, the officers recovered ten grams of cocaine, two grams of marijuana, and various objects used for sexual stimulation.

Beck, Nabwangu, and Irvin were indicted on drug possession charges. But Irvin's trial was abruptly halted following the court appearance of twenty-four-year-old Rachelle Smith, a third topless dancer and an associate of Beck and Nabwangu. Prosecutors had granted Smith immunity in exchange for her testimony about the three women's relationship with Irvin.

Smith testified that she, Beck, and Irvin had spent three successive Monday evenings in February at the Residence Inn, smoking marijuana laced with cocaine and engaging in group sex. According to Smith, she and Beck would reserve a hotel room, and Irvin would show up with the cocaine and marijuana. Smith added that she had flown with Irvin to New Jersey to meet other Cowboys, and that she and Beck had slept at Irvin's Dallas home. When asked by prosecutor Mike Gillett if there had been any sexual activity on the evening of February 12—one of the nights Smith had alleged being in the hotel with Beck and Irvin—Smith responded, "Yes."[2]

"Did this involve all three of you?" Gillett asked.

"Yes," said Smith.

Under cross-examination by Irvin's attorney, Don Godwin, Smith conceded to engaging in lesbian sex with Beck, but denied having sex with Irvin. Before testimony could be offered to clarify the trio's sexual relations, court adjourned for the day. The following day, July 13, Irvin pleaded guilty to the drug charges he had been vehemently denying, cutting off any further exposure of his nightlife.

Although the Irvin case centered on illegal drugs, it opened a window on the sordid sexual terrain at the pinnacle of sports celebrity. As an athlete's status rises, his behavioral license expands, and opportunities for deviant conduct increase—nowhere more abundantly than in the area of sexual promiscuity. In a culture in which women are often reduced to sexual prey, self-gratifying deviance easily spills over into criminal abuse, only to be dismissed by the athlete-perpetrators as mere incidental contact.

The Irvin incident occurred less than one year after his teammate

Erik Williams, another millionaire star, was charged with sexually assaulting a seventeen-year-old topless dancer in his home. Williams, who along with a male friend had taken the juvenile to his home for sexual purposes, was accused of confining her against her will when she attempted to leave. When police arrived at his mansion in response to the girl's telephoned plea for help, Williams assured the officers no girl was being detained in his home. After a search failed to cast doubt on his claim, police were preparing to drive off when they noticed the girl peering out of an upstairs window. Williams was charged with kidnapping and sexual assault, but a grand jury later declined to indict him after he agreed to pay the teenager an undisclosed amount of money as part of an out-of-court settlement.

The association of members of "America's Team" with illegal drugs, prostitution, and charges of sexual assault begs for an explanation. Yet the circumstances surrounding the arrests of Irvin and Williams are consistent with the growing trend toward illicit sexual behavior among highly regarded athletes. In any attempt to explain the growing number of athletes who are reported for abusing women, the natural starting point is their eccentric social environment, which spawns numerous opportunities for players to deviate from traditional sexual mores. The temptation to indulge becomes acute for players who are routinely relieved of responsibility by their coaches and agents, while simultaneously being lauded and rewarded for doing what they desire most—to play ball. Moreover, the unnatural wealth suddenly lavished on players further insulates them from established behavioral norms.

On learning of Irvin's arrest, the Dallas Cowboys personnel director, Gil Brandt, was perplexed by the apparent absence of any past conduct by Irvin that would have indicated a potential for criminal behavior. Six years earlier, Brandt had investigated Irvin's reputation at the University of Miami, and had encouraged the Cowboys to draft him. "We did as thorough a check on Irvin's background as you could possibly do," Brandt told *Boston Globe* columnist Will McDonough. "We checked with everyone when he was at Miami and the answer was the same. No problem. But the same thing happened with [former Dallas Cowboy players] Harvey Martin [arrested for drug charges and multiple assaults against a woman] and Duane Thomas [arrested for drug use] and Hollywood Henderson [convicted of illegal drug use and rape]. Great kids when they were in college, and then, for some reason, it all changes."[3]

To the contrary, membership in the professional ranks does not suddenly transform "great kids" into criminals. It merely provides a bigger stage, with higher drop-offs, for those inclined to indulge in illicit behavior. Despite countless college sports scandals—recruiting violations, grade fixing, illegal payments to players, and steroid use— many of the criminal violations by college athletes, particularly sex crimes and physical assaults, go unreported to police or the press. A study of campus police records and internal judicial affairs documents from thirty NCAA Division 1 institutions with basketball and football teams that perennially finish among the top twenty revealed that in general, crimes against women were far less likely than others to be reported to police—particularly when the perpetrator was an athlete.[4] For example, campus police data revealed that student-athletes were reported for acts of domestic violence and rape at a rate equivalent to the rest of the male student body, while internal judicial affairs data— which are not released to the police or press—revealed that they represented 19 percent of the reported perpetrators of sexual assault, though they composed just three percent of the student population. Press reports of college athletes' violence against women, which are overwhelmingly reliant on formal complaints, merely scratch the surface, revealing only those rare instances in which a victim files an official complaint with the police.

In sum, by the time the athletically gifted make the transition from college to professional sports, they have been conditioned, through a gradual reduction in accountability and social standards, to behave without fear of the consequences.

Anthony Jamison* is black and was raised in a single-parent home in a crime-infested section of a large East Coast city. In March 1994 he completed his fourth year of college basketball at a Division 1 institution in the eastern United States. At age twenty-three, after failing to be selected in the National Basketball Association's annual draft, he received an offer to play in the NBA's summer league. Jamison, who has now graduated from college and has fathered his first child, is still pursuing a career in professional basketball.

Kevin McDonald is white and was raised in an affluent suburb by well-educated parents, both of whom held full-time jobs. After a prestigious college basketball career, he was drafted by an NBA team and went on to enjoy a successful professional career. At age forty-four he earns a lucrative income conducting basketball camps, and remains associated with the league.

At their request, the identities of both men have been concealed through fictitious names; neither their places of residence nor the institutions and teams they played for have been revealed.

*The basis for most of this chapter is the experience of two male basketball players, one a college player attempting to turn pro, the other a recently retired NBA player. I interviewed both men at length. Their names have been changed to protect their identities.

Los Angeles, July 1994, the ASICS Southern California summer pro league:

As the pilot's voice sounded through the cabin, announcing the plane's approach to Los Angeles International Airport, Anthony Jamison stuffed his *USA Today* sports section into his gym bag, then shoved the bag under the seat in front of him. Adjusting the headphones on his Walkman, he glanced at the sun-drenched city below, recalling his first flight to Los Angeles following his senior year in high school. The Junior Olympics were being held in Long Beach that year, and Jamison had been chosen to participate before beginning his college basketball career. Despite having traveled all over the United States during his four years in college basketball, Jamison had never made it back to LA. Now he was there once more, hoping to catch the eye of a professional coach or scout.

Walking through the airport, Jamison convinced himself he was on the verge of the big break he so badly needed. With his final year of college ball behind him, and plans to marry his longtime girlfriend in the works, Jamison had dropped out of school temporarily and begun working full time. After failing to be selected in the draft in June 1994, he stood little chance of making the NBA. Nonetheless, he had received an encouraging phone call later that month from the director of Southern California's summer pro league. Sanctioned by both the NBA and the Players Association, the twenty-five-year-old summer league had gained a reputation for bringing together some of the world's finest players to showcase their skills for three weeks before coaches and scouts from the NBA, the Continental Basketball Association, and the European professional leagues. His highly productive college career had led to Jamison's being offered one of the coveted roster spots on a summer league team. In addition to receiving great exposure playing alongside high-profile players, he would be reunited with many friends he had competed with and against during college.

As he climbed into the back seat of a taxi, Jamison glanced at the tabloid left behind by a previous passenger. With O. J. Simpson in jail, awaiting trial for the murder of his wife and her friend, chilling 911 tape transcripts and photographs of Nicole's bruised face dominated the front page. "Everyone on that God-level gets brought down," Jamison thought as he told the driver he needed to go to the Radisson Hotel in Irvine. The moment the cab pulled into the hotel parking lot, a bellboy approached to take Jamison's bags. With players from all over the country checking in for a three-week stay, the hotel staff was out in full force. Fans, too, milled around the lobby entrance, in hopes of meeting the stars. A royal welcome awaited any man who stood over six feet tall. "You're no longer in the lower class," Jamison observed. "All of a sudden you're gettin' looked at."

The accommodations at the Radisson quickly relieved the pressure Jamison was feeling to secure an offer from a pro team. The league had spared no expense in assuring that players would enjoy their stay. "We were spoiled for a whole month," said Jamison. "It was unreal the things that went on. Poolside . . . it was crazy. Basically, it was fantasy."

Making his way to the reservation desk, Jamison made eye contact with a woman. As she struck up a conversation with him, his mind wandered back to the road trips he had taken in college, and the women he used to meet. "Most of the time you prepare for the game, but at night it's out and open. A lot of people want to see what they can get. Certain types of women that you see come up and want to talk to you. They know you play ball and they get into it. All the truth, we're out of town for a couple of days at a time. What other intentions are there? We're not trying to get a relationship going in most cases unless you find that special woman in that forty-eight hours."

The woman followed Jamison to the elevator and asked his name and room number. Introducing himself by his first name only, he decided not to reveal which room he was staying in. As the elevator door was closing, the woman assured him she would be around later. "If you stood over six-foot-two or six-foot-three, you were pretty set," Jamison said. "It was like picking apples out of a barrel. Pick which girl you want, which one was the ripest. It had to be four-to-one odds on women to men."

Though he had yet to don a uniform, Jamison had graduated from college to the pros. "A lot of things happened [at the Radisson]," he said. "It was drama. 'What can you do? What can you get away with?' "

The crop of players that left college that June with Jamison included top prospects Glenn Robinson, Jason Kidd, Grant Hill, and Juwan Howard. Although none of them were in the summer league, numerous other first-round draft choices were. The public spotlight these players attracted required a certain outward appearance of all the league participants. Yet Jamison was careful not to let his public demeanor compromise his on-court legitimacy in the eyes of the players against whom he would compete. "You're trying to be two different people," Jamison explained. "You want to be upstanding, but then you want to be hard. I came from the streets. I have street in me, but I have the knowledge of being able to go out and present myself in a well-mannered way in which I won't be considering myself a sellout."

Just hours away from taking the court with members of the Los Angeles Lakers, the Phoenix Suns, and other NBA teams, Jamison was unable to sleep that first night. The following morning he rose early, stopped quickly at the hotel's lavish breakfast buffet, then made his way to the University of California at Irvine. He was accompanied by a small group of rookie free agents like himself, all seeking job offers.

Jamison had no trouble picking out the rookies who had just been drafted in June. Their brash confidence conveyed the newfound freedom that comes with a pro contract. "They know that the name they have and the money that they're making [allows them to] do anything they want," explained Jamison. "They feel that they don't owe anybody anything because they got to this place all by themselves. Now they can carry themselves the way they want to carry."

As the first day's games got under way, Jamison felt lost in a sea of star players putting on an exhibition for the coaches and fans. By the time his game ended that evening, he was physically exhausted, content to write the day off as a transition. On returning to the hotel, he checked for messages at the front desk and discovered that the woman he had met the previous day had left a note. She was hoping to meet him in the lounge. Meanwhile, a small group of women who had watched his game had made their way back to the hotel—a practice that continued throughout his stay.

With games scheduled every other day, and two-hour practices on off-days, players had abundant time to take advantage of the carnival atmosphere. Some reveled in their status among the starstruck women. "They say, 'Damn, I have so much control,'" Jamison explained. "'I can get this girl to do this, I can get that girl to do that for me and not even care about waking up and having any headaches.' They have total control over their own lives."

Although they were not bona fide NBA players, Jamison and others like him nonetheless received the same celebrity treatment accorded the others. Players who were not likely to receive a contract offer from a pro club at the conclusion of the league made the most of their stay in LA. "A guy might try and feed a woman a whole bunch of lies," explained Jamison. "'Yeah, I'm going to stay in touch.' But basically, the player only stays in touch if he comes back out there to that state again or if he lands a job out there. Then he'll stay in touch with her until he can find somebody else. That's how the cycle goes."

Jamison's room was next door to that of one of the more prominent players chosen in the recent draft. Aware that the player had been married a week before the summer league started, Jamison was quite surprised to find that the new bride was staying in the hotel. "I thought that had to be pretty tough, because it seemed like he didn't even have a honeymoon," said Jamison.

Over the course of the next few days, Jamison noticed that the women who exited the room were different each night. "Mmm, I guess it has to be good being in the NBA," he thought. The millionaire player had not brought his new bride after all. "The women just kept coming and coming," Jamison explained. "It was crazy. They didn't care that he had a [marriage] relationship going."

The routine taking place next door to Jamison's room was nothing new to former NBA player and current coach Kevin McDonald. "A lot of players get married young, maybe twenty, twenty-one, or twenty-two," he explained. "They're in this atmosphere or environment where women are present all the time. A lot of times the wives put up with it. The attitude is, 'I know he may be sleeping with these prostitutes, with people who are less than women, but as long as he's a good husband, doesn't beat me, and brings me a huge paycheck, I'll live with it.'"

Having married since his retirement from the NBA, McDonald had settled into a more traditional lifestyle. Although basketball was still a central part of his life, he had little desire to return to his days as a player. "It's a different [kind of] fidelity," he said, as he mused over the marriages he had watched his teammates struggle through. "If you think of matrimony [as] being holier-than-thou and a sacred institution, it sounds awfully prosaic. But it's there and it's been there. It's something I never wanted to deal with, which is probably why I said I would never marry while I was doing it."

As Jamison pondered his own upcoming wedding, he conceded the difficulty of remaining faithful amid teammates who were taking advantage of carefree sex. "If I was going out of town," he reasoned, "and there were women just flocking on me or whatever and . . . boom! I know I have a woman at home, but I won't see her for a couple of days. And it's not like I can't wait, but it's the fact of immaturity just among the fellas and the pressure. A lot of guys that get out there sometimes don't want to get involved with that, but they're associated with trying to be like everyone else. It's the in thing, the fad thing to do."

Insisting that professional athletics left little room to nurture spousal relations, McDonald maintained that delaying starting a family was appropriate. "When you're a pro athlete, you're just so obsessed and subsumed in your lifestyle that it's very, very tough to maintain a relationship," he insisted. "I just did not think it was the proper lifestyle to get married in. There's a better balance in the mainstream nine-to-five life, with a wife and potentially children there."

By the end of his first week in Los Angeles, Jamison's game had improved consistently. One of the highlights came when his team confronted a team organized by Laker legend Magic Johnson. Playing before five thousand fans, Jamison gave one of his most productive performances. Afterward he was invited with all the other players to a huge reception thrown by the league. Social events were standard procedure for league participants. "When we had parties there were groupie girls," explained Jamison. "They will get out at night [with a player] and then they'll see him again [the next day] and they feel that they have some type of relationship going. But they don't have a relationship. It was just a one-night stand. 'You did something for me—I be gone. I'm going to have to move on.' That's how it is. There's no love behind it. It doesn't mean anything."

Elaborate parties offered the easiest way to arrange sexual encounters. "The opportunities were always there," McDonald recalled.

"Women want to meet you and form relationships with you. Women are handing over their bodies to me. It's mine for the taking. They're there, why not? So you have the mentality of, 'Hey, it's not like I went out and roped her or grabbed her. She just presented herself on my lap, that's what I'm doing.' That's sort of thinking with your loins, not thinking with your brains, but sports, professional and otherwise, is terminal adolescence."

Although he had been raised in a home where promiscuity was sternly frowned upon, McDonald found that the constant presence of casual sex overwhelmed his traditional upbringing. "Hanging around too many locker rooms with too many overheated adolescent men, I started talking like your average normal jock," conceded McDonald. "I was single. I had my fun, but I didn't go overboard and I recognized it for what it was."

As he waited for two teammates who were going with him to the ballroom, Jamison surveyed the scene in the lobby. "There wasn't a day or night that it wasn't close to fifty women down there in the lobby, just waiting to see us come out," he observed. "A lot of the times the players are successful because the women leave themselves so out in the open, and they're easy targets because they just allow themselves to be targets."

Jamison was embarrassed by one player, who in the presence of other players and women referred to the woman holding his arm as his "piece" for the night. The woman merely laughed it off and followed him out of the room. "There's tons and tons of good women, but there's a lot of women out there that just aren't worth Jack," said Jamison. "It's a shame that it just brings down all the other women. But from an athletic standpoint, we're going to take what they give. And what they don't give we'll get from someone else that's willing to give."

Sipping a cocktail and noting which women were already spoken for, Jamison knew that the following day he would hear boasting about who scored the quickest and most often—not on the basketball court, but with the women. "It's a bragging tool," he explained. "It's just a fact, I think a man thing, machismo. Like, how-many-girls-can-I-get-type figures. It's like a fraternity amongst men."

Secluded in a world of playing and partying, many players relied on body language to communicate with the opposite sex. Women who attended the parties thrown by the league were seen as advertising their availability. "They know what's involved," Jamison insisted. "They know what's going down. It's not like you're seeing these women at church or in the supermarket or whatever. Those are not spots where you will catch a typical athlete. No disrespect to religious beliefs or shopping for food, but shopping is something that you really don't have to do because everything is basically handed to us. Most of the spots you see women are at nightclubs or some type of sporting event or social event."

In the few years since McDonald retired, he has observed the increasing opportunity for crossed signals in this environment. "Given the judgment and perspective young players lack, and given the pampered life of these kids, because they've essentially been on scholarship for the last seven or eight years, even if they get to the pros at twenty-one, would they even understand if a woman was trying to be a friend to them?" McDonald asked. "So much of their lives, 100 percent of it, is wrapped up in 'me,' which is all that sports is as an athlete. 'How's it affecting me? What can I do to make me better or get me this?' These [players] who are sleeping around or who have the women thrown at them, I'm not sure if they could form a platonic relationship. I don't even know what they would do, if they could even understand or comprehend if a woman was trying to be a friend to them."

Jamison shook his head as one of the players staying on his floor headed to the elevator with a woman he had met earlier in the day. "Most of the time it's going to be a sexual thing," he insisted. "It's not a thing where they're going to fall in love. Most guys that go up there are either married, about to get married, or have a steady girlfriend."

The players just out of college most often went to the extreme in their exploitation of the environment. "The only thing they care about is what's going to satisfy them for the next time," Jamison said. "'Who am I going to get next?' Like they're going to commit a murder. 'Who am I going to get this time? Will it be this one? Do I want a short one, tall one, black one, white one, or Chinese?' It doesn't make a difference. Whatever's clever. Depends on the mood. That's how the mentality is."

The devil-may-care approach to women extends to their reckless disregard for sexual habits. "So many athletes have unprotected sex," claimed Jamison. "That Magic Johnson episode [the announcement that he had contracted HIV] doesn't mean anything. That was just irrelevant. Even at the college level, you'd be surprised how many athletes have unprotected sex. It's like they roll the dice, playin' craps."

McDonald confirmed Jamison's statement. "These groupies are sleeping around with several players," he said. "Who knows who's catching what from whom? And it's in every city. There's a cadre of women, catch them all as they come in—sleeping around with half the NBA."

Jamison noted, however, that not all players at the Radisson had a revolving-door policy toward women. "A lot of the guys are uplifting and good citizens that just don't indulge in [frequent sex]," he explained. "They have [participated to some degree], but they just realize that the cons outweigh the pros.

"The majority of it has to do with upbringing, the moral standpoints of what your parents and family members implanted in your life. If your parents brought you up with respect for other people's feelings and beliefs, you'd be able to incorporate that. But a lot of the guys don't have an upbringing that's stable and they end up gettin' into that lifestyle. They didn't have the foundation at home, but they were so gifted that they just moved on and became a great athlete . . . became someone."

Unfortunately, the players most vulnerable to the intoxicating excesses of celebrity athletics are also the most immune to any sense of wrongdoing or responsibility. "I'm not sure, given the opportunities, that these players who want to partake in voluminous sex, one-night stands, can tell the difference [between force and consent] anymore," said McDonald. "Especially if it's happened so much and they've been doing it since they've been sixteen years old. How would you know? If you've been to bed with so many, can you clearly define what you think is consent or what someone else thinks is rape? It just becomes so natural and happenstance to you."

After the final party thrown by the league, a woman came forward and claimed she had been abused. Her allegations involved an NBA player whom Jamison had seen with the woman during the party. "The only thing women are doing at these functions is getting a one-night stand, or they might get abused or assaulted," he reacted.

Yet he remained convinced that determining a woman's wishes took little effort on the part of players. "If you see any type of disfigure or discomfort out of a woman, you've got to know something's wrong," he said. "You don't continue to keep doing it. This is your upbringing. You are just supposed to know when to say when. A lot of guys get carried away. '[Expletive] what they think' or 'the hell with how they feel. Do you know who I am? My name is such and such.' They think they're on that God level. Assaults shouldn't happen, but both sides allow it to happen."

When the woman's charges were reported publicly, Jamison expressed little surprise. "He [the accused player] is the type of person that has to have his way or no way," he said. "He wanted everything, and I ain't saying he didn't deserve it or earn it, but if he snapped his fingers he wanted it. And that's why . . . it [the incident] happened out there at that party. His ego was hurt."

The player's decision to resort to intimidation of an uninterested woman, despite being in an environment ripe with other opportunities for companionship, seems to defy logic. But Jamison explained that the woman's cold response had triggered a sudden shift in the player's desire, from obtaining a sexual favor to saving face amongst his peers. His petty anger over being spurned contrasted sharply with his public persona. Ultimately, formal charges were not filed against the accused player, and the case disappeared from public view.

By the time the summer league wound down, Jamison's performance on the court had earned him an offer from a CBA team, as well as interest from teams in Spain and France. More important, an NBA team was considering extending an invitation to its training camp. In a telephone call to his fiancée from the airport, he could hardly restrain himself from sharing the news, but he wanted to tell her in person.

Boarding the plane for his return flight home, Jamison felt a sense of accomplishment in having resurrected his dreams, and a sense of achievement at having resisted the daily messages left for by him the woman he had met the day he arrived. "Why spoil something that I have that is good at home to deal with something that's only going to be there for a day?" he reasoned. Beneath his practical approach to the temptations of stardom was a sincere desire to secure a happy marriage and work with his wife toward a family and financial security. He placed the responsibility for making his dream a reality squarely on his own back. "The women out there allowed you to feel that you couldn't have enough," said Jamison. "That's the life of being a star, men just constantly letting it go—and it doesn't mean anything. A lot of those relationships out there absolutely, positively meant nothing. It's unreal. Basically, all you're doing is getting [expletive]. That's the bottom line."

Longing for the familiarity of home after three weeks at the Radisson, Jamison found his fiancée waiting for him at the airport gate. "When I stepped off the plane, I felt comfortable," he said. "Home turf. A lot of people get caught out there in LA. Everything is so free. Everything is just like free caring, just scary. It would be hard for me to relocate and just stay out there. You've got to have a lot of discipline.

"I can see how a person like O.J. got carried away, but I don't justify what he did as far as the battering and beating and all that stuff. A lot of women out there leave themselves open, tremendously open."

The groundwork for professional athletes taking exceptional liberties with women is laid in high school and reinforced in college, where student-athletes are held to a lower standard of accountability. Particularly for young men from violent homes or undisciplined backgrounds, an athletic scholarship can serve as a license to act out free of consequence. When surrounded by women, these players' unfamiliarity with behavioral boundaries can easily lead to sexual assault.

5

unreasonable doubt

IN SEPTEMBER 1993, SUN BONDS, WIFE OF NATIONAL LEAGUE MVP Barry Bonds, placed a 911 call to police and claimed she had been physically assaulted by her husband. When police arrived at the Bondses' residence, they found her "crying and holding her neck."[1] The police report indicated that "Barry Bonds threw her against the car and grabbed her around the neck," and that "she was thrown to the ground and was kicked in the buttocks by Barry Bonds."[2]

To avoid the scrutiny of the media, Mrs. Bonds declined to press charges, but she did file for divorce. Despite earning nearly $5 million per season, Barry Bonds appeared before San Mateo County Superior Court Judge George Taylor in August 1994 and petitioned to have his family support payments reduced. Immediately after granting the request, Taylor requested Bonds's autograph, which Bonds readily granted. This incident has been widely cited to support the claim that athletes receive preferential treatment from the courts.[3]

The Bonds incident is the exception rather than the rule, however. In an attempt to counter the growing public perception that athletes receive preferential treatment, law enforcement officials often overcompensate in their efforts to maintain impartiality. Arrests are now frequent and prosecution is aggressive when athletes are accused of criminal behavior. Of 217 felony complaints alleging sexual violence by collegiate or professional athletes between 1986 and 1995, 172 of the accused (79 percent) were arrested, and 117 (54 percent) indicted. In comparison, a U.S. Department of Justice survey of three hundred counties found that only 32 percent of rapes reported to police resulted in an arrest.[4]

But while accused athletes stand a greater chance of being formally charged, they enjoy a significantly lower likelihood of being convicted. Department of Justice figures indicate that nationwide, more than half the arrests for rape result in a conviction. But of the 172 athletes arrested for sex felonies from 1986 to 1995, only 31 percent were successfully prosecuted.[5] Evidence that the paradox of high arrest and low conviction rates among athletes is not the result of preferential treatment by law enforcement officials is found in the outcomes of those cases that are taken to trial. Of the 66 professional and college athletes who were tried before a jury for felonious sexual assault between 1986 and 1995, 85 percent were acquitted.[6] Those figures hardly reflect a soft approach by police and prosecutors, but rather a reluctance on the part of juries to convict popular athletes.

The standard deterrents to successful prosecution of rape are magnified when a celebrated athlete is involved. Starting with a brazen admission of consensual sex, accused athletes profit from popularly held cultural images of the jock-female relationship. Citing the abundance of women available to popular athletes, accused sex offenders insist there is no need to resort to force. The influence of this argument on jurors can be seen even when groups of athletes are put on trial for gang rape. Relying on the consensual sex defense, college and professional athletes tried for gang rape are acquitted more than 75 percent of the time. The prejudicial association of athletes with women and sex often proves an insurmountable obstacle for juries, preventing them from overcoming the "reasonable doubt" threshold required for conviction.

Further impediments to prosecution are (1) the exceptional glare of the media spotlight and (2) the exceptionally high standard of defense counsel received by athletes, in contrast to the typical accused sex offender. The excessive media attention that surrounds athletes charged with rape ultimately works against the victim, discouraging her from going through with a criminal trial. Furthermore, the resources available to athletes attract legal defense teams who specialize in high-stakes cases. These high-priced lawyers are particularly adept at using the forum afforded them by the press to bolster their clients' images at the expense of the accusers. As a result, victims either withdraw their complaints to avoid further publicity, or suffer character damage that reduces ability to obtain a conviction.

A winter chill still in the air, Assistant District Attorney David Meier sat in his Lowell, Massachusetts, office, reviewing the state's rape shield law. As the lead prosecutor in an unusually brutal gang rape case that was attracting attention from the Boston media, Meier was preparing for an upcoming pretrial hearing that would determine how much of the victim's background the defense could introduce in court. The victim was a prostitute with a criminal record that included convictions for possession of heroin as well as common night walking. The four defendants, college students from an affluent Boston suburb, claimed to have been out for a joy ride after having too much to drink. The hooker they had picked up, they said, was now making allegations of rape in revenge for not having been paid enough.

On July 13, 1992, Albert Troisi had lured the prostitute, Dawn Berry, into his car by insisting that Berry's friend Karen, who had been badly beaten a couple of weeks earlier, was just up the street, and in need of Berry's immediate help. Although she had never seen Troisi before, Berry accepted his offer of a ride. Once she was in the passenger's seat, Troisi drove around the corner, and three of his friends jumped into the back of the car. Despite her pleas to be let loose, one of the men grabbed her hair from behind, while the others threatened her. Troisi drove to Dead Horse Lane, a deserted dirt road that runs along the back of the University of Massachusetts football field.

Amid the tools and other debris scattered about the folded-down back seat, each man took a turn raping Berry. Afterward they beat her, then pushed her from the car and left her bleeding in a vacant field. "She was punched with such severity that her false teeth were shattered, and we found various portions of her teeth in different sections of the dirt road," said Sergeant Brendan Durkin, who oversaw the police investigation of the incident.

Ironically, two of the men involved—Troisi, who drove the car, and Derek Larson, who inflicted the beating—had recently completed training to become police officers, and were awaiting their appointment. Both were standout football players at the University of Massachusetts at Lowell; Larson was the quarterback and captain. Like their accomplices, Greg Pineo and Sean Herbert, they never suspected that a prostitute with a criminal record would dare to report them to the authorities. Even after being arrested, all four remained confident that no jury would convict them. Their attitude, Durkin said, was, "So what if we did this? She's only a prostitute."

With no physical evidence of a rape other than some seminal fluid found on Berry's clothing, the reputations of the one woman and four men would be critical. But after reviewing the police reports, Meier decided to indict the four men, despite the contrasting backgrounds and reputations of the victim and the defendants. "The law protects every individual," Meier said. "Whether she be a prostitute or whether she be the girl next door."

The defense strategy of building the case around Berry's promiscuous past became apparent in the pretrial motions submitted to Judge Peter Lauriet. Court TV had decided to televise the trial. Sitting at his desk, contemplating how such media exposure might infringe on Berry's privacy, Meier heard a knock on the door. A fellow prosecutor needed some advice on a new sexual assault complaint that had the potential to become even more sensational than Berry's. A twenty-one-year-old female student from Emerson College had contacted the district attorney's office, claiming to have been raped by a player on the Boston Celtics basketball team, rookie Marcus Webb. Rape kit results forwarded to police from Boston's Beth Israel Hospital supported the victim's story. But though she had suffered substantial tearing and bleeding inconsistent with consensual sex, her case was complicated by her sexual relationship with Webb, which led up to the incident in question.

Although Meier seldom worked on sex crime cases, his involvement with the highly publicized gang rape case in Lowell, as well as his leadership position in the office, made him the person from whom to seek advice. As Middlesex County's top prosecutor, Meier supervised twenty deputy attorneys. He spent most of his time investigating and prosecuting homicide cases. In addition to trying murder cases, he was frequently assigned to cases that were likely to attract exceptional media coverage.

Meier recounted his decision to charge the four men in Lowell, despite the victim's background. "Her lifestyle never really entered into the charging decision," Meier said. "I spent a lot of time convincing [Dawn] that we were not going to let that lifestyle be an obstacle, but rather we were going to use that to an advantage tactically. We were going to put in front of the jury her entire lifestyle."

After the prosecutor in the Webb case left his office, Meier thought little more about that investigation. He was not assigned to the case, and the Berry case was his priority. But all that changed one week later when a series of events launched the Celtics and their troubled young player to the top of the newscasts throughout the region.

On March 15, 1993, just as prosecutors were wrapping up the preliminary investigation into the student's rape allegation, Webb was arrested for physically assaulting a woman at his home. Quientina Brown, the mother of Webb's thirteen-month-old son, had journeyed to Boston from her hometown in Alabama to visit Webb. At 2 A.M. she called police, claiming to have been the victim of a domestic assault. Police arrived and arrested Webb. He was held in a cell at a local police station for nearly three hours before being released shortly before 5 A.M., on condition that he stay away from Brown.

Hours later, in another part of the city, Ericka Gomes, the student who had filed the rape charge against Webb a week earlier, obtained a restraining order against him. She claimed Webb had threatened to assault her in a nightclub just days after she went to police and accused him of rape. With the Celtics scheduled to fly west that afternoon to begin a long road trip, Webb remained in Boston to resolve his legal issues. Three days later, he was working out at the Celtics practice facility at Brandeis University when police arrived with a warrant and arrested him for the rape. Webb was escorted from the gym in handcuffs and transported to the Middlesex County courthouse jail. Later that day, Celtics head coach Chris Ford issued a press release from Denver announcing that Webb had been cut from the team.

The trouble had begun on March 3 at 1:30 A.M., when Webb was dropped off at his condominium by some teammates. The Celtics had played the San Antonio Spurs at Boston Garden that evening, and Webb had gone out with some other players following the game. Earlier in the day he had told Gomes that he was breaking off their three-month-old relationship. Brown and his infant son were due to arrive for an extended visit later that weekend.

When Webb returned home and found Gomes still at his apartment, he opted to have sex with her one last time. In the process, a dispute ensued, and Webb forced Gomes down on her stomach and sexually assaulted her from behind. Despite her protests, Webb continued to press on top of her from behind while she screamed and cried into a pillow.

Arrested and thrown in jail, Webb had no one to turn to. His agent was in Israel, and the Celtics had gone to Denver. Despite having earned nearly $140,000 in his short stint with the Celtics, his bank account contained just $5,000, leaving him far short of the $50,000 bail assigned by Judge Robert A. Barton.

When the Celtics returned from their West Coast trip, the county courthouse took on the circus atmosphere that often accompanies celebrities. Webb's teammate Xavier McDaniel paid $25,000 cash for his release. McDaniel was accompanied by his fiancée, Michelle Anderson, and teammate Sherman Douglas's girlfriend, Carol Ford. Both women took the opportunity to speak to the press and criticize Judge Barton's assigned bail. "I think he's being punished for being a high-profile person," said Ford. "He's a very sweet person at heart." Outside the courthouse several other women carried placards voicing their support for Webb.

The team of lawyers assembled to represent Webb included former superior court judge J. Owen Todd, who had opened a private practice following his retirement from the bench. His cocounsel in the case was Howard Cooper, a highly competent and experienced trial lawyer. Todd and Cooper had formerly been partners in the prestigious law firm of Hale & Dorr, which represented the Celtics in most legal matters. It was through that connection that Webb had landed such high-caliber representation.

Webb's first appearance in court before Judge Barton, Todd's former colleague, typified the culture clash between the free-for-all celebrity world and the criminal justice system. Having seen his share of criminal defendants, Barton immediately detected an air of arrogance in Webb. "He was a very cocky individual through this whole legal proceeding," Barton said. "He couldn't believe it was happening, and it was all a little bit ridiculous to him."

A Boston native who had attended the famed Boston Latin School before going on to Dartmouth College and eventually to Boston University Law School, Barton had been a standout baseball player with college and semiprofessional teams. He had completed a tour of duty in the Marines before coming to the court, and took a no-nonsense attitude toward criminal behavior. As the regional administrative judge, Barton was responsible for assigning all the felony cases in Middlesex County.

Although Webb was not the first Boston-area athlete to be charged with a violent felony, Barton had never presided over a rape case involving a professional athlete. Nonetheless, the sexual assault charges came as no surprise to him. "Athletes are spoiled as men because they have women throwing themselves all over them," Barton pointed out. "After a while they begin to believe that they personally are something special. They can't believe that anybody would ever say no to them. Even though they have the inner discipline as athletes, they don't have the inner discipline to comport their behavior to what society expects."

In over fifteen years on the bench, Barton had seen politicians, police officers, clergy, and entertainers tried for serious crimes. "People who are in positions of power—and athletes are in positions of power monetarily and as far as hero worship—have more control and feel that they're above the average human being and therefore can get away with more," said Barton. "I'm sure the last thing Mr. Webb ever thought was that this woman would ever make a complaint against him."

After Webb's release from the state's custody pending his trial, the Boston media's daily coverage of the case signaled to the district attorney's office that his trial would be a magnet for the media. A lot was at stake for the two parties involved—not to mention that the Boston Celtics, one of the most storied and revered franchises in professional sports, had seen a member of their team arrested and taken from their practice site in handcuffs. With the pretrial arguments in the Lowell gang rape case complete, and the trial not scheduled to begin for another six months, Middlesex County District Attorney Thomas Reilly put Meier in charge of the Webb case.

Despite the victim's timely report to police, and the presence of corroborating medical evidence that a rape had taken place, Webb's fame made the chance of winning the case marginal at best. In addition to the victim's intimate involvement with Webb prior to the assault, the lawyers who had been hired to cast doubt on her story were not the run-of-the-mill public defenders typically assigned to represent accused sex offenders. "As a prosecutor you're going to face the best defense available because [athletes] have resources," explained Meier. The victim's reputation would be the sole target of these resources. Knowing this, Meier met with Gomes and set out to learn everything he could about her past.

"I approached the case similarly to the way I approached the [gang rape] case, in the sense that . . . everything that I could have laid out about the victim I intended to lay out in front of the jury," Meier said. "She had a number of things about her background and her relationship with Marcus Webb that needed to be put out in front of the jury."

The roots of Gomes's relationship with Webb extended back to her California home. Her neighbor and childhood friend had been Brian Shaw, a standout basketball player who had attended the University of California at Santa Barbara and become the Celtics' top draft choice in 1988. Gomes followed Shaw's career with enthusiasm, and ultimately resumed her relationship with him when she moved to Boston after being accepted at Emerson. Through Shaw, Gomes had met numerous Celtics and become quite familiar with players' favorite nightspots. Webb had signed his rookie contract with the Celtics shortly after they traded Shaw; he and Gomes were introduced soon thereafter.

Although defense attorneys insisted that Gomes had been sexually involved with more than one pro athlete in Boston during her stay at Emerson, her involvement with Webb was not casual. Though it began as merely a physical relationship, Gomes eventually fell for Webb to the point of writing him love letters and making herself available at his beck and call. Then, on a day that included intense sexual involvement, Webb abruptly told her that their three-month relationship was over. Leaving her behind at his apartment, he departed for a game at the Boston Garden. In a desperate attempt to salvage the relationship, Gomes remained at Webb's apartment awaiting his return. When he arrived home after midnight, Webb saw her presence as an opportunity for one more sexual fling. The result was a sexual assault.

While Meier was attempting to build a case on the testimony of a victim whose past might not stir a jury's sympathy, Webb's past was being dissected, and his credibility slowly destroyed, in the pages of the local press. Before his savvy defense lawyers could stifle him, Webb was interviewed by *Boston Globe* reporter Lynda Gorov. An experienced beat writer accustomed to covering urban crime, Gorov exposed a candid side of Webb that threw his claim of innocence into serious question. Webb told Gorov, "Of course, I'm going to say I didn't do it. Even if you got a picture of me robbing a bank, I'd say I didn't." Suggesting his attitude toward women, Webb claimed, "Northern women are a hell of a lot different, more wild and loose. Once, in a club, a woman tried to undress me on the dance floor. I couldn't believe it."[7]

Gorov also traveled to Webb's hometown in Alabama to interview many people from his past. She discovered that he had been a poor student throughout high school and college. Nonetheless, he had received scholarship offers to play both football and basketball. After accepting a full scholarship from the University of Alabama and playing basketball there for three years, Webb had been kicked off the team for repeatedly failing to attend classes. Unable to play basketball, he had dropped out of school immediately. But before leaving Alabama, he had impregnated Quientina Brown; been hit with a paternity suit by another woman, LaTangelia Sanderson; and become the subject of a third woman's claim to be carrying a child he had fathered. And he had been arrested twice for repeated motor vehicle violations that caused the state of Alabama to revoke his license.[8]

Though Gorov's investigative reporting failed to reveal a malicious or violent side to Webb, it demonstrated a pattern of irresponsible behavior that a career in professional sports had only exacerbated. Just months after signing with the Celtics, Webb had made highly inflammatory accusations of racism against police officers from the suburban Boston towns of Brookline and Newton. Having been late for various team functions, Webb had failed to show up for a practice and for a mandatory appointment with the club's physician on January 8, 1993. Rather than risk Coach Ford's ire, Webb told team officials that he had been pulled over by police on Route 9, near the Brookline-Newton town line, detained without cause, and had his license confiscated. But once the police officers realized he was a Celtic, he claimed, they had let him go.[9]

When news of the alleged incident became public the following day, Brookline and Newton police emphatically denied having pulled anyone over at the time and location Webb described. Webb's tale followed an incident in Wellesley, an almost exclusively white suburb, in which police had forced the Celtics' Dee Brown and his fiancée out of their car at gunpoint and ordered them to lie facedown on a sidewalk in broad daylight. Brown had been mistaken for a black male suspect in a recent bank robbery.[10]

The incident, which was witnessed by many, had resulted in a public admission by Wellesley police that Brown and his fiancée were innocent victims of a police investigation. But there were no witnesses to Webb's allegations, despite his insistence that the traffic stop had lasted for over an hour and had occurred on one of Boston's busiest highways. Furthermore, to Webb's charge that an "Officer Smith" had pulled him over before three other patrol cars arrived, Brookline and Newton police departments replied that neither force employed an officer named Smith. They also discovered that Alabama had not issued a temporary license to Webb since his driving privileges were revoked in 1991.

Newton's mayor, Theodore Mann, suspected that the Celtics were withholding information, and demanded an apology to the police. "There have been serious implications made about the treatment afforded to Mr. Webb, and we want to get to the bottom of it," said Mann. "We deserve to have the matter cleared up."

Meanwhile, after conducting their own investigation—which turned up a report by one player's wife tending to corroborate Webb's story—Celtics officials claimed in a press release: "The Celtics are convinced that, although some evidence indicates Marcus Webb was stopped by police on Route 9, no police department or any police officer acted in any way detrimental to the rights of Webb." Adamant that none of his officers had pulled Webb over, Brookline Police Chief Howard A. Brackett responded to the release. "I think it's a complete cover-up," he said. "I think they're trying to blow it off, cut their losses and run. I just don't buy their story."[11] Yet Webb never apologized, and the Celtics dropped the matter after fining him $250 for being absent from practice.

Seldom does a prosecutor have the luxury of seeing a defendant's credibility so vividly demolished before a trial even begins. But though Webb had a well-documented history of problem behavior, none of that information was relevant to the case at hand, and little was admissible as evidence. Thus, despite the prospect of cross-examining a public liar, Meier knew that the only issue that mattered was what took place in Webb's bed on March 3. And Gomes's voluntary presence in Webb's bedroom posed a huge stumbling block. "There are definitely inherent obstacles in these types of cases because the public has held [athletes] up to higher esteem than the guy in the alley," said Meier.

That point was not lost on Webb's astute lawyer Howard Cooper. "This was not a case where you had a guy standing in a dark alley waiting for a stranger," said Cooper. "These were two people who had a very intimate relationship, and the jury was going to hear about some very difficult things that you don't typically hear about going on between two people."

Cooper's attempt to capitalize on Gomes's relationship with Webb was apparent from the start. "It is striking how large of a guy Marcus Webb is," he pointed out. "Basketball players really tower above people. As a result, when Marcus Webb or his teammates go out to a bar, they can't fade into the woodwork. In a bar, where it's a singles event and people are there to meet each other, that clearly is a factor. The other thing is that there's only twelve guys on the Celtics roster, and basketball is king in this town. Everybody knows who the Celtics are. I question whether this woman ever would have been interested if he wasn't a pro athlete of such high visibility."

Meier did not disagree with Cooper's argument that Gomes pursued Webb because of his status. Furthermore, he knew full well that if jurors could not get beyond that fact, they would never even consider whether her will had been forcibly violated. "The challenge was getting the jury to believe that a woman who sought out a relationship with a star athlete . . . was all the same a vulnerable person who was taken advantage by someone who had no intention of maintaining a romantic relationship with her," Meier explained. "No matter what her station in life, no matter what her lifestyle or her motivation in getting into that relationship, she still had her God-given right to say no."

While Meier was preparing to educate jurors on what constitutes force, Webb's attorneys were peppering Judge Barton with motions in an attempt to introduce unsavory aspects of Gomes's background. They requested permission to present evidence of her bias and motive to lie, as well as proof of her sexual involvement with other athletes. "It was clear to me that she had had a sexual relationship with Brian Shaw, and that she had possibly had other relationships with other professional athletes," Cooper said. "There was a lot there that would have put her credibility into very serious question. Things that would have come out would have been terribly ugly. This was a woman who sought out Marcus Webb. There was no way she could be portrayed as anything other than a sports groupie who got involved in a relationship with Webb."

Even if Judge Barton denied those motions by the defense, there was still the undisputed fact that Gomes had maintained a voluntary, intensely physical relationship with Webb for two to three months. "She knew that Marcus Webb was going out with other women," Meier conceded. "She knew that he had a child in Alabama and a former girlfriend who was the mother of his child. She told her friends how much she was in love with Marcus Webb, or admired him, and how happy she was with him. There was a lot on the facts of the case itself, which had nothing to do with Marcus Webb whatsoever, which suggested there was a real downside to the likelihood of conviction."

While Meier was required to convince the whole jury of Webb's guilt, Cooper and Todd needed to raise doubt in the mind of only one juror to prevent a conviction. "I have to get twelve ordinary people to the stage where they feel emotionally that they're doing the right thing," Meier said. "It's difficult enough for a jury to convict anybody of any crime. It becomes all the more difficult when the person [being accused] is within a class of people that society has held out to be on a pedestal." The lifestyles of Gomes and Webb raised the reasonable doubt threshold a notch, while making Cooper's job that much easier. "The whole lifestyle in and of itself is somewhat unique," explained Meier. "Part of the job of the prosecutor who's trying to prove beyond a reasonable doubt that any sexual relations that occurred were nonconsensual is to recreate that lifestyle to a jury. That's a challenge, a real challenge."

As both sides awaited the judge's decision on how much of Gomes's prior sexual history and other background information could be introduced by the defense at trial, Barton weighed her rights against Webb's. "I have a whole page on the rape shield law, and I can tell you all the exceptions that have been carved into it because of the right of confrontation and cross-examination," said Barton. "Anything that relates to bias, the defendant is entitled to inquire into. So the rape shield law gives way when it faces bias or motive for lying. . . . It seems the more ingenious lawyers become, the more and more exceptions are carved into rape shield laws."

With the trial just four days away, and Barton scheduled to render his decision on the first day of arguments, the defense grew restless. "The biggest roll of the dice in this case was that no one knew what Judge Barton was going to do with the evidence, whether he was going to let it in or not let it in," Cooper explained. "And there was evidence which we felt was absolutely critical to Marcus's defense. I firmly believe that Judge Barton was not going to let in the majority of what we were looking for. It would have been very difficult for him to let it in."

Barton's pending decision was not the only risk Webb was facing. "On the one hand you had a fairly attractive, fairly petite young woman who was college educated," Cooper said. "A trained actress and singer trained at performing in front of crowds. In order to acquit Marcus, a jury would have had to believe she was making the charges up because she was a scorned woman.

"We had an inarticulate, not well-educated, gigantic black man who would be accused—in front of a Middlesex jury that probably would have been mostly white—of raping a very light-skinned woman. The simple realities of it were that a rape conviction carried with it a potential twenty-year sentence. A conviction would have meant that he would have no possibility of playing basketball during his twenties, as a practical matter. That type of time, no matter how small the risk, would have ended the opportunity that he had to earn a living."

On the eve of the trial, Webb's lawyers contacted the district attorney's office in hopes of reaching a compromise that would spare sending the matter before the jury. While the defense was looking to reduce the charge to a misdemeanor and eliminate jail time, the state insisted that the crime remain a felony, and that some prison time be part of any plea agreement. Ultimately, the defense agreed that Webb would plead guilty to indecent assault and battery, a felony crime that would carry a thirty-day prison sentence. The plea would not include an admission of forced penetration, and there would be no appeals.

It was apparent to Meier that the motivation behind the offer was to preserve Webb's ability to play pro basketball, and to minimize the public embarrassment of a messy trial. At the same time, the offer guaranteed Meier a victory without the risk of trying the case before an unpredictable jury. Furthermore, it would preserve Gomes's privacy. "Her confidential records . . . would have become presumably public in terms of her physical condition, mental condition, emotional background, psychiatric and psychological background, which could have created in the jury's mind a real reasonable doubt as to what happened," Meier stated.

For Gomes, Webb's willingness to plead guilty to a lesser crime provided a way to have her assailant convicted without subjecting herself to public humiliation. "I wasn't going to try to make her out to be the girl next door, because she wasn't," explained Meier. "I was going to portray her as she was: a basketball groupie who went to the Harbor Club to seek out professional athletes. She engaged in sexual relations with Marcus from the get-go, adored him, kept a scrapbook for him, was at his beck and call, and when he snapped his fingers she would be there. But on this particular occasion he had gone too far."

Because of the potential impact of her questionable behavior on jurors, Gomes understood why Meier was going to emphasize the strong medical evidence. "I had blown up a very large diagram of a human's anal cavity," Meier explained. "The doctor was going to show very graphically where he saw the tears and where he saw the bleeding and how far up the anus it was."

Taking these harsh realities into account, Gomes agreed to accept

Webb's offer to plead guilty. Following her meeting with Meier, she drafted a letter to be delivered to Judge Barton at Webb's sentencing. The following excerpt includes most of that letter:

I've decided to accept the guilty plea of a lesser charge because the name of the crime is not important to me. The facts are the same. Rape *is* an indecent assault. Whether the crime is called rape or indecent assault and battery, Mr. Webb is still a sex offender. The difference for me is closing this horrible chapter without a trial and to finally see the brighter side of things again. For Mr. Webb it means freedom and plenty of help in the form of counseling.

No mother wants to imagine her daughter having been raped. On the other hand, no woman wants to know that her son violated another woman. I would much rather come to this compromise, than to subject myself, Mr. Webb, and the people that love us to a gruesome trial in which the details of our private lives would be mapped out for all to see.[12]

On July 20, 1993, Marcus Webb appeared before Judge Barton to plead guilty to indecent assault and battery and be sentenced. The following excerpt is taken from the records of that proceeding:

Barton: *It is my understanding, sir, that you are going to offer a plea to the lesser included offense of indecent assault and battery, which would essentially allege that on or about the fourth day of March of 1993 at Waltham, you did assault and beat Ericka Gomes indecently. Do you understand what the crime of indecent assault and battery alleges?*

Webb: *Yes, sir.*

Barton: *As far as the elements of indecent assault and battery are concerned, assault and battery is an intentional, offensive, unprivileged, unconsented to touching of another. Do you understand that, sir?*

Webb: *Yes, sir.*

Barton: *As far as an assault and battery being indecent, it is indecent if it involves touching of the genitals, buttocks, or female breasts. It is done by a defendant with the intent to arouse, to appeal to or to gratify the sexual desires or passions of either the victim or the defendant. Do you understand that, sir?*

Webb: *Yes, sir.*

Barton: *What is your recommendation on a plea of guilty, please, Mr. Meier?*

Meier: *Your Honor, the Commonwealth's recommendation is a sentence of three to five years at MCI Cedar Junction, thirty days of that sentence to be served, the balance to be suspended for a period of some three years with supervised probation. . . .*[13]

The sentence proposed by the state was a first for Judge Barton. "I've been a superior court judge for sixteen years," said Barton. "I can't remember a single case where someone has pled guilty to rape and ended up receiving a split sentence with the committed part being thirty days. Other cases come to mind. People do serious time. It was a very unusual plea bargain. You've taken a fellow who was charged with rape, that's a twenty-year felony, he ends up doing a month? He ends up doing thirty days because he had a damn good lawyer and that's a tough case to prove."

Although he could have rejected the plea and ordered the trial to go ahead, Barton accepted the state's recommendation. "In this state I cannot exceed the district attorney's recommendation," said Barton. "The only thing I can do is not accept it and order the case to trial. Under the circumstances, seeing where the government was coming from and where the defense was coming from, it didn't upset me *that* much that I wouldn't accept it."

Webb's attorney J. Owen Todd requested an opportunity to speak on his client's behalf. "Marcus Webb, a twenty-three-year-old young man, grew up in Alabama, is the sole support of his son, one-and-a-half years of age, his mother, [and] his grandparents," said Todd. "He's a young man who is just starting out on a professional basketball career which promises are great [sic]. I've explained to Mr. Webb the potential sentence of twenty years for a rape case. What was important to Mr. Webb was that it be acknowledged that he had not raped, that he not be branded a rapist and that he be permitted to resume his basketball career. . . ."[14]

Having heard all the parties, Judge Barton asked Webb to stand.

The clerk: *Marcus L. Webb, as to indictment 93–533, indictment number one, this indictment now charging indecent assault and battery on a person over 14 years, what is your plea now?*

Webb: *I plead so much of that sentence as indecent assault and battery but not rape.*

Barton: *You plead what, sir? You have to say the words.*

Webb: *Guilty.*[15]

Despite Webb's jail sentence for committing a felony sex crime, Cooper viewed the disposition of the case a success. "Pro athletes are these young guys who have the attitude that the world is their oyster for plucking," said Cooper. "They're young, generally in their early twenties. They have money. In Marcus Webb's case, for the first time in his life he had some money. There's an attitude out there that this is just a woman who is known to hang out with pro athletes and be available for them sexually. That's the way of the world, *their* world.

"Does he carry that label with him as someone convicted of an indecent assault? Absolutely! But there are others in the NBA, even who have rape convictions, that are playing. So it just looked like a smart decision."

As Webb's attorneys distributed a press release outside the courtroom emphasizing that Webb had not pled guilty to rape, Meier stated he was pleased with the results, under the circumstances. "He was willing to admit that he had been involved in some sort of forcible sexual contact with this woman," said Meier. "And that's what she wanted. She was vindicated in the sense that he was held accountable, and he admitted publicly that he had physical contact with her in a sexual way against her will."

Meier had spent a great deal of time with Gomes, and it was clear to him that in addition to inflicting serious physical damage on her, the incident had greatly injured her psyche. "If she had said, 'Listen, David, I want to go to trial. I don't want to see him plead guilty to anything other than what he did to me. What he did was rape me,' then the case would have been tried," Meier insisted. "Ericka Gomes wasn't Desiree Washington [Mike Tyson's rape victim] and she wasn't Miss Nebraska [Nebraska football player Christian Peter's sexual assault victim]. Had she been, maybe I would have been in a better position to evaluate the case and say, 'We should go forward and we should convict him of rape.' "

While presiding over previous highly publicized rape trials, Barton's view on the crime emerged quite clearly. "A man could say to a woman, 'Listen, you let me round second base . . . round third base . . . and all of a sudden you say I can't score? Well, you can't do that to me. I'm a male and I'm all aroused. And if you let me go this far you can't say no now.'

"Well, that isn't the law. The law is that women can consent to first base, second base, third base and say, 'That's it. You must stop.' And men can't justify it on the basis of arousal or anything else."

While serving his brief jail term, Webb was released for a day to stand charges for physically assaulting Quientina Brown. The case was heard by a judge rather than a jury; Brown was flown up from Alabama to testify against Webb. "She was very emotional on the witness stand, quite a good witness for the commonwealth," said Cooper. "Clearly something had happened, but as I said to the judge, this was a situation where both of them were extremely upset."

The judge found Webb guilty and sentenced him to an additional fifty-nine days in jail. Nonetheless, Webb's lawyers took advantage of a provision in Massachusetts law that permits a defendant who is found guilty by a judge to appeal and have his case heard before a six-person jury. "The practice amongst defense lawyers is always to use the first trial as discovery, which is effectively what we did," explained Cooper.

Rather than go through a second trial, which would have required flying the victim back to Boston to testify again, the state accepted a plea from Webb that stipulated "no admission of guilt but a finding that there are facts from which he could have been found guilty." It was a watered down conviction that allowed Webb to avoid any additional jail time.

At the end of Webb's case, David Meier returned to the Lowell gang rape case, opening arguments in which were only weeks away. While he had been working on Webb's case, Dawn Berry had been arrested again. Each of the defendants had retained his own attorney, all of whom were gearing up to exploit the contrasting backgrounds of their clients and the victim. But Meier had no intention of making the victim out to be anything she wasn't.

"I told the jury in my opening statement exactly who Dawn Berry was, what type of life she had led, what type of record she had, and what type of problems she had," Meier said. His unconventional strategy of emphasizing to the jury all the victim's flaws angered defense attorneys. Their objections led Judge Peter Lauriet to call a conference in which the defense lawyers insisted they wanted to be able to cross-examine Berry so as to bring her prostitution and drug use to the jury's attention. But Meier pointed out that the state was not prohibited from bringing this information out first. "She had absolutely nothing to hide in front of the jury," retorted Meier. "She told it exactly the way it was: that she was addicted to heroin, that she used heroin, that she turned to prostitution to earn money for heroin. That didn't make this case any less of a rape."

The distinction between the victim and the four men she had accused was visually evident in the courtroom. Berry came without the support of family or friends, her thin frame and uncustomary clothes indicative of her life on the streets. When she took the stand to testify, she had to walk past rows of short-haired, muscular, young white men dressed in white shirts and ties, who lined the gallery of spectators in support of the defendants. "She would see, as I saw, this sea of large white-shirted people out there," said Judge Lauriet. "They were all young and strong and healthy. They weren't interested because they wanted to see justice done or because they were taking Civics 101. They were clearly there to help their friends."

In the end, the trial boiled down to a social outcast pitted against four young men with promise written all over them. "There was no physical or medical evidence of a rape," pointed out Meier. "It was ultimately her word against theirs. Proof beyond reasonable doubt is no small burden. I didn't know how the jury was going to rule."

On September 27 the jury began deliberating and the following day returned guilty verdicts on all four men. The substantial beating Berry had sustained, and her unwavering testimony about what had occurred, had persuaded the jury. The reading of the verdicts prompted outbursts and tears from the young men's families, and Troisi tried to bolt from the courtroom. Four court officers were required to subdue him while Larsen struggled to resist being handcuffed. Outside the courtroom, Larsen's defense attorney, Ralph Champa, said to a *Boston Globe* reporter, "I wonder what the jury will think when they find out that she is HIV positive. You know she is, don't you? All the four boys have been so informed."[16]

On October 20, 1993, Judge Lauriat faced the four men and prepared to sentence them. He had received 140 letters of support on their behalf from teachers, Little League coaches, community leaders, and friends. "The sentences imposed by this Court must reflect the norms and the values of the society that it represents,"[17] said Lauriet before sentencing Larsen to five years in prison, Troisi to four, and Herbert and Pineo to three years each.

"I was obviously pleased with the verdict, not because it was a matter of winning or losing," said Meier. "I felt bad for these four guys and their families, particularly their parents and their brothers and sisters. But I felt very gratified in the sense that this woman had stood up to these four guys. She had told her story and laid herself out for the jury. Four people were held accountable for what they did."

As the four men entered the Massachusetts Correctional Institution at Cedar Junction to begin serving their prison terms, they passed through the same steel doors that Marcus Webb had exited two months earlier, after completing his thirty-day sentence. Webb was already in France, where he resumed his basketball career and became a premier player.

6

it takes Miss America to convict an All-American

BETWEEN FEBRUARY 1991 AND DECEMBER 1994, TWELVE UNIVERSITY OF Arkansas football and basketball players were investigated for felony sex crimes. In three separate incidents, several athletes had been accused of sexually assaulting women who had willfully entered a dormitory designated for male athletes. The University of Arkansas campus police, who were fully vested with the same powers of arrest held by city and state police, had jurisdiction over the investigations, since all the complaints originated in campus housing. Because the three cases yielded a total of just three arrests and one conviction, a public perception grew that police actions had been influenced by the athletic status of the accused. Most notably, the school's standout basketball star, future NBA player Todd Day, and three of his teammates went uncharged after being accused of raping a thirty-four-year-old woman, the daughter of a local criminal prosecutor.

At 4:00 A.M. on February 27, 1991, campus police discovered a coatless woman walking alone, looking somewhat bewildered. An officer asked her if she was all right, and if she needed a ride. The woman insisted she was fine, but accepted an escort to her car, which was parked off campus. En route to the vehicle, she began to cry. Sitting in the back seat of the police cruiser, she indicated she had been raped by some university basketball players she had met at an area bar. The campus police immediately brought in a female officer from the city police force, to talk with the victim and accompany her to a local hospital, where a rape examination was administered.

To avoid any impression of favoritism toward the athletes, the campus police chief, Larry Slamons, took the extraordinary measure of bringing District Attorney Andrew Ziser into the investigation from the start. "This involved a nationally ranked team and more than one athlete," said Slamons. "I knew this was going to be a big deal."

Although protocol did not mandate that campus police work with the district attorney from the start of an investigation, Slamons wanted to bolster his department's integrity as it investigated the university's most prominent students. "Any university has a problem, in that when you're a university police department, there is a tendency to believe that you report to the administration, who therefore can control what happens in an investigation," said Slamons. "This may be done on some campuses, but in our instance it is very clear that no one in the university, including the chancellor, will ever call me and tell me how to handle a criminal case. If you have a police department on campus, in order to protect the school and the department's credibility, there can be no interference. Otherwise, our integrity and ability to be perceived as a viable police department goes out the window."

Less than a week after the police began their investigation into the incident, the victim opted not to press formal charges. Nonetheless, campus police went ahead with the investigation, ultimately turning over a three hundred-page report to the prosecutor's office. Day and his teammates had conceded sexual contact, but denied using force. Ziser reviewed the report and decided against charging the players. "The evidence in this matter simply does not prove that a crime has occurred," said Ziser.[1]

Following Ziser's announcement, the prosecutor's office came under intense criticism for what was widely interpreted as preferential treatment of the athletes. The appearance of impropriety was exacerbated two months later, when the university's president, B. Alan Sugg, overturned the one-year suspensions that had been handed down by the university's internal judicial court. On reviewing the players' appeals, and in light of the district attorney's determination that insufficient evidence existed to support criminal charges, Sugg had concluded that the four players "did not participate in sexual acts with an adult woman without her consent."[2]

Sugg's executive decision opened the way for the players to return to school in time for the upcoming basketball season, further darkening the cloud over local law enforcement and campus authorities. "It is a scam and a shame when athletes are put above the rest of society," said Barbara Middleton, state coordinator of the National Organization for Women in Arkansas. "Had this incident happened in any other dorm on campus, there would have been very strict and swift action taken."[3]

When a university's most visible students are repeatedly investigated for criminal actions, yet routinely escape discipline, authorities can become the prime targets of public outrage. Ironically, law enforcement officials, unlike other self-interested parties, are often the most vigorous in their attempts to hold athletes accountable. "You have to be more aggressive on athletes," said Slamons. "You are protecting your entity. If I get a call that involves an athlete, I handle it personally.

Normally, I don't ever get involved in investigations, but in an athlete's case, it is so sensitive and so spontaneous that anything can happen." Arkansas prosecutor Terry Jones concurred: "They [campus police] are rabid because of the experiences they've had in the past. They work these cases very hard."

Jones, who succeeded Ziser as Washington County's prosecutor shortly after the Day case, later brought charges against Arkansas athletes in two cases, despite circumstances unfavorable to their prosecution. "The inference is always there that athletes get special treatment," said Jones. "I know that no matter what I do, if it's short of hanging them at dawn, it's not going to be a good decision."

In January 1993, Jones unsuccessfully tried Razorback football players Freddie Bradley and Derrick Martin for statutory rape and sexual assault. The two victims, a thirteen-year-old and another teen beyond the age of consent, went voluntarily to the players' room, where sex ensued. Despite needing to find only that sex had occurred with a minor in order to render a guilty verdict, the jury voted to acquit the two players on all counts. "That didn't make any difference to the jury, who said, 'They're doing it voluntarily,' " said Slamons, who oversaw the investigation, which concluded that sex did indeed occur. "The jury ignored that particular part of the law."

Both defendants benefited from their appearance in court, where they projected an image superior to that of their accusers. "Bradley and Martin were two very handsome, clean-cut, soft-spoken, nice kids, except for what they were doing," said Jones. "We're still in the Bible Belt here, and there's one theory about those kind of cases, that the women tend to blame the victims a lot. If you have a particularly well-developed thirteen-year-old who's had a sexual history, then they become much less effective witnesses. Juries down here will give you forty years if you look like you're nine years old. But if you look like you're eighteen and out on the town, then they're not that blaming."

Jones also presided over the 1994 investigation into the case of six Arkansas football and basketball players accused of raping a woman. Five of the players were not charged after the victim confirmed that though all six were present, only one, DeAnthony Hall, had forcibly assaulted her. "[Hall] sat upon her chest while trying to force his penis into her mouth," said Jones. "When she resisted by screaming and fighting back, he violently threw her back onto the bed several times. Then, in a further attempt to force her to engage in oral sex with him, he sat his bare bottom upon her face."[4]

Charged with attempted rape, Hall offered to plead guilty if the charge was reduced, but Jones wanted nothing less than the maximum penalty. "I held out for a felony conviction," said Jones. "The trouble is that these guys [athletes] are smarter than the average bear. They're good-looking kids. They come to court and they're cleaned up and they look good and make great defendants.

"As the time for trial came closer and closer, it became apparent that my victim was getting nervous. She had a wide and varied sexual past. She had to be recommitted to the hospital for treatment, and she was getting very nervous about the trial. She had a past that would have haunted her a bit." As a result, Hall succeeded in getting his attempted rape charge reduced to public sexual indecency, a misdemeanor that carried a six-month prison term. He was able to finish serving his sentence in time to compete the following football season.

Although accused athletes often have more notorious sexual habits and histories than their victims, it is the accuser's credibility that counts in a rape trial. Over the course of a trial the victim's character is eroded, and the veneer of a revered athlete becomes a distinct advantage. "It's very difficult when you have willing females, who go out of their way to make dates with or arrange liaisons with athletes to go up in their bedrooms and have whatever happens to them, to not have the blame placed on the girls for a considerable amount of what happens to them," said Jones. "They're not regarded as innocents anymore. And it's very tough to convince a jury that they either were not victimizing the athletes or that they were not willing participants in the sexual activity that ensues.

"My frustration with these cases is that I'd like to get a good one, one of these days. I'd like to have one with substantial evidence and credible witnesses."

Cruising through Lincoln, Nebraska, at speeds that exceeded the posted limit, Natalie was having difficulty steering as the strange man in the passenger's seat gripped her right arm, shouting out instructions. "Turn right," he demanded, forcing her to swerve into the other lane to make the turn. "Go, go, go, faster," he demanded, before she had even rounded the corner. "Faster, I said."

"You can't tell me where to go," she cried, as tears ran down her face.

"Shut up," said the passenger, as he squeezed Natalie's arm.

"You can't do this," she retorted, unable to escape his grip.

When he ordered her to turn left across oncoming traffic, Natalie suddenly lurched forward in bed. The room was dark, and she was dressed in her pajamas. The clock on the nightstand read 2:45 A.M. For the second consecutive night, she had had the same nightmare.

"This is trivial. It happened. I'm OK. Big deal," she tried to convince herself, as she sat up in bed, clutching her pillow.

As the reigning Miss Nebraska, Natalie Kuijvenhoven was one of the most recognizable women in the state. She had spent the past eleven months serving as Nebraska's ambassador at public functions around the nation. In her own state she had spoken to over two hundred school and civic groups. Wrapping up her final month as the state's beauty queen, and just having graduated from the University of Nebraska, she had landed a job as a television news anchor in Lincoln. Then, unexpectedly, a stranger had destroyed her self-confidence in a sexual assault.

On Thursday evening, May 13, 1993, Kuijvenhoven and three friends were on their way to a college graduation party when they stopped to pick up two more friends at the Brass Rail, a popular hangout for students of the University of Nebraska. Summer was just around the corner, and the bar was packed, wall to wall. Coeds sporting summer attire were being scouted by men guzzling brews.

A nondrinker who was unaccustomed to the crowded college bar, Kuijvenhoven followed closely behind her friend Donald as he slowly zigzagged through the maze of people. Suddenly she felt a forceful hand push between her legs from behind. Startled, she spun around quickly, and found an imposing man with a crew cut and large muscles showing through his ripped T-shirt. "C'mon. I know you like that," he said, grinning too close to her face.

Before she could respond, the man and his equally large friend pushed past her. "Hey, do you know who that person is?" Kuijvenhoven asked, as she turned back and tapped Donald on the shoulder.

Looking behind her, Donald replied, "Oh, that's Christian Peter. He plays football for the university."

"Well, he just put his hand between my legs," Kuijvenhoven reported.

Although she was personally acquainted with a number of the more popular football players, Kuijvenhoven did not recognize Peter's name. "Are you sure that's who that is?" she asked.

"Oh, yeah. Why don't you just stay over here and don't go near where he is and we'll leave," Donald said.

But after locating their friends and heading for the door, Kuijvenhoven and her friend found themselves confronted again by the six-foot-two-inch, 305-pound defensive lineman. Blocking the door, he placed his hand on Kuijvenhoven's crotch and squeezed, leaving his hand there for a few seconds. Drowned out by the noise, Kuijvenhoven demanded, "Keep your hands off me!" and tried to push his arm away.

Peter brushed her off and made his way back into the crowded bar. Kuijvenhoven reached for his companion and said, "Tell your friend to keep his hands to himself."

With a smirk, Peter's friend replied, "Well, I've told him that before. It doesn't ever seem to help."

On the many occasions when Kuijvenhoven had been in the company of members of the Nebraska Cornhuskers, she had never felt at risk. "I never felt like I would have to defend myself against someone much bigger, larger, and with such ideas as he had," Kuijvenhoven said. "These are the kinds of guys who should protect you. I knew some of these people and they were my friends. I never had a feeling of being scared, being nervous around these types of people."

Her closest friend on the team was an All-American and a team captain. Kuijvenhoven decided to seek him out for advice. As she informed him of what had occurred, his facial expression and nodding head indicated little surprise.

Prior to being offered a scholarship to the University of Nebraska, Christian Peter had flunked out of the Christian Brothers Academy in New Jersey. He had also briefly attended Tilton School in New Hampshire, where he performed very poorly in the classroom. As a result, he was not heavily recruited by colleges, despite his exceptional physical strength and athletic talent.

Nebraska had decided to offer him a football scholarship and an opportunity to be tutored in its highly touted academic assistance program for athletes. But because he failed to meet the NCAA's minimum eligibility standards, he was forced to sit out his first year at the school. In his second season he was redshirted, and so spent his first two years on campus without having played a down. Since arriving on campus he had been arrested six times—once for threatening to kill a parking attendant. At the time he assaulted Kuijvenhoven, there was a warrant out for his arrest.

Stunned that a player who had demonstrated such disregard for the law, and particularly for women, would be tolerated on campus, much less allowed to represent the state on a scholarship, Kuijvenhoven complained to her close friend, a team captain.

"Well, we hear things on the team all the time about him. I've heard worse," he conceded.

"I just can't believe he did that," Kuijvenhoven repeated.

"I'm sorry. I don't know what you think you're going to do about it, but whatever it is, you'll never get it over the football team," he assured her. "The best thing to do is just forget about it."

Kuijvenhoven felt her heroic impression of the Nebraska football team, so prevalent when she was growing up, had been betrayed. "My image and my feelings of safety have changed dramatically," she said. The message was clear: *If you wear the red and white, the law can't touch you.* Her instincts told her to seek justice.

On Sunday, less than three days after the incident, she turned to her father for help. A wealthy entrepreneur and lifelong supporter of the team, he was outraged, and immediately contacted his attorney, Bruce Wright.

A well-respected Lincoln lawyer, Wright was a former Cornhusker and a passing acquaintance of coach Tom Osborne. Sensing Kuijvenhoven's bitterness over the mistreatment of his daughter, he offered to telephone Osborne to discuss the matter with him.

On Monday, without disclosing that the accuser was Miss Nebraska, Wright informed Osborne that Christian Peter had grabbed a woman. Osborne immediately asked if the accuser was "the girl from Wyoming."

"No," Wright replied. "She's not from Wyoming. That must be someone else."

Osborne insisted that he needed to know the identity of the accuser and the location of the incident, in order to confront Peter. When Wright refused to identify the victim by name, Osborne offered a simple solution. "I would be happy to have Christian, if he did it, apologize," said Osborne.

That was not what the victim had had in mind. "That just blew my mind," Kuijvenhoven exclaimed. "The last thing I wanted to do was to see Christian Peter, let alone sit and talk with him and Coach Osborne."

Osborne's offer to discipline Peter privately did little more to convince Kuijvenhoven. "I didn't believe that would happen, and wasn't satisfied with that, because I had heard that other women had been assaulted by him," she said.

In the rare event that a victim's complaint against an athlete reaches the courthouse, defense attorneys and supportive coaches usually argue for leniency, citing the accused's clean record. Police reports and other accusations that cannot be substantiated in court are discarded as having no merit. Kuijvenhoven explained, "I wanted it to be on his record so that if it happened again, it would be documented that he had been accused and convicted of this before."

Surprised by Osborne's treatment of the complaint, Kuijvenhoven's father said to her, "You need to do what you feel is right here, because you can go to the prosecutor's office according to what Bruce has said." Leaving her father's house on Sunday evening, Kuijvenhoven looked at her pocket calendar and saw that she was scheduled to visit six schools in the coming week. Working with the Lincoln police department, she had been speaking to students about the DARE program, designed to keep students from using drugs. On Monday she would return to her old high school, to speak for the first time since her graduation four years earlier. Her advice to the students would be: "Believe in yourself and do what's right." Her message to avoid the peer pressure that accompanies teen drug use was enthusiastically received, causing her to confront her own tough choice: whether to press charges against Peter.

Having grown up in Lincoln, Kuijvenhoven was well aware that in Nebraska, football was the state religion. "It's hard for people who aren't from there to understand that on football Saturday, you can't go anywhere without everyone wearing red in Nebraska," she explained. "It's the *only* thing. We don't have anything else to do. There's farming and there's football."

Bringing charges against a Cornhusker was sure to attract a great deal of negative publicity for the entire football program. Furthermore, her status as Miss Nebraska would only magnify the attention. "I don't know if this is the right thing, because I don't want to hurt the football team's fanfare," Kuijvenhoven thought. Even some of her friends were cautioning her to consider how the complaint might tarnish the team.

"I could have very easily backed down and said that it is easier to just forget about it. No one wants their past to be put out on a plate for everyone to see," she explained. "But I didn't have anything to hide. I didn't have anything in my past that I was afraid of people knowing. A lot of women don't have that courage because they're afraid of other people finding out some minuscule thing they did years ago."

"Lancaster County district attorney's office," the voice on the other end of the phone said.

"I need to speak with the district attorney," Kuijvenhoven replied.

"What is this pertaining to?" the receptionist responded.

"My name is Natalie Kuijvenhoven, and I was assaulted by a member of the Nebraska football team, and I need to speak with the county attorney," she stated firmly.

That afternoon, Kuijvenhoven met with Lancaster County District Attorney Gary Lacy. He and Kuijvenhoven were joined by the deputy attorney who handled sex crimes. Although Peter's name had surfaced in the prosecutor's office in connection with other criminal matters, Kuijvenhoven was the first woman to go there with a complaint of sexual assault.

As Kuijvenhoven told her story, the deputy prosecutor put her and her statement through the threshold drill. Because the state of Nebraska's jury instructions included a requirement that prosecutors prove the victim of a sexual assault resisted to the utmost of her ability, it was not uncommon for a prosecutor to reject complaints of acquaintance rape. "I find date rape more difficult to prosecute, regardless of who the defendant is," the deputy attorney conceded. "I don't care who it is, whether he is famous or not, those are just tough cases to prosecute. I've done a lot of sexual assault jury trials, and juries are very hard on victims."

In less than fifteen minutes, Kuijvenhoven's statement was finished. The deputy prosecutor asked herself, "Can the jury believe her? . . . Sometimes you can just judge that the jury is going to like her. And when you have jury trials, that's a factor. . . ."

Kuijvenhoven was a college graduate with a job that required her to be in the public spotlight, a beauty queen with no prior involvement with her assailant. "She could accurately remember what had happened, and her stories were consistent," the prosecutor reasoned. "She didn't seem to have a motive to lie. There was no reason for her to put herself through this."

Kuijvenhoven listened anxiously as the two prosecutors said confidently, "You need to go press charges. We wouldn't agree and tell you to go on with this if we didn't think you would win this case. You need to go ahead and press charges." Although they would be required to prove both the presence of force and "conduct . . . reasonably construed as being for the purpose of sexual arousal or gratification," they were confident the case was a winner.

At 4:00 in the afternoon Kuijvenhoven completed her meeting at the county attorney's office and headed for the police department. The prosecutor telephoned Sergeant Kawamoto to inform him that a victim of sexual assault had just left his office, and had been sent to the station to file a report.

The Lincoln police had arrested their share of football players over the years. But the players were seldom convicted. Critics had complained privately that prosecutors were dropping the ball.

Kawamoto was waiting for Kuijvenhoven when she arrived thirty minutes later. Having interviewed hundreds of sexual assault victims during his career, Kawamoto knew how to make Kuijvenhoven comfortable from the moment she entered the station. He escorted her to the interview room. With a tape recorder running, Kawamoto began to ask her pointed questions, and it suddenly hit Kuijvenhoven that she had passed the point of no return. Stopping in mid sentence, she said, "I'm nervous about this. I don't know if you know that I'm Miss Nebraska."

Kawamoto responded without hesitation, "Yeah, I knew that." Although he had not previously heard of Kuijvenhoven, Kawamoto had been informed of her status.

After expressing concerns about the media, Kuijvenhoven was assured that precautions would be taken to maintain her privacy. When she finished her statement, Kawamoto explained, "If we can't get someone like you, who has the courage and the status that you have, to come forward with a third-degree assault, how can we expect a five-year-old girl who is being molested by her father to ever tell anyone?"

Soon after making her statement, Kuijvenhoven was introduced to the victim witness unit at the police department. Each year the unit works with 150 to 200 victims of sexual assault. A source there insisted that most years there are only one or two cases involving university athletes. "There's more of a fear level there than people have been told. Victims have been told by their friends, 'Well, you know he's an athlete, maybe you shouldn't report this. Are you sure?' " The source added, "I think victims [of athletes] feel that they're stigmatized, more so than other rape victims. They feel they may be ostracized at school. They've been approached by other athletes, telling them, 'You'd better rethink this.' Those types of things . . . make it much harder, because our campus is rather small, and people tend to know each other. All of a sudden they start losing their friends who may be close to the athletes."

When Kuijvenhoven began working with an advocate at the unit, she was told there had been numerous complaints about Christian Peter, but that none of the women had wanted to file formal charges. A month after she filed her report, Peter was arrested in connection with an outstanding warrant from another assault case. While he was being detained at the Lancaster County jail, it was discovered that he was wanted in connection with the third-degree sexual assault against Kuijvenhoven.

The investigating officer asked Peter if he recalled being at the Brass Rail on May 13, 1993. Peter admitted to having been in the bar, but he could not recall being present on that particular night. Asked specifically if he recalled touching a female in the crotch while in the bar, he stated that he had never touched any female in that way. Furthermore, he denied ever being confronted by a woman in that bar. When Peter asked what was going to happen, the officer informed him that he would be issued a citation for third-degree sexual assault, a misdemeanor. After being told what a misdemeanor was, Christian said, "So basically, some chick can say [she was] touched by you and you're going to arrest [him]."[5]

With a sexual assault charge added to his arrest for failure to appear in court to answer charges of threatening a parking attendant, Peter obtained the legal services of the prominent defense attorney Hal Anderson. Accustomed to representing Nebraska football players, Anderson succeeded in delaying Peter's court appearances. As a result, Peter was able to play through the entire 1993 season without answering the charges brought by Kuijvenhoven. During the fall, Kuijvenhoven's victim advocate notified her about the delay. "Wait 'til after the football year," Kuijvenhoven was told. The defense had worked within the bounds of the law to postpone Peter's court date and keep him on the field. The prosecuting attorney confirmed, "He [Anderson] was delaying because of that. He had tactics. First he set it for jury trial and then he couldn't beat it one jury term so it got moved to the next jury term."

Less than two months into the season, police were called to respond to another sexual assault complaint at Peter's residence. On October 24, 1993, Peter and six friends spent the evening at BJ's Hideaway, a strip bar outside Lincoln. Peter paid particular attention to Melissa DeMuth, a dancer at the club. At the conclusion of her shift, DeMuth agreed to let Peter drive her home. On the way, Peter indicated he needed to stop by his apartment. His friends had already driven there in another vehicle.

Once inside the apartment, Peter's roommates offered DeMuth a drink, while Peter went off to his room. One of the guys informed her that Peter wanted to show her something in his bedroom. When she walked in, Peter was sitting on his bed with his shirt off. Soon they began kissing. DeMuth claimed that "he was getting very aroused and that he then pulled his underwear down to below his knees and pulled hers off at the same time." Momentarily, Peter stood up and attempted to engage Melissa in oral sex. Then the door to the room suddenly opened. All of Peter's roommates were standing in the doorway, with nothing on but their underwear.

DeMuth began screaming hysterically, prompting them to leave the room, and angering Peter. Without bothering to recover her underwear, she ran out of the house with just her sweatpants, and immediately drove to a friend's house, where she called the police.

When police arrived at Peter's apartment, they were aware of the sexual assault charge pending against him. Peter met them at the door, claiming that his accuser was crazy. His white briefs and T-shirt matched DeMuth's description of what he was wearing. Once inside, the officers recovered DeMuth's headband, which according to the report filed later, police "believed to contain [Peter's] dried sperm."[6]

In the bedroom, Officer P. J. Schneider asked for Peter's version of what had transpired. Admitting to participating in various sex acts with DeMuth, Peter insisted that she had initiated everything. In his words, "Melissa went crazy and started screaming" after they had both put their clothes on, and an unexpected knock came on the bedroom door.[7]

During the questioning, Schneider stepped out of Peter's bedroom to talk with his partner, Sergeant Gade. Agreeing that they did not have a strong case at that point, Schneider and Gade decided to turn it over to the county attorney without making an arrest.

Worried about the perception that Nebraska athletes received preferential treatment from the courts, the sex crimes prosecutor carefully reviewed the police reports and Peter's and DeMuth's contrasting stories. "I believed her version," the prosecutor admitted. "I thought his sounded goofy, and I thought he had a temper."

Nonetheless, the prosecutor concluded, "I have to judge a case. Is there a reasonable basis to take this to trial? Is there a possibility of a conviction here?" The only physical evidence in the case was semen found on the headband DeMuth was wearing that evening.

"Take the facts as true," the prosecutor offered. "Say I give this to a jury. Did I prove that there was forcible sexual contact? Taking it just as her version, I didn't think I could prove it."

Besides, it was her word against his. Despite the ever-growing list of criminal complaints against Peter, it was her character that was going to be under a microscope. "Let's face it, the jury's going to know what she did for an occupation, and she goes with him to the house voluntarily. And I just didn't think there was any way a jury would convict based on those facts."

Another one of Peter's lawyers, New Jersey-based Gary Fox, dismissed DeMuth's story out of hand. "Let's set up the two poles," Fox said. "I think that clearly would make the difference. I think that's the way society works. That's the way our legal system works.

"People's reputations for truth and veracity are clearly taken into consideration. And when somebody says something to you, you look at the person that's saying it to you and you make a judgment based on what you know about them or what their reputation for truth and veracity is in the community in which they live. . . ."

Simply put, the accused was a prominent football player, and the accuser was a stripper. Peter's attorney concluded that DeMuth was "not of high moral character. Not somebody that you would say is a credible witness. And a person who is not to be believed."

It was a classic he-said, she-said case involving two individuals whose conduct and credibility could easily be called into question. Although the credibility and behavior of both the accuser and the accused were open to criticism, Fox explained, "The scales would be equal, so . . . my guy walks."

Feeling compelled to dismiss the case, the prosecutor commented, "I don't have a lot of respect for Christian Peter. And if I felt I had a good case, I would have filed it . . . [but] the burden's too great."

Meanwhile, Kuijvenhoven's case remained unresolved. Tired and frustrated by the delays, she called the victim witness unit and was told to hold on until after January. The Huskers had been invited to compete for the national championship in the Orange Bowl on New Year's Day. Peter's lawyers had succeeded in pushing his trial date back, but when it looked as if the case would end up interfering with the Orange Bowl, the defense decided to withdraw Peter's right to a jury trial and have the case heard by a judge. "When it [Peter's case] looked like it was going to get called up, then he [Peter's lawyer] waived jury to take it out of the jury term," said the prosecutor. "So he used delays to continue it."

Although prosecutors had resisted previous defense motions to delay the case, this time they gave their support. Peter's lawyer approached the lead prosecutor, saying, "Look, he is going to plead." The prosecutor responded, "If you're telling me this is a plea and you are not going to have a jury trial, OK, I'll continue it for that reason." The prosecutor stated, "It was an intentional delay on the part of the defense attorney to begin after football season, no doubt." But, she added, "If you do a jury trial you risk losing. And if I've got a guarantee of a plea, I'm sure I'm going to say, 'OK, I'll continue it for that reason.' "

Two weeks before the Orange Bowl, a third woman came forward with sexual assault charges against Peter. This accuser alleged she had been raped. Kathy Redmond was a student-athlete in her junior year at the University of Nebraska. Her academic advisor was one of Osborne's assistant coaches. Because she was personally acquainted with Osborne, she decided to take her case directly to him before going to the police.

Redmond was introduced to Peter in the first week of her freshman year on campus. His dorm was located next to hers, and she met him through friends. After accompanying Peter to his dorm room, she charged, he prevented her from leaving and ultimately raped her. According to Redmond, Peter showed up at her dorm a couple of nights later, intoxicated, along with a couple of friends. While one of his team-mates listened from a nearby room, Peter raped her a second time.

Listening to her describe a series of incidents that had occurred two years earlier, Osborne asked Redmond, "Why did you wait so long?"

Getting little response, he then asked, "Well, are you absolutely sure of who it was?"

"Yes. It was Christian Peter," she insisted.

"Well, I will have Christian here . . . and if you can identify him as the person who did this, then we will go forward and certainly take this to the authorities," Osborne explained.

Having Redmond come back when Peter was present was consistent with Osborne's preference for handling matters internally. "I realize that a lot of rape victims don't like to confront the rapist, but I knew her pretty well, and if she expressed any dismay or concern about it, then I would certainly not have expected her to come," he insisted.

Osborne added, "Since we were reasonably well acquainted, I assumed that she would be willing to do this if her statements were accurate."

Rather than return to Osborne's office with Peter present, Redmond took her complaint to the University of Nebraska campus police on December 16, 1993, just two weeks prior to the Orange Bowl. Three months later, Redmond's father called the campus police and demanded to know the status of the complaint. He found out that it had not yet been sent to the county prosecutor for review. On March 25, 1994, the sex crimes prosecutor finally received the complaint.

The circumstances surrounding Redmond's complaint posed insurmountable obstacles to the county prosecutors. Because the incident had happened over two years before, there was no physical or medical evidence to support Redmond's claim. More disturbing was the fact that the alleged second rape took place inside her dorm room, after she had allowed him to enter. "Frankly, I just didn't find that there was sufficient evidence on that one," the prosecutor said.

Nonetheless, the prosecutor was compelled to approach Peter's attorney Hal Anderson regarding Redmond's complaint. "Look, I'm not filing it, but I think he's got a problem and you ought to do something about it," the prosecutor said.

"She [Kuijvenhoven] is different from the others," said Peter's attorney Gary Fox. "The only reason that anybody listened to her is because of who she is, and that's the only reason it got as far as it did."

March turned out to be a busy month for the Huskers at the Lincoln courthouse. Peter finally entered a plea of no contest in the Kuijvenhoven case. He was sentenced to eighteen months' probation.

Meanwhile, Peter's defense lawyer, Hal Anderson, received a new client—Peter's teammate and future Heisman Trophy candidate Lawrence Phillips. Nebraska coaches had plucked Phillips from a halfway house in Los Angeles, where he had been living since age thirteen. His mother had thrown him out of the house following a violent episode. An exceptional talent, Phillips, like Peter, was brought to Nebraska despite academic skills so poor that he was virtually unrecruited by other schools. Like Peter, Phillips wasted no time running afoul of the law.

Phillips faced assault charges, but the delay process shelved the case for a year. Despite their legal problems, neither Peter nor Phillips saw any change in his status on the football roster. On the contrary, both were permitted to play the entire 1994 season. They led the team back to the Orange Bowl and helped it to capture the national championship against Miami on New Year's Day, 1995.

From her new home in a western state, Kuijvenhoven watched on television as the Cornhuskers were the honored guests of President Clinton at the White House on March 13, 1995. In keeping with tradition, the president had invited the college football champions to a private ceremony in Washington. "They are given an immediate status by being a part of the football program," Kuijvenhoven said. "A celebrity-type status without earning a moral status. It doesn't mean that they're very good and trustworthy people and that you can hang out with [them] and trust that they are not going to do these types of things to you."

Because of the status afforded to athletes, women who accuse them of rape come under exceptional scrutiny. The contrasting backgrounds of DeMuth and Kuijvenhoven, as well as their results within the justice system, indicate the importance prosecutors place on a victim's credibility—regardless of the athlete's character.

7

the appearance of respectability

I always instruct my clients upon arrival at the courthouse to get out in a normal manner, walk next to me in a slow and deliberate way, to have a look of confidence and acknowledge with a nod those who are familiar and supportive. . . . If your client is in custody, take special care to make sure that he or she appears neat, well groomed and in civilian clothes, even for perfunctory appearances.[1]

—Robert Shapiro, defense lawyer for O. J. Simpson

AT 8:00 P.M. ON NOVEMBER 2, 1994, TOM OSBORNE'S PRIVATE PLANE touched down at Boston's Logan Airport. Across town, at the Park Plaza Hotel, over six hundred dignitaries from sports, politics, media, and higher education were eagerly awaiting his arrival. Earlier that week, the Nebraska Cornhuskers had taken over the number-one rank in college football, but on this night Osborne was being honored by the Center for the Study of Sport in Society for his exceptional leadership in the community, particularly his advice to players to encourage youngsters in making positive life choices.

After rushing the coach and his small traveling party from the airport runway to the hotel's side entrance, the limousine driver waited outside the hotel. He had been informed that Osborne was due to exit the hotel just fifteen minutes later, and needed to return to his private plane for an immediate flight back to Lincoln, Nebraska.

Before Osborne was introduced, a sixty-second video clip prepared by the University of Nebraska's athletic department highlighted both the team's contributions to the community and its academic successes. The audience looked on with approval as Osborne was lauded for producing scholar-athletes while at the same time managing to compile an unsurpassed win-loss ratio. These qualities were in short supply in successful college sports programs. The coach then delivered a one-minute acceptance speech, expressed his thanks for the great honor, and exited the ballroom to rousing applause.

Ironically, as Osborne was accepting the prestigious humanitarian award, he was being rebuked in the press for his refusal to hold his players accountable when they broke the law. The criticism continued through the remainder of the 1994 season and on into the 1995 season. His attempts to justify using players who were under criminal investigation, and his pattern of reinstating players even after they had been convicted, produced a firestorm of criticism. *Sports Illustrated* deemed it "prairie justice,"[2] dubbing Osborne "coach and jury." The *New York Post* ridiculed the situation as "Tom foolery."[3] And *USA Today* asked, "What exactly does it take to get a Cornhusker suspended for the season?"[4]

With Nebraska the top-ranked team in the nation, the situation resembled the familiar scene of a college champion undergoing scrutiny for rules violations. Sports champions are seldom pure, but the Cornhuskers were coming under fire for matters far more serious than infractions of NCAA regulations. During the 1994 and 1995 seasons, seven of the team's starters and one key reserve player had been charged or convicted of serious crimes of a violent nature. Beginning with the decision in March 1993 not to suspend defensive tackle Christian Peter for even one regular season game, despite his being convicted of sexually assaulting Natalie Kuijvenhoven, Osborne excused a litany of highly public felony charges levied against his players:

• In 1993, after sitting out his freshman year because of academic ineligibility, defensive back Tyrone Williams was voted the Big Eight Newcomer of the Year. Weeks after the season ended, he was arrested for firing a gun into an occupied car. Lawyers successfully delayed the case for two years. After the charges were filed, Osborne stated publicly that he believed that Williams was innocent. While awaiting trial, Williams established himself as the best defensive back on the Cornhuskers, playing through the 1994 and 1995 seasons to complete his career at Nebraska. At the conclusion of the 1995 season he was drafted by the Green Bay Packers. On September 9, 1996, with his trial scheduled to begin in the first week of the NFL season, Williams pleaded guilty to an assault charge and a lesser charge of unlawfully discharging a firearm. He began serving a six-month jail sentence on February 24, 1997.

• Receiver Reggie Baul was forced to sit out his first two years at Nebraska due to academic deficiencies. But in his junior year he established himself as the team's number-one receiver. On November 29, 1994, he was arrested for theft, but Osborne allowed him to keep his starting position without missing any games. Baul later pleaded guilty to receiving stolen goods.

• Baul's counterpart, wide receiver Riley Washington, was arrested in 1994 after assaulting a man. He suffered no disciplinary action from the team. Later the criminal charges were reduced, and Washington was fined $100. Then on August 2, 1995, Washington was charged with attempted murder for shooting a man at a Lincoln convenience store. He spent thirteen days in jail until

$10,000 was raised to pay his bail. Osborne permitted him to retain his football scholarship and remain on the team while he awaited his trial, scheduled for fall 1996. "I think there is a very, very good chance that Riley didn't do what he's accused of," said Osborne. This statement came after a preliminary hearing in which two witnesses positively identified Washington.

• After playing for a junior college in Kansas, defensive tackle Jason Jenkins joined the Nebraska team. In April 1993, soon after arriving in Lincoln, he was charged with first-degree assault for smashing a beer bottle in a man's face, causing him to lose his eye. Jenkins faced twenty years in prison if convicted. His lawyer, Hal Anderson, negotiated a $25,000 settlement in exchange for the victim's agreement not to testify against Jenkins, who was allowed to plead guilty to lesser charges carrying a penalty of probation. Jenkins continued to play for the Cornhuskers. When Nebraska captured the national championship in January 1995, Jenkins graced the cover of the *Sporting News*.

• The defense attorney for Lawrence Phillips, the team's star running back at the start of the 1994 season, fought successfully to have the assault charges pending against him dropped in exchange for Phillips's entrance in a pretrial diversion program. But Phillips failed to complete the program, and within six months he was arrested for brutally beating his ex-girlfriend, Kate McEwen. Osborne initially suspended Phillips and told reporters, "Lawrence and I have agreed on what happened, and there's no question—I wouldn't call it a beating—but he certainly did inflict some damage to the young lady. She was dragged down some stairs and there were some injuries." Osborne suspended Phillips from the team on September 11, 1995, announcing publicly, "We have told all our players that abusive behavior such as this will not be tolerated." Osborne conceded, "There are occasions every four to five months when [Phillips] becomes a little explosive." Nonetheless, after just six games, Osborne reinstated Phillips after he pleaded no contest. "It wasn't a difficult decision for me to make," Osborne insisted. "It's like going for two points against Miami in '83. It was something I didn't have to think about."

• Less than twenty-four hours before Phillips attacked his ex-girlfriend, the team's other starting running back, Damon Benning, was arrested for assaulting his former girlfriend. After meeting with Benning, Osborne explained publicly, "We're sorry about it, but if it's like he says . . . certainly we're not going to fault him for what he did." Benning faced no disciplinary action from the team, and the charges against him were later dismissed.

• At approximately 5 A.M. on September 23, 1995, a woman was escorted to an area hospital, where she reported she had been raped hours earlier by a Nebraska player. Osborne was notified by his assistant coach that the player was likely to be charged later that day. The unnamed player and the alleged victim had met at a party following Nebraska's game against Pacific College. On Osborne's advice, the player contacted a defense attorney. The county attorney's office declined to press charges, and the case was dismissed.

• Only two weeks after Phillips was reinstated, a third running back, James Sims, entered a pretrial diversion program after being arrested for a July 3 incident involving his ex-girlfriend. He was charged with disturbing the peace and vandalism. Sims lost no time on the team.[5]

In the midst of this series of incidents, Osborne explained his recruiting policy to the *Omaha-World Herald*. "If we find a history of drugs or serious criminal activity, we don't touch them," he said. "But yeah, we'll take a kid who comes from a no-parent family. And we'll take a kid out of a tough neighborhood. You don't win football games with choirboys. You've got to be tough to play."[6] Bringing kids from troubled backgrounds to Nebraska and thrusting them into an environment where there were no boundaries was a dangerous game. "Generally, all college students are faced with freedoms that they typically have not had in high school," said Peter's lawyer, Gary Fox. "Beyond that, for the college athlete, particularly in a high-profile sport, those freedoms are exaggerated. There is sex, drugs, alcohol. . . . You better think about the potential consequences of what . . . typically . . . does occur to athletes, especially if they become successful, after partaking in some of the temptations that are there."

Seven of the Huskers' crimes reported to the police between 1993 and 1995 involved violence against women. Fox said, "The athlete gets more attention from girls. Whether it's a rock star or football star . . . people, for whatever reason, want to get closer to them and somehow be part of them and hook on to them. It clearly has the potential to affect their view [of women].

"Problems occur in any human relationship when two people have a different idea of where that relationship is going. The star's perception of where the relationship is going may be a whole lot more short term. . . . That creates a classic opportunity for a problem."

Osborne portrayed Phillips's eventual reinstatement as an attempt to reform the player, claiming that Phillips needed the structure of football to become "a pretty viable human being and a guy that does well down the road."[7] He added, "When the event first occurred, I felt that probably he should be dismissed permanently, because I thought it was more of a stalking case. But when I got to finally talk to him about the particulars and the details of the whole thing, I realized that wasn't the case at all.

"I asked him what I thought was the key question. I said, 'Were you in control, or were you out of control?' And he said he was out of control. And I knew at that point that he needed some help. Because he knew, and he had been talked to so extensively about the consequences of his actions. So we felt at that point something needed to be done, and the best way to get him to do it was to keep football in the equation."[8]

But a closer examination of Christian Peter's reinstatement suggests that Osborne's decision to reinstate Phillips was inevitable. In Osborne's view, the commission of a crime does not warrant a player's dismissal from the team. This conclusion is apparent when one considers the four-step process through which Osborne puts every criminal allegation. Ultimately, it serves as an endurance test that few complaints can withstand.[9]

Step 1: Gathering evidence

Because public figures are the subject of so much scrutiny, whenever an accusation is made against a Nebraska player, Osborne begins with the premise that "An awful lot of rumor and innuendo . . . has no substance in fact." More specifically, when the accusation involves a sexual assault, Osborne takes a lawyerly approach. He explains, "Sexual assault, it could mean rape, it could mean assault, it could mean touching a person inappropriately, it could mean verbally abusing someone of the opposite sex. There's a lot of gradations there."

In the case of Christian Peter, Osborne was forced to deal with all kinds of allegations. Feeling a responsibility to shield young players from sensational coverage, Osborne prefers to conduct his own interviews in an attempt to judge the merits of an accusation. Why? Osborne explains: "The main thing is that you want to make sure that whatever comes down is accurate, that you're not dealing with rumor and innuendo. That if someone is guilty, that they pay the price for it, but you want to make sure that you're not involved in witch hunts. And a lot of times people are pilloried publicly for things that really didn't happen.

By meeting personally with an accuser, Osborne can begin to form judgments on her credibility as well. He explained, "You certainly . . . have to look at the situation . . . the seriousness of the charge . . . and secondly you have to look at the charges. Are they timely?" Finally, he insists, you have to ask, "How reliable does the source of the information appear to be?" In Osborne's mind, none of the three women who filed police reports against Peter passed muster on all three questions.

Kathy Redmond's complaint lacked, among other things, *timeliness of reporting*. Osborne stated publicly, "I assumed the charges were rather suspect." With little evidence, it was difficult to substantiate the claim. "In other words, is this something that happened in the last few days, or is this something that happened four years ago? And if it happened three or four years ago, then why the time lag, and what are you going to really be able to find out?"

The reliability of the source was the problem in Melissa DeMuth's case. Although she reported the assault just hours after the incident, her occupation as a dancer in a strip bar threw her account and her credibility into question. Besides, six of Peter's friends and roommates had confirmed his version of the events.

Natalie Kuijvenhoven, on the other hand, had both credibility and a timely report. But Osborne was unimpressed with the *seriousness of the charge*. Kuijvenhoven was grabbed in the crotch twice, once from the front and once from behind, by a man she had never seen before. Osborne explained, "I mean those types of things happen, I would assume, almost every weekend in almost every college town . . . where somebody grabs somebody inappropriately in a bar or something like this. It's not an unusual type of event." Although there is a state law prohibiting this type of abuse and intimidation, Osborne's position was that the incident would be better resolved quietly in his office. Kuijvenhoven and prosecutors saw it differently.

After Kuijvenhoven rejected Osborne's invitation to meet with him and Peter in his office, Osborne pursued the facts in the case independently. "I never was able to talk to the young lady, so I don't know what her story was," said Osborne. "I did talk to Christian and one or two other people who were apparently present."

Not only did his methods anger the victim; his hands-on approach bordered on evidence tampering, a felony. A prosecutor handling the Kuijvenhoven case complained, "They're tampering with witnesses. I'm not saying that they're trying to get them to change their story or anything, but usually you're not to have contact with [potential witnesses]."

Osborne's meddling with the evidence in criminal investigations went beyond merely interviewing potential witnesses. After defensive player Tyrone Williams was identified in connection with a shooting, Osborne locked away the gun he was suspected to have used in the crime. County attorney Gary Lacy told *Sports Illustrated,* "That's Osborne using his influence to disrupt the criminal justice system . . . and he should stay out of the criminal justice system."[10]

Step 2: Handling law enforcement

Osborne maintains that his heavy involvement in criminal matters early on does not impede justice, but rather ensures fairness. He explained, "I guess if I'm convinced that something happened, and if it was serious, then, of course, we'd go to the authorities, and we'd have to ride it out and let people collect all the evidence they can, and see what happens."

The qualifiers Osborne placed on allegations that deserve the attention of law enforcement come from his genuine belief that athletes are at a disadvantage once they enter the criminal justice system. "It has been my contention for some time that it is almost impossible for an athlete to get a completely fair shake in the courts if there has been a great deal of publicity concerning the case," he asserted. This position is based partly on his belief that law enforcement bends over backward to avoid the stigma of being soft on athletes. "In many cases that have come to my attention, once an athlete receives a certain amount of publicity, you find that the city attorney, the county attorney, or whoever is looking at the case feels some pressure to press charges—to bring the case forward in the courts—in view of not wanting to appear that somehow he's soft on athletes or he's not doing his job. It becomes very difficult for law enforcement people to put them [athletes] in pretrial diversion or to give them probation or to say, 'We don't have enough evidence to push the case.' "

A prosecutor who has handled numerous cases against Nebraska players conceded, "I think we may treat the male athletes more harshly than non[athletes], because everybody is worried about being accused of giving them preferential treatment. So I think, actually, in Lincoln it's more likely they get filed on. Not that we're making up charges or anything like that, but I think we worry about the appearance of giving them a break."

While this statement seems to support Osborne's suspicions, it says nothing of the tremendous impact Osborne has on whether a charge filed against one of his players ultimately results in a conviction. Osborne's outstanding reputation, combined with the abundant resources available to accused athletes, plays a major role in deterring prosecution of his players. Filing a charge against a player is one thing; convicting him is another.

The prosecutor confirmed, "[Athletes] get good representation, and they have a lot of resources available to them that other individuals don't, so I think after it's filed, they certainly have lots of opportunities for them to assist them in their defense that maybe the regular Joe on the street doesn't have."

How does this situation affect the prosecutor's approach to a case? A prosecutor who has reviewed numerous complaints against Nebraska players explained, "I suppose you just want to make sure you have your ducks in a row. Just prepare yourself for the onslaught that's going to come. So you might prepare the case better or . . . be more prepared on what you have to face, and make sure everything is in order when you file it.

"The coaching support over there is a huge support system for these athletes, and I think that they feel like these students are here without parents or family, and so they assist them in lots of ways . . . going to bat for them, writing letters, or whatever."

This support system was not lost on the sex crimes prosecutor when she reviewed the three complaints against Peter. She admitted, "I was aware of this presence"—a history stretching back to a criminal case that had a negative impact on both the police department and the prosecutor's office.

In January 1992, Nebraska running back Scott Baldwin was charged with first-degree assault against a woman and third-degree assault against a police officer. Following a dispute with a police officer at an on-campus basketball game, Baldwin had begun jogging home to his apartment. When two of his teammates saw him and offered him a ride, without provocation Baldwin attacked the player in the passenger's seat, choking him. While both players were attempting to get Baldwin under control, he jumped on the hood of the car and shattered the windshield with his fist.

When Baldwin threatened one of his teammates with a jagged piece of glass, his other teammate wrestled him to the ground. Once subdued, Baldwin got up and removed all his clothing. As he stood there stark naked, a woman in her early twenties emerged from a nearby apartment to take her dog for a walk, unaware of what had happened just minutes before. Suddenly, Baldwin lifted her off her feet and slammed her violently down on the pavement. He then dragged her across the street and smashed her head against a nearby car, picked her up again, and repeatedly banged her head on the concrete.

The victim was bleeding into the frontal lobe of her brain as well as her sinus cavity. Her skull was fractured and blood ran along the brain sack, ultimately draining into her spinal column. Her recovery from the savage attack required two months of hospitalization. A former graphic artist, she had lost all her basic motor function, and had to relearn skills like brushing her teeth and combing her hair. Her short-term memory capacity, counting ability, and vocabulary all had to be rehabilitated.

Hal Anderson defended Baldwin, challenging the prosecutor's request for $500,000 bail. The judge set Baldwin's bail at $10,000—still far more than he could muster. Yet "an anonymous source" paid the fee, allowing Baldwin to be released. Osborne explained, "The only thing I know is that [the anonymous source] had been out of the state for some years and had recently returned. It was a stroke of good fortune, because no ticket holder or anyone connected to the team could pay it." He went on to remind the public, "I would hate to see Baldwin painted as a villain. This was not a voluntary act. . . ."[11]

With the support of the university, Osborne was instrumental in establishing a private fund to help pay for Baldwin's legal and medical fees. The university also obtained clearance from the NCAA to pay for Baldwin's medical expenses directly. In addition, the athletic department worked within NCAA rules to pay for the transportation of Baldwin's family to Nebraska. Finally, a judge granted Osborne's request to assume personal care of Baldwin while he awaited trial. Baldwin was allowed to move in with the coach.

This show of support for Baldwin led one police officer to write a letter of protest to the NCAA. He called Osborne's plan "offensive," insisting that portraying Baldwin as the victim was misguided. Responding to the letter, Osborne told the *Daily Nebraskan,* "After visiting with [the officer], I was alarmed because he didn't seem to be able to distinguish the difference between someone who is a criminal, who premeditates an unprovoked attack, and someone who might have a psychological problem. The concern I had was that someone in law enforcement was objecting to somebody getting a medical checkup. I thought that was a dangerous attitude for a police officer to have."[12]

Osborne then sent a letter to the chief of police. "I just thought the letter to the police chief might be a good idea, to let him know that maybe this is a topic that might be discussed with some of the officers," Osborne said. "If [the complaining officer's] perception is a common one among police officers, maybe it is a matter that needs to be addressed." Osborne went on to tell the *Daily Nebraskan,* "I can understand how frustrating it can be for the police to arrest someone, then see them let go. But I felt a person in a law enforcement position would respect the rights of the accused, and would want to find out what the problem was."[13]

All this begs the question: If Baldwin was so unstable mentally, what was he doing on the football team? Nonetheless, Baldwin, through his attorney, entered a plea of not guilty by reason of insanity. Osborne dedicated the annual spring football game to raising money for the victim's medical bills. In a press conference he announced, "We're doing this because we feel it's the right thing to do and because of commitments we made to [the victim] and her family. It's not because of anything that's happened in the last couple of months, the public pressure or outcry."[14] Osborne had been criticized for being more concerned about his player than about the victim. The game raised $34,000 for the victim.

Baldwin was eventually acquitted on all counts by reason of insanity. Under court order to take the drug Lithium twice daily and check in with his psychiatrist once a week, Baldwin was allowed to return to school under scholarship while receiving outpatient treatment. Less than three months later, two female Omaha police officers responded to a series of phone calls regarding a disturbance involving Baldwin. When they arrived at the scene, they found Baldwin, who was naked, attempting to crash through a glass door. In their struggle to subdue him, a gun was discharged. Baldwin was hit with a bullet and paralyzed from the chest down.

Recalling Baldwin's case, the sex crimes prosecutor who was reviewing the complaints against Peter explained, "There was a lot of support by the university and coaching staff on that one. Osborne took an active part in terms of appearing with [Baldwin] and things like that." A police source added, "I saw how much they [intervened] for Scott Baldwin. And that was an eye-opener for me."

Step 3: Determining appropriate team discipline

Osborne's presence, the exceptional legal representation available to Christian Peter, and public support for the Nebraska football program did not prevent Kuijvenhoven from obtaining a conviction in her case. Because Peter's conviction placed Osborne in a must-punish situation—a player had been found guilty according to law—he kept Peter out of the annual spring exhibition game. But he took no other action. The following exchange from a July 1995 interview illustrates the complete power Osborne exercised in deciding what was appropriate punishment for a player convicted of a third-degree sexual assault.

Question: *Did you have a role in that [the decision to suspend Peter from the spring game], or was that completely independent of your jurisdiction?*

Osborne: *How would somebody suspend him if I didn't do it? I don't understand.*

Question: *Is that something that the athletic department had input on, or was that a sole . . . [interrupted]*

Osborne: *I had input!*

Osborne, then, controls the penalties handed down to his players; no disciplinary measures are made without his approval. His approach is, "If I'm thoroughly convinced it's a serious matter, then we're naturally going to take some disciplinary action, which usually involves suspension of some kind. It may be permanent. It may be for a game. It may be for whatever." Convincing Osborne that a suspension is in order is no small chore. Defending his decision to allow Riley Washington to remain on the team while he was facing a charge of attempted murder, Osborne said, "He is, by law, innocent until proven guilty, and that is our stance, also."[15]

In Peter's case, there had been a conviction. "He was convicted of a sexual assault in court, so I didn't feel I could ignore that," Osborne acknowledged. Nevertheless, Osborne's opinion of the conviction was reflected in his decision to suspend Peter from only one practice game. "I realize that there was still, even though he was convicted, that there was some question as to what exactly did happen . . . there was never unanimity that Christian even did it. So I didn't feel real great about it," said Osborne.

"There was one other person who claimed that he did it and that it wasn't Christian," Osborne maintained. "I'm not even totally convinced that we absolutely got the right guy. She turned around and claimed Christian was standing there, but it was never a real clear-cut thing. . . . No one ever saw him do it. The girl did not even see him. . . . She knew somebody grabbed her from behind, in an inappropriate place. And she turned around, and she said Christian was standing there. Well, there were a lot of people standing there."

Peter had had a chance to contest Kuijvenhoven's allegations in court, but chose not to, in part because of the presence of at least one witness who had confirmed that Peter had assaulted Kuijvenhoven. Nonetheless, Osborne managed to find a flaw in the witness's statement. "I believe that her [Kuijvenhoven's] boyfriend was the guy who had tried out for the football team and that had decided to quit. And I'm thinking he was a person who was not real friendly toward our program. And he may have been involved, too," Osborne explained. Peter's defense attorney, Hal Anderson, had stated publicly that the victim was engaged to a man "who was anti–Nebraska football." In fact, the man who was with Kuijvenhoven and had witnessed the assault had never tried out for the Cornhuskers. Furthermore, Kuijvenhoven had never been engaged.

Another one of Peter's lawyers, Gary Fox, tried to minimize the importance of the conviction by insisting, "No court of law ever determined any facts in that case." Fox explained, "The court accepts that the complaint is not being contested and finds [him] guilty. There was never any testimony under oath given by Natalie. There was an unpermitted touching and he pled guilty to that. In the plea, they tried to establish a factual basis and [Christian] said, 'I don't remember what occurred, but from what I've been told by friends of mine that were there, apparently I did touch her.' So did he ever admit specifically and exactly what she makes in her statement? No!"

Osborne incorporated Fox's line of reasoning into his decision not to suspend Peter. "Christian has denied ever really remembering that particular event." said Osborne. "He just chose not to dispute it." Nonetheless, Osborne recognized, "Some disciplinary action was certainly due and forthcoming. We did suspend him. In view of all the publicity and the uproar and the furor, he paid a pretty good price for it. He was given all kinds of negative publicity which most people don't receive . . . nationally. He was suspended from the football team at a time when his parents came out to watch him play."

Step 4: Convincing the public

The weekly press conferences that sometimes transform Osborne from a football coach into a legal advocate are not altogether unwelcome to the coach. "The accuser ofttimes has free reign in the press, and yet the person being accused, many times, is on legal advice not expected to say anything," he said. "So it becomes a one-sided conversation in the papers. And that's kind of a disconcert[ing] situation." As a result, Osborne takes it on himself to level the playing field.

Insisting, "I did what I thought was right," Osborne closed the book on the Kuijvenhoven case. But his public advocating had just begun. Encouraged by Peter's conviction, and dissatisfied with the court's treatment of her rape complaint, Kathy Redmond filed a civil suit against both Peter and the University of Nebraska in August 1994. Her suit compounded the sensational coverage surrounding the arrest and reinstatement of Phillips the following month.

With the Phillips incident pushing Peter's conviction out of the spotlight, Osborne attempted to garner support for his decision to return Phillips to the playing field. Despite Phillips's conviction in a criminal court, the university had decided not to suspend him. Instead, it mandated his attendance at all his classes, completion of anger counseling, and probation. "I don't think that the university or the football program has done what is the easy thing," Osborne explained to the national press. "The easy thing would have been to dismiss him, probably permanently. But basically, after examining all the factors involved, many of which you will never be privy to, and shouldn't be, we simply feel it was the right thing to do."[16]

Although this approach failed to persuade many, the campus community and the state of Nebraska embraced it at face value. Chancellor Joan Leitzel endorsed Osborne's position in a public statement. "Both the student judicial process and judgments made by the football program have been difficult," said Leitzel. "I feel that the sanctions assigned to Lawrence Phillips are substantial and appropriate. They provide him with a highly structured and supervised environment.[17]

NCAA secretary-treasurer Phyllis Howlett also emphasized her trust in Osborne's judgment. She told USA Today, "Certainly, Tom has a great reputation, and I have no reason to question that it's well-founded. Based on that, I have to assume he's got information I don't."[18]

Those in the campus community who disagreed with Osborne refrained from speaking out. Phillips's victim, Kate McEwen, was a player on the Nebraska women's basketball team. Her coach, Angela Beck, held back tears, stating publicly, "Tom has made a decision. As part of the university and part of the athletic staff, I'm going to support Tom."[19] The following day she conceded, "The process, itself, I'm very uncomfortable with . . . the fact there aren't stricter guidelines. But I have to be professional about how I act and what I say. I think most people who know me, they know what I feel internally. But it's not my team. It's not my player. It's not my university."[20]

Only the university's women's groups condemned the decision publicly. Referring to the condition that Phillips had to attend all his classes as part of his reinstatement, the director of the university women's center, Judith Kriss, asked, "Since when is going to class at a university a punishment?"[21] Meanwhile, the chairwoman of the women's caucus, Mary McGarvey, stated, "The main point is that we don't want students who are assaulting people to represent the university."[22] When the caucus submitted a proposal to amend the student code of conduct to require suspension from extracurricular activities of students convicted of violent crimes, the school's vice chancellor for student affairs, Jim Griesen, said that though the cause was noble, it was not one he supported. He added, "There are unique circumstances to every situation and every case should be looked at on its own merit."[23]

A source close to the criminal cases against Cornhusker players, whose daughter attends the university, offered an explanation of why so many people there refused to speak out against giving scholarships to criminals. She said, "People from all over Nebraska, or any state, they're trusting the university. They're sending their children to the university to live away from home, maybe sometimes for the first time. We want to project that as a safe environment. . . . The school obviously has to present that image that the campus is safe, 'We take care of our students.' "

Just as he had trivialized Peter's attack on Kuijvenhoven, Osborne split hairs to justify his leniency toward Phillips. But the beating McEwen sustained at Phillips's hands was a vicious assault.

A native Kansan, McEwen had begun dating Phillips shortly after he arrived in Lincoln. The relationship was quite abusive; Phillips beat her on numerous occasions, ultimately prompting her to break it off. In the summer of 1995 McEwen was seeing a Stanford University transfer student, Scott Frost, who was scheduled to become the Huskers quarterback after sitting out a year. McEwen was at Frost's apartment, watching television, when Phillips came looking for her.

After trying unsuccessfully to enter Frost's apartment through the front door, Phillips scaled the wall of the three-story building and forced his way through a sliding glass door on the balcony. Fearing for her life, McEwen rushed into Frost's bathroom. Following her into the bathroom in a rage, Phillips grabbed McEwen, shouting, "Why did you lie to me?"[24] In a flurry of pulls and pushes, he dragged her from the bathroom and began to beat her mercilessly in Frost's living room.

"What about football, Lawrence?" Frost shouted, as he futilely attempted to fend Phillips off. "What about football?"[25] Osborne had spoken to Frost about Phillips's run-ins with McEwen. Frost was aware that Phillips had been warned not to have any further contact with her, or risk being throw off the team.

Ignoring Frost, Phillips dragged McEwen by the hair down three flights of stairs, slamming her head into the lobby wall. McEwen's hair and shirt were soaked with blood. But not until numerous female students, a residential supervisor, and two men had rushed to the lobby, roused by the noise, did Phillips leave McEwen alone. She was taken to the hospital, where she received stitches on her head and treatment for various other wounds.

In his book *On Solid Ground,* released after the 1996 season, Osborne described the attack as follows: "Lawrence then dragged her down three flights of stairs. He grabbed her by the hair and at times by her shirt. When Lawrence and the victim reached the bottom of the stairs, Scott tried to separate Lawrence from the victim. . . .

"When Lawrence pulled the victim away from them [the two men trying to rescue McEwen], she hit her head on the wall. At some point, the back of her head was cut. Lawrence became somewhat distracted and Scott and Matthew helped her reach the safety of a neighbor's apartment. At that point, Lawrence beat on the mailboxes with his hands and cut them quite badly."

Minimizing the severity of McEwen's injuries, Osborne went on to write: "The victim did receive several stitches on the back of her head. She received bruises and scrapes from being dragged down the stairs. Her shirt was torn and bloody, so she left it with a person who lived in the apartment complex. Although she was treated and released from the hospital in a short time, she was understandably traumatized by the event."

Sandy Worm, who witnessed the portion of the assault that took place near the mailboxes, said, "I saw Lawrence Phillips at the time of his assault pounding the victim's head against the wall." Osborne wrote, "It became clear that [Worm] only saw Lawrence holding [McEwen's] head against the wall with his hands, and did not see any movement to or from the wall."

The absurdity of Osborne's efforts to diminish the brutality of Phillips's actions toward McEwen reached its peak in August 1996. On August 16, less than two months after Osborne's book was published, McEwen filed a lawsuit in Jackson County circuit court in Kansas. It outlined the full scope of Phillips's excessive violence, which went unchecked throughout his career at Nebraska. Although the suit was filed under seal, Judge William F. Mauer lifted the seal temporarily, and the *Kansas City Star* obtained a copy. The *Star* reported the following excerpts from McEwan's suit:[26]

• In October 1994, "Phillips shoved her head into a wall so hard it broke through the wall, then choked her and would not allow her to leave his apartment."

• In April 1995, "Phillips asked her whether she was dating anyone else and threatened her, saying, 'I'm going to shoot you in the kneecaps and then shoot you in the elbows. This is Los Angeles gang style of dealing with people.' "

• On May 10, 1995, "Phillips slashed her car tires and threatened to kill her. That came after he demanded a glass of water and McEwen told him to get it himself."

• On August 24, 1995, "McEwen agreed to drive Phillips, who was drunk, home to his apartment. He forced her to stay there and sexually assaulted her."

• On September 10, 1995, "Phillips beat her and kicked her while she was at a friend's house. She contends he then grabbed her hair 'caveman style,' pulled her down three flights of steps and slammed her head into a wall."

Soon after the *Star* published these statements, Phillips's lawyers succeeded in removing the case to the federal court in Kansas City. After holding private hearings in his chambers on September 17, 18, and 19, U.S. District Court Judge D. Brook Bartlett ruled against keeping the suit under seal. "No human being should treat another one the way he [Phillips] allegedly treated her," said Bartlett, "and no respectable university should be condoning this kind of behavior. . . . This matter should result in a substantial investigation into the University of Nebraska as to how they—what are they in the business of doing up there?

"Are they in the business of making money off the football team, or are they in the business of providing an atmosphere where students can get, on a fair and equitable basis, an education and are protected in their physical well-being from other students?

"And if outrageous behavior occurs, assuming, I'm not concluding it did, then the university has an obligation to the victim not to make it worse, not the make the victim suffer, but to make the wrongdoer suffer."[27]

Immediately after Bartlett's ruling, Phillips reached an undisclosed settlement with McEwen. To Bartlett's remarks Osborne responded, "I know what happened here and we have no apologies for anything we did."[28]

Revenue-generating college athletics is no place for young men who display criminal tendencies—particularly violent behavior toward women. The environment of big-time college sports facilitates recidivism, not reform. "Deterrence requires that potential offenders think about the consequences of their actions," Northwestern University law professor Paul H. Robinson has said. "More important, deterrence requires that those who do think about the consequences see some real risk that they will be caught and punished."[29] To continually excuse criminal violence by troubled athletes simply nourishes their proclivity for abuse. The willingness of coaches to maintain scholarships for athletes with a clear disdain for the law serves the athletic program, but hurts the athlete and puts the community at risk.

Just days after Nebraska won its second consecutive national championship, Lawrence Phillips announced that he was dropping out of school and entering the NFL with Peter. Both players left the University of Nebraska without graduating, and both were arrested before the summer. On March 2, Peter assaulted twenty-one-year-old Janelle Mues in a bar following a football banquet. He was reportedly with Jason Jenkins and Reggie Baul—both well known to the courts—when he grabbed Mues around the neck, shouting obscenities at her. Peter pleaded guilty and was sentenced to ten days in prison. On August 22, 1996, after losing his appeal of the sentence, he entered a Nebraska state prison.

Phillips was arrested on June 13, 1996, after a California highway patrolman spotted him driving 80 miles an hour in a gold Mercedes-Benz with a flat tire. Phillips's blood-alcohol level was twice the legal limit in California.

Osborne's players' troubles continued. On February 24, 1997, Green Bay Packer Tyrone Williams began serving a six-month jail sentence in Nebraska in connection with the shooting incident during his junior year. After pleading no contest in December 1996 to driving under the influence in California, St. Louis Ram Lawrence Phillips was arrested on February 16, 1997, for disorderly conduct at a hotel in Omaha. Four days after his arrest, he and his ex-Nebraska teammate Clinton Childs were sued by Lisa Bateman and her boyfriend, Arthur Stallworth, who were present at the hotel when Phillips was arrested. The suits alleged that they were assaulted, battered, and falsely imprisoned by Phillips and Childs. Bateman's lawsuit also alleged that Phillips touched intimate parts of her body with his hands and a champagne bottle.[30] Additionally, on February 20, 1997, St. Louis police charged Phillips with property damage, leaving the scene of an accident, and driving with a revoked license in connection with an incident in which he left the scene of an accident: he had driven his Hum Vee into a pillar at the entrance to his Forest Hills Country Club neighborhood in late January.[31] On March 11, 1997, Phillips was sentenced to thirty days in jail for violating his Nebraska probation in connection with the beating of Kate McEwan. And in February 1997 the Board of Regents for the University of Nebraska reached an out-of-court settlement with Kathy Redmond in connection with her civil suit in which she alleged rape at the hands of Christian Peter. Meanwhile Peter, after completing a brief jail sentence in Nebraska for the assault on Mues, was signed by the New York Giants at the close of 1996.

As noble as Tom Osborne's words may sound, his repeated recruitment and support of criminal players is reprehensible. It is difficult to imagine any other scenario in which so many citizens would not only stand behind, but actually cheer for, thugs who abuse women and commit other violent crimes. But Osborne's status as a coach allows him to defend socially deviant behavior without serious criticism or consequence. Moreover, the failure of universities to address coaches' tolerance for athletes who commit rape, battery, and gun-related crimes is equivalent to complicity.

8

the price
of justice

The average rapist gets three and a half years. Most victims get life.

—United Way public service announcement

THE GUILTY VERDICT RETURNED AGAINST MIKE TYSON IN 1992 FOR THE rape of Desiree Washington was a rarity in criminal jurisprudence. In general, juries hesitate to believe women who claim rape at the hands of male acquaintances. When athletes are involved, it is virtually unheard of. Tyson was the most celebrated of the few athletes who have been convicted and imprisoned for rape.

On the surface, Washington's triumph in court would seem to bode well for other victims of date rape by a well-known athlete. Nonetheless, the ordeal Washington experienced in the aftermath of Tyson's conviction sends a chilling message to women who are raped by prominent athletes: Even when an athlete is convicted, he will often regain his fame and fortune, only to run afoul of the law again. Meanwhile, the victim's actions are scrutinized and her character maligned long after the verdict.

Washington watched helplessly as appeals lawyer Alan Dersho-witz impugned her reputation throughout Tyson's three-year incarcera-tion. On his release from jail in May 1995, Tyson immediately returned to professional sports, earning a reported $40 million for his first fight. He also went back to frequenting strip joints, and was reported to police for abusing a woman less than one year after his release.

At 3:30 A.M. on July 20, 1991, Desiree Washington walked into the emergency room at Methodist Hospital in Indianapolis and reported that she had been raped. The on-duty physician, Dr. Thomas Richard-son, attended to her. Because Washington arrived at the hospital more than twenty-four hours after the attack, Richardson did not collect fin-gernail scrapings, comb for pubic hairs, or administer a vaginal wash-ing—all standard procedures that would have yielded little, if any, evidence at that point. Instead, he performed the uncomfortable yet critically important physical examination. He discovered two abrasions, both an eighth of an inch wide and three-eighths of an inch long, at the opening to Washington's vagina. Richardson's attempt to insert a speculum in order to search for internal injuries caused Washington to wince and squirm. From his experience in conducting more than two thousand pelvic examinations, some of which he had performed on rape victims, Richardson was sensitive to Washington's pain, and refrained from completing the full pelvic exam. Police later recovered the panties Washington wore on the night of the rape. They contained two blood stains corresponding to the abrasions Richardson found in her vaginal area.[1]

After counseling Washington on the possibility of pregnancy and disease, Richardson injected her with an antibiotic to prevent her from developing gonorrhea. He also advised her to undergo an HIV test. After completing the exam, he documented his findings and forwarded his report to the sex crimes unit of the Indianapolis Police Department.

The nature of sex crimes is such that the victim and perpetrator are typically the only people with direct knowledge of the assault. Without witnesses, medical evidence corroborating the victim's version of events is of paramount importance. Documentation of bruises, blood, and other trauma to the most intimate areas of a woman's body is crucial, but it requires victims to submit to a humiliating medical examination on the heels of being sexually assaulted. When the perpetrator is a relative of the victim or a person of public note, self-blame and confusion often dissuade a victim from coming forward until the physical evidence of sexual violence has been lost.

"The guilt trip that the woman puts herself on causes the passage of time to elapse, letting the trails get cold and the sheets to get washed and the wounds to heal and the bruises to dissipate," said Greg Garrison, the prosecutor in Washington's criminal complaint against Tyson. When an athlete is the rapist, "It's worse, because not only are you dumb for going out with the wrong guy, but you are really dumb for not knowing that a jock was going to try to get you," Garrison explained. "Washington struggled awful hard with that." Investigators would later discover numerous other women whose allegations of abuse at Tyson's hands closely resembled Washington's. Fearing reprisal and disbelief, those women had remained silent about their encounters with the fighter.

On July 22, Washington's medical report landed on the desk of Tommy Kuzmik, sex crimes investigator for the Indianapolis Police Department. On reading Dr. Richardson's findings, Kuzmik assumed it was the last he would ever hear of Washington's complaint against Mike Tyson. He knew that countless victims avoided going to the police after seeking medical treatment for rape. Victims of sexual violence are understandably averse to public disclosure of their trauma. By filing a formal complaint against an athlete of Tyson's stature, Washington had opened herself to intense media scrutiny. "There is a proclivity toward sensationalism which attends the charges of any athlete, cutting more against him than her initially," said Garrison. But defense lawyers can manipulate the media and their attraction to athletes. "It is the time-honored tradition of character assassination," Garrison explained. Women who are raped by famous men risk having their reputations smeared in the pursuit of justice.

Nonetheless, one day after setting aside Washington's medical report, Kuzmik was surprised to hear her voice on the telephone, seeking an appointment to press charges. Accompanied by her parents, Washington went to the station and told her story to Kuzmik. Shortly after she delivered her thirty-minute formal statement, Marion County District Attorney Jeffrey Modisett asked Kuzmik matter of factly, "What do you think?"

"He did it," Kuzmik assured him. His unequivocal assessment carried great weight with the district attorney, because of his extensive background in interviewing both the victims and the perpetrators of sexual assaults. "I think she's going to make an excellent witness," he continued. "She's intelligent, she's articulate, she's attractive—easy to look at, easy to understand, easy to believe. Given her background in public speaking, you're not going to fluster this girl. She's going to sit up there and she's going to tell her story. She's going to stick to it. It's believable, it's factual."

"Can we win?" Modisett asked.

"It's as good as any case I've ever taken to court," said Kuzmik.[2]

Given the public's limited awareness of the social myths that defense lawyers so easily exploit in cases of acquaintance rape, prosecutors are skeptical of jurors' ability to get beyond the reasonable doubt standard in he-said, she-said disputes over consent. A jury's image of the victim can play a far more influential role in a trial's outcome than the subtle dynamics of a man's use of force on a female acquaintance. Not only would Indianapolis jurors be asked to judge a classic case of date rape. The accused was Mike Tyson, a notorious ladies' man with a clever argument: Why would I resort to rape when I can have almost any woman I want?

The reason for prosecutors' trepidation is apparent in the comments of juror Michael Wettig, a computer maintenance worker and sports enthusiast who, prior to serving on the Tyson jury, had no knowledge of the prevalence of acquaintance rape. "I didn't hear much about date rape until this trial," said Wettig. "I read a lot of stories in the paper about rape on the street, but not about date rape."

Kuzmik's assessment of Washington proved on the mark; the jury found her appealing and persuasive. From the moment Washington entered the courtroom to testify against Tyson, jurors' eyes were riveted to her slight, 102-pound body, which contrasted starkly with Tyson's thick, 260-pound frame, seated just a few feet away. "She was cute," said Wettig, sizing up Washington's appearance. "She was very intelligent. She didn't seem like the type of person who went to parties . . . just for sex. The way she acted and talked, she seemed very innocent."

Although they were genuinely impressed by Washington's appearance, jurors were convinced of Tyson's guilt by her graphic recital of what had occurred in suite 606 of the Canterbury Hotel on July 19, 1991. "He put his hand into me, his fingers in my vagina," she testified before the court, as Tyson looked on. "He grabbed my legs, and he lifted me up . . . and he licked me from my rectum to my vagina; he pulled his penis, exposed his penis. . . . He jammed it in my vagina."[3]

At Garrison's request, Washington recounted Tyson's words as he climbed off her after the brutal ordeal. " 'You're just a baby,' " she recalled him saying. " 'That's all. You're just a crybaby. You're crying because I'm big.' "[4]

Mesmerized by Washington's testimony, Wettig called her "a trouper." Garrison would comment later, "She had the guts and courage to say what the law required. A kid with less courage than she had would have folded up like a cheap card table. In fact, a person with less courage than she had would never have made it to the trial."

Perhaps anticipating the impact of Washington's unwavering, precise responses to such intimate questions, Tyson's handlers attempted to dissuade her from testifying against the champ. Just before the trial started, Washington was offered $1 million to drop the charges and settle the case privately.[5] Such tactics are not unusual; most wealthy athletes who are accused of violence desperately want to escape criminal prosecution and conceal their deviant lifestyles. In 1995, a seventeen-year-old alleged sexual assault victim was persuaded not to testify before a grand jury after Dallas Cowboy Erik Williams paid her an undisclosed sum. In 1994 University of Nebraska football player Jason Jenkins paid a student victim who had agreed not to testify against him $25,000. And as many as ten members of the Cincinnati Bengals contributed to the payoff of Victoria Alexander, out of fear that the incident might become known to their wives as well as the public.

Instead of taking Tyson's money, Washington opted for criminal prosecution. Although she had already endured the assault, a difficult rape exam, a statement to police, and testimony before a grand jury, her decision to accuse Tyson in open court meant exposing herself on a new level. "They had this big oversized picture of a woman's vagina with her legs spread, and it was facing the jury for two days," recalled Wettig. "I wouldn't want to look at that with men around for two days."

By submitting herself to the cruel process of reliving her rape before the eyes of the jury and the public, Washington placed Tyson in a position accused athletes rarely encounter: having to testify under oath about their behavior and attitudes toward women. A crucial contributor to the unusually low rape conviction rate among athletes is the fact that jurors are seldom exposed to players' warped sense of what constitutes appropriate treatment of women. Boasting of their consensual contact with their accusers, athletes rarely need to testify, as their victims shrink under the relentless character attacks of high-priced lawyers. But in this case, Washington managed to step down from the witness stand with her reputation intact.

"The truth of the matter is that if they don't have forensic evidence, expert opinion testimony, alibi, or character evidence—none of which Tyson had—somebody's get to get up there," said Garrison. "In every violent crime, the jury wants to look at [the defendant's] eyes and they want to see if he is a liar or telling the truth. If you don't give them that chance, they may assume, 'Well, hell, the scales look very one-sided. What choice have I got? All the evidence is one way.'

"Tyson can't sit there like Mortimer Fud who they picked up down in the alley somewhere for caving up some wino. He can't sit there like a bump."

Tyson's blunt admission of frequent, crude sexual exploits proved devastating to his case. "He didn't have a motive," concluded Wettig. "He's been with all these other women and they've wanted it. Why should Washington be any different? After a while you get used to it. Every night you're going to bed with somebody different. All these women are willing. Maybe in his mind he didn't think he was doing it, but if this lady says no and tries to fight you, you're guilty of rape whether you think you are or not."

The jury needed less than ten hours to deliberate before reaching a unanimous guilty verdict. "All the men voted guilty right away, first vote," said Wettig. "The first thing out of the four women's mouths was, 'I wouldn't put myself in that position.' But all of us thought that she was credible. Any discussion that came up in the jury room was not toward her, it was pointed at him. We all agreed that he was guilty. When he got on that stand, that clinched it for me."

On March 25, 1992, the day before Judge Patricia Gifford sentenced Tyson to six years in prison, Harvard law professor Alan Dershowitz filed a twelve-point appeal at the Indiana Court of Appeals. After spending an estimated $2 million for his trial defense, Tyson was sparing no expense in an attempt to reverse his conviction. In enlisting Dershowitz, Tyson assured that Washington would pay a hefty price for her determination to hold him accountable. Before ever appearing in court to argue Tyson's appeal, Dershowitz began to chip away at Washington's reputation.

"Had I been the defense lawyer in this case, I would have focused on the groupie phenomenon, and would have concluded that Desiree Washington was a groupie," said Dershowitz, who felt that Tyson's initial defense team had done a poor job of discrediting Washington. "Certainly she acted like a groupie. She behaved like a groupie. And in some respects, she should have know that when you go to the room of an athlete at three o'clock in the morning, who is used to groupies, you better make it very, very clear that you are not a groupie. And she didn't make that clear."

Although she had survived the invasion of her privacy that accompanied the trial, Washington was unprepared for the ensuing frontal attack on her character. Dershowitz took his message to outlets ranging from CNN to pornographic magazines. Exploiting popularly held notions about women who seek out famous athletes, Dershowitz fashioned an image of Washington as a scorned woman motivated to lie. "My own sense is that she was prepared to use sex as a way of getting more than just a one-night stand with Mike Tyson," said Dershowitz. "And she wanted his money. That was her goal from the beginning. She couldn't get it by the first route, so she decided to go the second route. The second route was crying rape." Ironically, Dershowitz made this argument despite the fact that Washington had turned down an offer of $1 million to drop her charges against Tyson.

Using the media as a forum, Dershowitz widened the attack to include constitutional issues such as improper jury instruction, procedural error, and denial of due process. He charged that Washington's presumed motive to lie had been obscured from the jury at trial. After compromising Washington's credibility in public, Dershowitz laced his appeals brief with suggestions that the jury had been denied crucial background evidence about Washington which may have led to a different verdict if it had been included. "The jury might have concluded that what happened in that room was very different from what either of them testified to," Dershowitz suggested. "And they might have come to a conclusion, for example, that she wasn't *anxious* to have sex with him, but was *willing* to have sex with him if she thought that was necessary to become his friend and his lover and perhaps his wife . . . that she never said no, but she was coy . . . went along with it. Since the judge didn't instruct the jury properly on what they could consider, we have no idea what the jury decided."

Eventually, the jury's stamp of approval on Washington's credibility eroded under Dershowitz's barrage. Just two weeks after Tyson was convicted, the search for jurors with second thoughts began. Despite attempts to protect the privacy of members of the jury, a team of private investigators hired by Tyson's handlers managed to track down every juror. "They didn't even call me, they just showed up at my house," said Wettig after being approached on a Sunday evening by a man from

Indianapolis and a private investigator from New York City. "They were looking for a juror who would say, 'I went with the crowd just to get out of there,' things like that," Wettig said.

In their initial response to these heavy-handed tactics, all twelve jurors took the unusual step of signing a document affirming their unanimous verdict. Yet some jurors, who were not warmly received on their return to their communities and workplaces, soon recoiled in the face of mounting pressure. One male juror, a UPS driver who was being harassed at work and in his neighborhood as a result of the verdict, warmed to the tireless investigators. His peers saw Washington as a deceitful woman whose only purpose for going to Tyson's room was sex. "They [his male coworkers] didn't want anything to do with him [the UPS driver]," explained Wettig. "Talk of the trial was better left alone. Not long after this is when he started changing his mind."

Ostracized at work, the juror publicly recanted his guilty vote in a radio interview, insisting that information unavailable to the jury at the time of trial had since led him to conclude that a woman had raped a man rather than vice versa. Dershowitz had been stating publicly that newly discovered evidence revealed that Washington had once fabricated a rape claim to spare herself from her father's wrath after she had become sexually involved with a popular student-athlete in high school. "She falsely accused somebody of rape once before, and used a false accusation to try to get herself out of a problem with her father, which is what we submit happened here," Dershowitz said. Although this claim was never substantiated, it implied some evidence for Dershowitz's thesis that Washington was an athlete groupie.

Soon thereafter the disgruntled juror appeared on the *Montel Williams Show* with Dershowitz, and then began phoning other jurors. "He [the juror] has been taking things that he's heard and passing them on to Dershowitz," said Wettig. "He [the juror] called me and asked me a few questions. He wanted to know if our jury instructions were written or oral."

With numerous talk shows and television analysts pursuing the jurors, Dershowitz's savvy media skills were reaping benefits for Tyson and taking a toll on Washington. "Dershowitz would say something to the effect, 'I've got evidence of this.' And some of the jurors said, 'Well, if he's got this evidence, then it must be true,' " Wettig said. Within six months of the sentencing, six jurors had expressed doubt over whether Tyson had received a fair trial.

"Thank Alan Dershowitz for that," said Garrison. "Cured testimony. I can't tell you that they got paid, but something made them change from when they were getting nothing for it and they were swearing before God to do the right thing to what happened later. Go back and dump a bunch of stuff on them and fan the flames and put them on TV and put them up in the Ritz Carlton. Or treat them like kings for a while and nod your head at them a few times and get them to second guess."

Jurors were solicited by NBC News, ESPN, Ed Bradley's *Street Stories,* Maury Povich, and other TV personalities examining the case. "A lot of the interviews were not looking at whether we made the right decision," said Wettig. "They wanted somebody to change their mind. Depending on how you handle situations, you could easily be talked into things without realizing that this is contrary to what you said you swore to in the jury room, especially when he's pushing you. You're a big star now, more or less, at least for a short period of time. Everybody's calling you.

"It is not just the media, it is your peers, your friends—especially amongst the black jurors. They got all kinds of hell when they got out. One guy changed his phone number constantly. He ended up moving because he was getting harassed by his old friends. It didn't take him long to turn around [his original decision]. He has since convinced [a female juror] to change her mind."

On February 15, 1993, Dershowitz presented his case before the Indiana Court of Appeals, putting forth a wide range of theories cleverly designed to obscure the truth. "I don't ever tell an appeals court what I think the truth is because I don't know what the truth is at this point," admitted Dershowitz after filing his brief on Tyson's behalf. One issue Dershowitz vigorously pursued was that the court had erred when it refused to "instruct the jury on the defense of mistake of fact as to whether the complainant had consented to sex . . . and as to the defendant's reasonable belief as to consent." According to Tyson's appellant brief, "Defense counsel could have argued that defendant in fact believed that the complainant had consented and that his belief, even if mistaken, was reasonable given the circumstances of their encounter."[6]

Capitalizing on the inordinate amount of consensual sex indulged in by some athletes, Dershowitz's argument implied that Tyson's routine random sexual relations may have led him to mistakenly perceive Washington as just another groupie. "She *appeared* to be consenting," said Dershowitz. "It sounds to me like he thought she was going to consent, not that she had consented but that she was going to consent. She has the right to change her mind at any time, but she has to do it in a way that communicates to him."

In fact, Tyson's trial testimony contradicted this scenario. When asked to explain how he had expressed his sexual intentions to Washington (in other words, how he had gained consent), Tyson told the court that he had bluntly told Washington he "wanted to **** her," and that she had replied, " 'Sure.' "[7]

If accepted by the court, Dershowitz's premise would make athletes virtually immune to criminal prosecution for acquaintance rape. "The law is incredibly confused," said Dershowitz. "The instruction [given to the Tyson jury] says all you have to do is conclude that she did not consent. That's not what the law is supposed to be. The law is supposed to be . . . it's a criminal defendant and a criminal defendant is on trial and it's state of mind that governs. It's *his* state of mind about her state of mind that ought to govern. Did he reasonably believe that she consented?"

However, rape, unlike murder, is not recognized as a specific-intent crime, but rather a general-intent crime. In other words, in situations in which an accused rapist claims to have mistakenly perceived the accuser's consent, juries must consider: Would a reasonable person in the defendant's position know that the woman did not consent?

Contrary to Dershowitz's position, which would prove most advantageous to accused athletes, the test for determining mistake of fact in disputes over consent is an objective, not a subjective, one. " 'What would a *reasonable person* in that position do?' Not, 'How'd Mike Tyson feel about it,' " explained Massachusetts Superior Court Judge Robert A. Barton, who has issued countless jury instructions in rape cases, and is familiar with the argument put forward by Dershowitz. "It has to be a reasonable person in the defendant's shoes, not this specific guy, be he an athlete or be he not an athlete.

"You're not going to find too many courts that are going to say, 'Oh sure, if this guy thinks in his own mind, because of his background and experience—because he's a great athlete and has got all these groupies falling all over themselves to go to bed with him—that every woman loves him and wants to have sex with a professional athlete, therefore that's going to be the divining rod as to whether he raped the woman or not, or whether she consented.' That doesn't make sense at all. Are you going to allow each individual, based upon his own back-ground and experience, to be able to say, 'Criminal intent should be decided by how *I* look at it?' "

The Court of Appeals rejected the notion that the Tyson jury had been improperly instructed with regard to mistake of fact on the matter of consent. Nevertheless, before the ruling from the appeals court was handed down, Dershowitz stepped up his attack on Washington by framing a disparaging image of her in the pages of one of the world's most widely read pornographic magazines. The cover of the May 1993 issue of *Penthouse* contained a menacing close-up of Tyson, with a caption reading " 'The Rape of Mike Tyson,' by Alan M. Dershowitz." Taking advantage of his position as a contributing writer for *Penthouse,* Dershowitz dressed up his smear campaign as a sophisticated attempt to expose a gross injustice. Offering sleazy and unsubstantiated claims, some of which the court had previously barred from evidence because they were without merit, the article also flashed photographs of Wash-ington in bathing attire, taken when she modeled at the Black Expo in Indianapolis. An excerpt from the article reads:

At least five of the jurors have recently urged that Tyson be given a new trial, at which the false evidence that was presented to them can be cor-rected, and the excluded evidence can be submitted. As one of the jurors put it, "We [the jurors] felt that a man raped a woman. . . . In hindsight, it [now] looks like a woman raped a man." Another juror, Rose Pride, now believes that Desiree Washington "has committed a crime." On the basis of new information, which was kept from the jury during the trial, Ms. Pride has concluded that Washington "isn't the innocent young girl pre-sented in court."

Two other jurors recently called me out of the blue to tell me that after hearing about this new evidence they also believe that Tyson deserves a new trial, and they doubt they would have voted to convict if they had known the whole truth about Desiree Washington. And a fifth juror appeared on the Maury Povich show to tell the world that he, too, would have voted for an acquittal had he known then what he knows now.[8]

Although he was unsuccessful in persuading the Indiana Court of Appeals that Tyson deserved a new trial, Dershowitz nonetheless fueled a media campaign against Washington that obscured the jury's verdict. "I had the privilege of having a glass of wine with Vince Fuller [Tyson's trial lawyer] one day in Washington about a year and a half after the trial," said Garrison. "I asked him what the thought about that [jury tampering after the fact]. He was as mad about those people being required to second-guess their verdict as I was. That impugns the whole idea. You try a case on sworn testimony at the time. Why did the stuff that Dershowitz talked about not get into evidence? Because it wasn't admissible. Because it was conjecture. And because it was irrelevant.

"Does it matter that some kid made up a lie that she accused him of rape in high school? The boy never had come to court, raise his right hand, and swear. But Alan can take these people [ex-jurors] and tell them these alleged facts and make them go, 'Oh man. I didn't know that. Gee. Wow. Gosh, if I'd known that . . .'

"But it is bullshit. It wasn't true in the first place. It's not true when he's telling it to them, and it's not going to be true later. But it causes these people, who worked so hard and had the integrity to do the hard thing, to question themselves. And that is reprehensible."

The media frenzy generated by Dershowitz at Washington's expense did nothing to further Tyson's quest to be exonerated. Dershowitz failed in his appeals, all the way up through the United States Supreme Court.

• On August 6, 1993, the Indiana Court of Appeals upheld Tyson's rape conviction.

• On August 26, 1993, Dershowitz argued for a new trial before the Indiana Supreme Court. On September 21, 1993, the court refused to consider the case. Following the release of the justices' one-page order, Dershowitz declared, "We will take whatever legal recourse is necessary to see that this injustice is finally brought to an end."[9]

• On December 15, 1993, taking advantage of an Indiana law that allows convicted criminals a second round of appeals, Dershowitz petitioned for and was granted a hearing before the Indiana Court of Appeals. The issue was whether prosecutors knew that Washington was considering suing Tyson.

• On March 7, 1994, the Indiana Supreme Court, without comment, turned away arguments that Tyson had been denied a fair trial.

• In April 1994 Dershowitz petitioned the United States district court in Indianapolis to overturn the conviction.

• On June 13, 1994, Tyson appeared before Judge Patricia Gifford to plead for a reduced sentence, showing no remorse for his actions. His request was denied.

• On July 11, 1994, Tyson sent Gifford a letter apologizing for what had occurred, and asked her to reconsider her decision to deny him early release.

• On September 8, 1994, United States District Court Judge Sarah Evans Barker denied Tyson's claim that he was wrongly held in jail. All the issues that were raised were dismissed as having no merit.

• On January 8, 1996, nearly a year after Tyson had been released from prison, the United States Supreme Court rejected arguments that Tyson had been denied a fair trial.

Despite a host of appellate court rulings affirming the jury's guilty verdict, by the time Tyson was released from prison on March 25, 1995, public opinion about both his guilt and Washington's credibility had shifted dramatically. A poll taken by the Indiana University Public Opinion Laboratory for the *Indianapolis Star* and WRTV television found that 67 percent of the black respondents and 28 percent of the white respondents believed that "Mike Tyson was unfairly convicted of the rape of a beauty pageant contestant."[10]

Posturing about Tyson's being a wronged man who would return to the ring with a vengeance had a magnetic marketing appeal. Within weeks of his release, the former champ had secured a $40 million offer for his first postprison fight. Two months before the scheduled fight, on June 21, 1995, Tyson appeared at a Day of Redemption ralley outside the Apollo Theater in Harlem, where he was greeted by two thousand fans. He pledged $1 million to charities.

Earlier that day, Tyson had skirted a final chance to contest the rape charge by quietly settling a civil suit scheduled to begin in the United States district court in Indianapolis one month later. On June 22, 1992, Washington had filed a multimillion-dollar civil suit seeking punitive damages from Tyson. At the time the suit was filed, Dershowitz had boasted, "We couldn't be happier, because it finally gives us a vehicle for bringing out the whole truth, for deposing Desiree Washington and for exposing her for what she is: a money-grubbing phony who has done this—as we suspected right from the beginning—for the money." He then told the *Boston Globe* that there was no chance whatsoever of Tyson's settling this case out of court. "Not for a dime," insisted Dershowitz. "If they have hope of a settlement they can forget it. We see this as an opportunity to reopen the case and include the matters that were not allowed in the first trial."[11]

Dershowitz conveniently avoided one key question likely to be raised at the civil trial: whether Tyson had infected Washington with a sexually transmitted disease. Washington's lawyer, Boston attorney Deval L. Patrick, was reportedly preparing to introduce evidence regarding two venereal diseases Washington tested positive for before the criminal trial. "We will have testimony from experts to help establish what the physical and emotional illnesses are," Patrick told the *Boston Globe*. "They may include sexually transmitted diseases."[12]

Contrary to Dershowitz's vehement insistence that Tyson would not pay a dime to settle, Washington was not challenged in court. She was instead paid an undisclosed amount of money in an out-of-court settlement.

Before completing the first year of his postrelease probation, Tyson was investigated by Chicago police for an alleged sexual assault. On April 7, 1996, LaDonna August went to a Chicago-area hospital and then to police following a run-in with Tyson at a popular nightclub. After police decided against charging Tyson in the matter, August's civil attorney, Charles Graddick, explained, "There was a confrontation between my client and Mr. Tyson whereupon, according to her, some inappropriate comments and statements were made, followed immediately by inappropriate touching and fondling, which included a suckling . . . of the left side of her face."[13] The incident led Judge Patricia Gifford to tighten Tyson's out-of-state travel. George Walker, chief probation officer for the Marion superior court, ordered Tyson not to attend any bars or strip clubs for the duration of his probation.

Meanwhile, Washington went on to complete four years of college and became an elementary school teacher. Her name continues to appear in articles and press reports regarding Tyson.

9

sexually transmitted disease

Some of us will call a hooker once in a while, when you just don't want to wait. It depends how many hormones are working. But most of the time, you go out to the bars. You like the challenge, the thrill of the hunt. When you go with a hooker or someone easy, it's like the hunter going to the store to buy dinner.[1]

— National League baseball player

ON FEBRUARY 10, 1996, JUST HOURS BEFORE HIS SCHEDULED TEN-round bout in Las Vegas, heavyweight boxer Tommy Morrison was eating his prefight meal when he was summoned to the room of his promoter, Tony Holden. On entering the room, Morrison discovered his personal physician, his trainer, his assistant trainer, and Holden assembled in stony silence. "I knew something was wrong," Morrison later told ESPN Radio. "I could tell by the look on everybody's face."

Morrison was no stranger to bad news. His reckless approach to life outside the ring—particularly with women—had frequently placed him in precarious situations. On two separate occasions he had learned that he had fathered children by women with whom he had had brief sexual encounters. Twice he had been investigated by the police for assaulting women, once in connection with the mother of one of his children. Pinpointing the root of Morrison's recurring problems with women, a close associate of his said, "There was a time period there when Tommy shopped for women like going into a candy store."[2]

Although such behavior would derail a career in most professions, it did not stop Morrison's meteoric rise to fame in the boxing community. Civil laws and social norms had failed to slow the blond-haired, muscle-bound athlete from the Midwest. But now, a microscopic virus had landed an unforgiving blow. Holden bluntly informed Morrison that he had tested positive for HIV. "My initial response was that there obviously had to be something wrong; this couldn't be," said Morrison, still unable to come to terms with the news two days later. "I'm perfectly healthy. I feel healthy. I work out daily and still continue to work out."

Seven days after his heavyweight bout was abruptly canceled, Morrison held a press conference in Tulsa, Oklahoma, with his fiancée, Dawn Freeman, by his side. There he announced that he was retiring from professional boxing, because he had contracted the AIDS virus. In part, he said:

[I] lived a permissive, fast, reckless lifestyle. I ask that you no longer see me as a role model, but see me as an individual who had an opportunity to be a role model and blew it. Blew it with irresponsible, irrational, immature decisions . . . that one day will cost me my life. . . .

I thought this [HIV] would be contracted by addicts who shared needles, and homosexuals. I was sure I had a better chance of winning the lottery than contracting the disease. I've never been so wrong in my life. . . . I've been trying to get in touch with all the people I contacted the last few years, the sparring partners, *especially the young ladies*. [emphasis added][3]

Candidly admitting to his indiscriminate sexual liaisons with women, Morrison followed in the footsteps of the legendary basketball player Magic Johnson, the first high-profile athlete to be forced out of sports by a sexually transmitted disease.

"If you listen to the nonsense that is transmitted by athletes like Wilt Chamberlain [Chamberlain claimed to have had sexual encounters with twenty thousand women] or Magic Johnson, and how many exposures they've had, players come to town to play basketball or football and they just go through as many women as they can get to," observed Greg Garrison, shortly after his successful prosecution of Mike Tyson on rape charges. "It just amplifies what's wrong with casual sex. On nonmoral ground, it is stupid because it has repercussions—people get pregnant, you can pick up diseases. There's all kinds of reasons not to do it, besides the right reasons, which are the moral reasons."

Like Johnson's, Morrison's public disclosure created uncertainty and fear among his previous sex partners. Nonetheless, the public discourse surrounding the two cases barely mentioned the scores of women who were exposed to the AIDS virus through consensual sex with the two athletes. Instead, the fallout from Morrison's announcement emphasized the need to protect other athletes from the risk of infection through the close contact of athletic competition. Within days of the fight's cancellation, state boxing commissions in Massachusetts and New York had mandated HIV testing for all boxers. The Pennsylvania state legislature introduced a bill requiring boxers to be tested thirty days before a fight. Under the terms of the bill, refusal to be tested would result in the immediate forfeiture of a boxer's right to fight in the state of Pennsylvania.

Some advocates lobbied for the implementation of mandatory AIDS testing in all contact sports in which athletes risk direct contact with an opponent's blood. Similar appeals for broad-based AIDS testing among athletes had been made in 1992, when Magic Johnson's attempt to come out of retirement prompted some players to express their fear of transmission publicly. Initially, the right of an individual athlete to be protected from unwarranted search and seizure had prevailed, and the sports community had settled for stepped-up measures when players began bleeding. For example, the NBA introduced a procedure for team trainers whereby any bleeding player is removed from the court immediately, and cannot return until the wound is closed and the bleeding stopped. But Morrison's announcement coincided with a reinterpretation of Fourth Amendment case law, which indicated that carefully crafted testing programs could be considered constitutional.

In *Vernonia School District v. Acton* (1995), the U.S. Supreme Court upheld random drug tests for student-athletes. The case had reached the Court after a student was denied the opportunity to play football after refusing to submit to the school district's newly adopted student-athlete drug policy. At issue was the Fourth Amendment's protection against "unreasonable searches and seizures," in this case the collection and testing of a urine sample without due cause. In a six-to-three decision upholding the random drug testing of athletes, the Court held, "A search unsupported by probable cause can be constitutional, we have said, 'when special needs, beyond the normal need for law enforcement, make the warrant and probable cause requirement impracticable.' "[4] Writing for the majority, Justice Antonin Scalia went on:

School sports are not for the bashful. They require "suiting up" before each practice or event and showering and changing afterwards. Public school locker rooms, the usual sites for these activities, are not notable for the privacy they afford. . . .

There is an additional respect in which school athletes have a reduced expectation of privacy. By choosing to "go out for the team," they voluntarily subject themselves to a degree of regulation even higher than that imposed on students generally. . . .

Finally, it must not be lost sight of that this program is directed more narrowly to drug use by school athletes, where the risk of immediate physical harm to the drug user or those with whom he is playing his sport is particularly high. . . .

It seems to us self-evident that a drug problem largely fueled by the "role model" effect of athletes' drug use, and of particular danger to athletes, is effectively addressed by making sure that athletes do not use drugs.[5]

Together with other rulings on random tests, the Court's ruling suggests that when a government testing program achieves an important public purpose with minimal intrusion of an athlete's privacy, testing programs are constitutional. Although the rulings apply specifically to drug testing, it follows that carefully constructed HIV testing initiatives for athletes would likely withstand constitutional scrutiny.

Even so, such measures are misguided, and will likely prove worthless in deterring the spread of AIDS among athletes. From a practical standpoint, athletic competition does not pose a risk of HIV infection.[6] Although numerous professional athletes have been diagnosed with AIDS—including some who have died from the disease[7]—there has yet to be a verifiable case of an American professional or college athlete contracting the AIDS virus through the exchange of bodily fluids during athletic competition. Theoretically, an infected athlete could contaminate a lesion, wound, or mucous membrane of another athlete, but leading AIDS researchers maintain that is highly unlikely.[8]

On the other hand, the indiscriminate sexual relations many college and professional athletes enter into pose a far more significant risk for contact with HIV—not to mention a host of more easily spread venereal diseases, including gonorrhea, syphilis, chlamydia, genital herpes, and hepatitis B. Exacerbating the potential for infection are an aversion to condoms, not uncommon within the ranks of college and professional athletes, and a multiplicity of sex partners—both proven factors in the spread of HIV and especially venereal diseases. Ironically, in the years between Johnson's announcement in 1992 and Morrison's announcement in 1996, athletes' attitudes toward high-risk sex have not only remained cavalier; in many cases have become more flagrant.

Mandatory AIDS testing of athletes misses the mark, precisely because it is predicated on protecting male athletes from a potentially infected competitor. The women in athletes' lives—wives, girlfriends, and indiscriminate sexual partners—are the ones who face the increased risk. In general, women suffer higher rates of infection than men as a result of heterosexual relations. In 1992, heterosexual intercourse surpassed intravenous drug use as a cause of AIDS in women.[9] Heterosexual intercourse poses an even greater threat to women through the transmission of more common venereal diseases, which have a disproportionate affect on women in the form of pelvic infections, infertility, and bacterial infection of the uterus, Fallopian tubes, and other organs.[10]

One of the more unjust consequences of the promiscuous social climate surrounding celebrity athletes, which often reduces individuals to sexual prey, is the indiscriminate nature of infectious disease, which fails to distinguish between those who willingly engage in high-risk behavior and the wives and girlfriends who do not. Thirty-five-year-old

La Gena Lookabill Greene, a former college honor student and beauty queen, was unaware that her former fiancé, famed race-car driver Tim Richmond, had AIDS until he died, and the cause of his death was reported in the newspapers. When Greene accepted Richmond's marriage proposal in September 1986, just months before he was diagnosed with AIDS, she was not cognizant of the many sexual partners he had had in the previous decade. A former college football player who became a celebrity auto racer on the NASCAR circuit, Richmond had sexual partners who "were like stars in the sky—too numerous to count," according to his friends. Following his death, the *Miami Herald* reported that one of Richmond's girlfriends had died of AIDS, and that two other partners had gone into seclusion because of the disease. After Greene's infection was reported in the press, no fewer than thirty women contacted her to confirm that they had been exposed to HIV via their sexual relations with Richmond.[11]

In addition to the tragic circumstances of sexually promiscuous athletes' wives and girlfriends confronting the fear of the unknown is the cruel injustice suffered by women who are sexually assaulted by athletes. Both ethical and legal considerations prevent the collection of reliable data on the frequency of infection of rape victims with HIV or venereal disease as a direct result of the rape. Nonetheless, certain characteristics of the perpetrators (frequency of sexual contact and a multiplicity of partners) as well as the type of sexual exposure (vaginal, anal, or oral) can increase the probability of a rape victim's becoming infected. Many of the athletes charged with sex crimes have high-risk profiles, including frequent casual sex, unlimited partners, failure to use condoms, and even participation in group sex. "All of those are risk factors," said Veronica Ryback, director of Beth Israel Hospital's rape crisis center in Boston. "Each one of them increases the risk and possibility of passing on sexually transmitted diseases." Thus, victims who are assaulted by sexually indulgent athletes bear an increased risk of exposure to disease.

A unique psychological factor further enhances the potential of sexually indulgent athletes to contract and transmit venereal diseases. A pervasive mind-set of invincibility characterizes the sports community, and is frequently carried over into the athletes' sexual relations. Following his HIV diagnosis, Magic Johnson noted, "In the age of AIDS, unprotected sex is reckless. I know that now, of course. But the truth is, I knew it then too. I just didn't pay attention. As often as I had heard about the importance of being careful, I never took it seriously. I couldn't believe that anything like this would happen to me."[12] Although that sentiment is not restricted to athletes, the safety net athletes enjoy in all aspects of their lives reinforces it in a unique way.

Though the frequency with which athletes transmit disease via sexual assault cannot be measured, case studies confirm that the victims they infect suffer in silence while the perpetrators routinely return to the playing field and to public adulation.

Madison, Wisconsin, January 24, 1986:

Taxiing down the runway just before takeoff, the 7:30 A.M. commercial flight from Madison, Wisconsin, to Minneapolis, Minnesota, was suddenly instructed to return to the terminal. Rather than potential mechanical failure, poor weather, or sabotage, police action had detained the plane. The pilot was informed that Madison police were requesting the plane's return as part of a criminal investigation. Three members of the University of Minnesota men's basketball team, passengers on the plane, were wanted in connection with an alleged gang rape that had occurred earlier that morning.

Nearly two hours before the team boarded the early morning

flight, an assistant coach had placed a wake-up call to the rooms of all the Gophers players, to ensure their presence on the team bus before 6 A.M. When the phone in room 308 rang shortly after 5 A.M., neither Mitch Lee nor his roommate, twenty-one-year-old junior Kevin Smith, was asleep. Instead, both players, along with a third teammate, nineteen-year-old sophomore George Williams, were watching each other take turns sexually penetrating an intoxicated woman they had lured to the hotel with promises of a big party involving many people. The coach's phone call sent the players scurrying about the room to gather up their things. With the victim still lying on the floor, Smith retrieved his wadded-up basketball jersey from a corner of the room. When the victim caught a glimpse of the words "Minnesota Gophers," she realized the men were college athletes.

In his haste to get out of the room, Lee inadvertently left behind his wallet. Not until the team was en route to the airport did he realize it was missing. As soon as they arrived at the airport, Lee phoned the hotel and asked a staff member at the front desk to retrieve the billfold from his room.

On entering room 308, the hotel attendant discovered a disheveled young woman curled up in a fetal position under a wad of sheets. When the attendant inquired, eighteen-year-old Wendy Slokolov* began to cry, saying she had been raped. Minutes later, hotel management contacted Madison police and reported that an alleged rape victim had been found in a room previously occupied by members of the University of Minnesota basketball team.

Aware that the suspects were preparing to fly back to Minnesota, police reached air traffic control and prevented the plane's departure. Slokolov was helped into a squad car and driven to the airport to iden-

*Wendy Slokolov is a fictitious name used to protect the victim's privacy.

tify the perpetrators. All the members of the team were asked to debark the plane and walk past the patrol car. From this makeshift lineup, Slokolov identified Lee on the first pass and Smith on the second. She was unable to identify Williams, because she had not seen his face. Williams had entered the room after the lights had been shut off, and had penetrated Slokolov anally while her face was pushed down toward the floor. Although he managed to escape her identification, Williams admitted his involvement while being questioned by police.

With a commercial flight postponed, a nationally ranked college basketball team detained at the airport, three players in police custody, and a victim who had just been whisked to a nearby hospital for a rape exam, the captain of detectives for Madison police placed an urgent call to the district attorney's office. By mid morning, sex crimes prosecutor Judith Hawley was involved in the case. Four years before joining the prosecutor's office in Madison, Hawley had worked in the U.S. Attorney's office, where she had handled sex crimes. Since coming to Madison, she had continued to prosecute sex crimes, as well as miscellaneous misdemeanor and felony cases. Despite having no previous exposure to a sex crime allegation involving an athlete, Hawley did have experience in prosecuting athletes. "Being that Madison is a college town and for much of the time the drinking age was eighteen, we had a lot of disorderly conducts, batteries, some thefts, some burglaries," said Hawley. "The athletes were in trouble a fair amount. It's not terribly unusual in college towns."

While the victim was undergoing a medical exam, which included the collection of cultures from the cervix, rectum, and oral cavity, since she had suffered penile penetration in all three areas, Hawley began to evaluate the players' versions of events. Smith had admitted to police that he thought his teammates were hurting Slokolov, conceding they "got a little rough with her and they weren't very nice with her." Yet he maintained his contact with her was strictly consensual. Williams claimed that he walked in on Lee and Smith, and had discovered Lee straddling Slokolov, who was lying face down on the floor. When Lee got up, Williams recalled him saying, " 'Now it's your turn.' So I just dropped my drawers, never said a word to the woman and she never said a word to me. And I had intercourse with her from behind."

Hawley viewed Williams's version as supportive of the victim's claim that she had been raped. "To me that was really an outrageous statement," said Hawley. "That's consent? That was his version. 'I didn't know the woman. I didn't know what those guys had been up to. I entered their room. I saw what was going on and I couldn't resist.' And then he left the room and felt guilty and called his girlfriend."

Nonetheless, Hawley knew she would have to explain to a jury why an eighteen-year-old college student had voluntarily entered the hotel room of a couple of college athletes. Slokolov, who had grown up in a very rural community in northern Wisconsin, was right out of high school, just six months into her freshman year at a technical school in Madison. She was not an athlete-groupie, but rather a free-spirit type with a diverse social circle. She shared an off-campus apartment with a group of gay men, some of whom were college students. On the night of the rape, she had gone out dancing at a club with her gay friends. That same night, the University of Wisconsin's game against Minnesota had added to the big-party atmosphere that surrounded the Madison campus on Thursday evenings.

As Slokolov and her friends were returning from the club, they encountered a carful of people on the way to a party. Slokolov knew one of the female passengers, and on a whim accepted her invitation to join her. The car Slokolov climbed into had just come from Zingers, a local bar where members of the Minnesota basketball team had congregated after defeating Wisconsin. Unbeknown to Slokolov, some of the women in the car had attended the game, met Lee and Smith at Zingers, and invited them home to party.

"These women were very sophisticated and involved with all of the basketball players," confirmed Hawley. "They saw these tall, young, black men come in from the University of Minnesota basketball team, and they were going to have a party that night. The victim didn't know any of these people, but she ends up at this party."

At the women's apartment, Slokolov met Smith and danced with him a few times. Ultimately, two of the women hosting the party decided to accompany the players back to their hotel. Slokolov accepted an invitation to attend "a party at the Concourse Hotel." Although the other women fully expected sexual activity, Slokolov was apparently too naive—and impaired by alcohol as well—to pick up on the agenda. "He [Smith] said that it would be a lot of fun," Slokolov later testified. "He said I would be able to get a ride home."[13] Hawley concurred, "She thought there was a party at the hotel because she was innocent enough to truly believe this."

When the group arrived at the Concourse shortly after 3 A.M., one of the women went into a room with one of the players, while Smith and Lee escorted Slokolov to their room. (It is not known what happened to the third woman.) Almost immediately after entering the room, both players began undressing her. "I was saying, 'Get your [expletive] hands off of me, what are you doing?' " said Slokolov. "I didn't know what was going on."[14]

In the early stages of the assault, numerous players entered the room. Finally Williams joined the fray, after returning from a booster party upstairs that had wrapped up in the early morning hours. When Williams opened the door to room 308 at approximately 4 A.M., he removed his pants and without hesitation began forcing his penis into Slokolov's rectum.

Although Slokolov never saw Williams's face, she was well aware that another person had joined the assault. "Another black man had entered the room, and he was holding my left leg," she said. "They were spreading my legs apart."[15] Before it was over, Slokolov had been penetrated no fewer than twelve times orally, vaginally, and rectally.

Reviewing the circumstances, Hawley's confidence in the chance for a successful prosecution grew. "We should be able to obtain convictions in this case," she reasoned. "Three guys and one woman and she doesn't know them. And she's eighteen years old. That's a lot to swallow to think that she's going to consent to be penetrated by all these guys. That's nonsense."

A few weeks after prosecutors began putting their case together, the lab results from Slokolov's venereal disease cultures came back. She had tested positive for gonorrhea both orally and vaginally. While the physician was collecting smears from her mouth, rectum, and cervix, Slokolov had reported smelling strong odors and seeing some form of skin infection in Lee's genital area. With the confirmation that Slokolov was infected, prosecutors subpoenaed urine and blood specimens from all three players. State health department tests confirmed that Lee was infected; Williams and Smith tested negative. A source closely associated with the medical exam confirmed, "Lee was very solidly positive."

Although the prosecutor's office was well aware that Lee had gonorrhea, and the victim was found to have gonorrhea, both orally and vaginally, they opted not to introduce that evidence in the case against Lee. "We knew it," said a source in the prosecutor's office. "The victim was clear that this guy had odors and that there was something the matter with him. She knew it just from what she was able to tell about the condition of his body. It was clear to the investigators when they did the exam that he was infected. It was confirmed by the state health department that did all of the testing."

Explaining the decision not to introduce the transmission as evidence against Lee, Hawley explained, "There would have been the whole 'Who gave it to whom?' and it would have opened up her prior sexual past, arguably. So we stayed out of it. Had we gotten a conviction, it would have been an aggravating type of a factor to justify a lengthier prison sentence."

The insult of infection took on an added dimension when Slokolov learned that Lee had previously stood trial for raping University of Minnesota student Lisa Jones on January 22, 1985. A Minneapolis jury had acquitted Lee on January 14, 1986—a mere ten days before her ordeal in Madison. The game against Wisconsin was only Lee's second since rejoining the team after sitting out the time leading up to his trial.

A cursory glance at the circumstances surrounding the first case (a penniless black male from out of town had made his way into the dorm room of a white woman in a virtually all-white college community, and sexually assaulted her) offered little prospect that Lee would remain in uniform a year later. But Lee was no ordinary rape defendant. Perhaps the most talented player on the team, he was represented by one of the city's most expensive criminal defense attorneys. Furthermore, instead of swiftly denouncing Lee's actions, university officials—some overtly and others covertly, by not cooperating with the police—had deterred the prosecution.

Within twelve hours after Jones checked into a local emergency room and reported being raped, University of Minnesota police detective Marge Phillips* was put in charge of the criminal investigation. From the outset, campus police chief Bill Hulls warned Phillips that she would encounter considerable internal resistance. "He told me, 'The athletic department is concerned and wishes not to make a big deal

*The true identity of the police officer has been protected at the officer's request.

about this,' " said Phillips. "There was an undercurrent of discussion on campus to the effect of 'We don't want this to get out' type of thing."

The most blatant interference came from the coaching staff. In their attempt to protect Lee, they went as far as to lie to law enforcement officials. When police tried to apprehend and charge Lee, they searched his dorm room and the basketball practice facility, then questioned the coaches regarding Lee's whereabouts. Each insisted he had no idea. "When it came time to arrest Mitch Lee on probable cause for criminal sexual conduct in the first degree, we couldn't find him," said Phillips. "It turned out that an assistant coach [Jim Williams] was hiding him and not making him accessible to us to make the arrest."

Sequestered at Coach Williams's off-campus home, Lee succeeded in eluding police for two days—long enough for distinguished attorney Phil Resnick to be brought on board. Resnick engineered the terms of Lee's surrender, negotiating directly with the captain of detectives. By virtue of Resnick's presence, police were shielded from obtaining a statement from Lee, who was notorious for his inadvisable and impudent remarks to the local media. Thus Lee was spared the likelihood of self-incrimination during unrehearsed interviews with the police. Furthermore, Lee's seclusion prevented the exposure of his severely deficient academic record, which would have raised embarrassing questions for the administration regarding Lee's admission and eligibility to play.

"We were not able to interview him or take a statement from him because he had gotten a high-buck attorney, which was surprising knowing that this young man came from a very disenfranchised and impoverished neighborhood, and both parents were not able to come up with that kind of money," said Phillips. "He should have had a public defender, but someone was footing the bill for the high-buck attorney to represent Mitch."

Attempting to ascertain who was funding Lee's legal defense, campus police soon realized that university support for Lee transcended the athletic department. When Phillips called on the president's office to provide an official list of boosters who had contributed money to the basketball team, she met delays, bureaucratic hurdles, and outright lies. "We were trying to find out how Phil Resnick could be defending Mitch Lee," said Phillips. "It must have been coming from the boosters, and I was being blocked on that."

With high-ranking administrators refusing to assist police in obtaining the list of financial contributors, Phillips finally acquired one from a staff employee in the president's office. "We did enough in-uniform assignments in the president's office that I got to know a lot of the people in there by first name, especially the support staff," said Phillips. "That's how I got the list. One of them said, 'Between you and me and the lamp post, here it is.' "

Although they were unable to establish clearly who had financed Lee's superior legal defense, investigators uncovered an informal network between the boosters, Resnick's office, and criminally accused athletes at the university. Besides being retained in Lee's first rape case, Resnick was dispatched to Madison, Wisconsin, for the second rape trial. His firm was also retained to defend one of the university's football recruits, who had been arrested and tried for sexual assault shortly after arriving on campus. Like Lee, the football player had serious academic deficiencies and came from a poor family.

In the first trial, Resnick's arguments established a sufficient degree of doubt in the minds of jurors, and Lee walked away a free man. He was immediately reinstated, in time for the next home game. Less than two weeks after his acquittal in Minneapolis, Phillip's secretary told her of an important call that had come in while she was out.

"Marge, you better sit down for this one," said the secretary.

"Why?" asked Phillips.

Without answering, the secretary handed her a phone message that read, "Call Detective Rob Lombardo. Mitch Lee and two other basketball players have been charged with rape in Madison, Wisconsin."

Instinctively, Phillips reached for the phone and called the victim in the first case. "It was just so compelling, I called her right away," said Phillips.

When the victim heard the news she was silent for a moment, then responded softly, "Oh, wow. . . . See."

Facing his second rape trial in as many years, Lee remained adamant about his innocence, suggesting that his athletic stardom was attracting false and unfair accusations. "People, they call me trouble," said Lee. "But it's not me. I don't know why, but ever since I got to Minneapolis I've tried to be positive and everything's turned out negative. People always are making accusations to me. I don't know why. But why should I travel two thousand miles from my home to rape some female? That's not me."[16]

Unable to see the fault in his actions, Lee's depraved view of women had twice spelled trauma for naive young college women. "They were similar," said Hawley, referring to the two victims. "They were physically similar, both from rural areas, and both new to the city. They were trusting people, therefore more vulnerable to the predators."

Striving to ensure Lee's conviction the second time around, Hawley called on law enforcement officials from Minnesota who had worked on the first case. They were eager to help. But Hawley found no such enthusiasm when she approached University officials. "We met with anybody that would talk to us, and there weren't a lot that would," said Hawley.

Despite the reluctance of most university personnel to talk with prosecutors, a few individuals risked the potential fallout associated with a candid discussion of the school's notorious basketball team. The picture that emerged from investigator's interviews was a bleak one of an athletic program rife with disciplinary problems. In a rush to achieve prominence in basketball, head coach Jim Dutcher and his staff had recruited basketball mercenaries who were woefully underqualified to assimilate to life on a major college campus, either academically or socially. Not only were some scholarship players grossly unprepared for the rigors of the classroom (Lee's ACT score was rumored to be in the second percentile nationwide), but their home environments virtually set them up for behavioral problems on campus. "I was a kid from the ghetto," admitted Smith, "suddenly playing in front of seventeen thousand people and having all these people trying to give me everything I could want. I took advantage of those situations.' "[17]

As a consequence of giving basketball scholarships to incorrigibles, the incidence of on-campus misconduct and off-campus crimes increased. "The coach did not have control of the team, and he was just sort of looking the other way," said Hawley. "He was just ineffectual. He knew he couldn't control these guys, but he didn't want to lose them."

Dutcher's attitude toward the charges filed against Lee, Williams, and Smith was telling. "I had information that the police, that few other people, had access to, and I believed they were not guilty," said Dutcher, in an interview published in the *Minneapolis Star Tribune*. "Does that mean they were right? No. We don't condone group sex. The troubling thing for me was the immediate assumption of guilt."[18]

In electing to frame the incident as a morally offensive but legally permissible incident of group sex, Dutcher legitimized the position of the accused players. All three later complained that their basketball careers had been forever injured because of false rape allegations. "There is a term for what we did that night for a reason—group sex—because it goes on," insisted Smith. "All of that [the trial] cost me my scholarship, my dreams. I was in a state of depression for a long time. I put myself in a position I shouldn't have been in and it cost me. But I've had to find a way to look at the bright side."[19]

Smith also praised Lee for enduring two rape trials. "He's [Lee] been through so much," Smith lamented. "I think about what we [Smith and Williams] just went through and the fact that he went through it twice. It was like everybody was anti-Mitch, like, 'We don't want you, Mitch. We don't need you, Mitch.' That's a helluva thing to deal with when the whole state thinks that way about you."[20]

Like those of many athletes charged with crimes against women, these views reflect the morally destitute, socially deprived outlook that has become a trademark of big-time athletics. The grossly inverted priorities criminally accused players often express are reinforced by coaches reluctant to demand discipline. In citing the assumption of guilt as his most troubling concern, Dutcher epitomized the ethical retreat common among college and professional coaches, who rely increasingly on players with criminal records to secure success on the field. Coaches downplay unlawful behavior as youthful exercises in poor judgment. They refuse to confront the sexual deviance and criminal violence that are increasingly entangled with college and professional athletics.

"The common assumption is that women are throwing themselves at the feet of these guys, that women want to attach themselves and have their fifteen minutes of fame," said Hawley. "A lot of it is just this sort of pedestal that people put athletes on. Their attitudes toward women, many of them, are extremely negative. If you are paying attention to what they say and you have the opportunity to see them, you are probably going to see that they think they can do whatever they want to women."

Hawley's efforts to hold the players accountable fell by the wayside when a second Madison jury acquitted Lee and his cohorts on July 25, 1986. The jurors' decision was based largely on the difficult-to-comprehend circumstances of the incident, which hampered their efforts to establish what had occurred. Although all three players later left the university, each ultimately resumed his career, either at another institution or overseas.

"I'll go somewhere else and play a different kind of basketball and try to attain the NBA, which is what I always dreamed of," said Lee immediately after the trial. "I've been accused of raping girls, and it's just not true. It's just a lie. Me? I'm not that kind of person. I think it's because I'm an athlete . . . people say things about you."[21]

After his premature departure from Minnesota, Smith received a lucrative offer to play professional basketball overseas. "I'm a free man," said Smith. "I have my health and I have a job that pays $50,000 a year. I'm not condoning the situation, but I see it as a blessing in disguise, really."[22]

Williams continued to play college ball for a short while in California.

After continued treatment for gonorrhea, Slokolov's infection was eventually eradicated. She dropped out of college and returned to her hometown in upstate Wisconsin.

Mitch Lee's two consecutive acquittals came at a time when the general public had yet to grasp the concept of acquaintance rape. In the mid-1980s, public understanding of AIDS and the manner in which HIV is transmitted was also rudimentary. In the decade since, the term *date rape* has become a household expression, and many of the myths associated with the crime of rape have been exposed. Furthermore, health officials have made great strides in educating the public about behavioral precautions that reduce the risk of contracting HIV and other sexually transmitted diseases. Society is now far better informed with respect to the prevalence of acquaintance rape and the prevention of sexually transmitted diseases.

But the current trend in sex crimes among college and professional athletes suggests that that segment of the male population remains mired in backward attitudes toward both the crime of rape and high-risk behavior associated with sexually transmitted disease. In the period from January 24, 1995, through July 25, 1996 (an eighteenth-month span that began and ended exactly ten years after Mitch Lee's second case, from point of arrest to acquittal), no fewer than forty-seven professional and college athletes were reported to the police for alleged sex crimes involving multiple perpetrators against single victims.[23] Of those forty-seven, forty-three admitted to having sexual contact in a group setting, insisting it was consensual. During the same eighteen-month period, multiple-perpetrator sex crimes accounted for more than 50 percent of the reported sexual assaults involving athletes.[24] The following examples are representative cases.

• On July 30, 1996, nationally prominent high school basketball star Ronnie Fields of Chicago was arrested along with two friends for raping a woman at the home of his coach. While a third associate was engaging in consensual sex with a woman, Fields and an accomplice emerged from a closet where they had been hiding and forced themselves on the woman. Prior to this incident, Fields had been a prized recruit at DePaul University, but his admission was subsequently revoked owing to severe academic deficiencies. All three men pleaded guilty and were sentenced to probationary work programs. They were also fined and ordered to undergo counseling. "Hopefully, this sentence will impress upon the defendants, especially Mr. Fields, that he's no longer thought of as a basketball star but as a sex offender," said prosecutor Thomas Epach.[25]

• In February 1996, three Arizona State University basketball players were arrested for forcing a woman to perform oral sex. After the victim had consented to sex with one, two teammates unexpectedly forced themselves on her. When the victim took exception to their advances, one of the players brandished a gun. All three players—George Gervin, Jr., Thomas Prince, and Rico Harris—were eighteen-year-old recruits who were sitting out their freshman season after being declared academically ineligible.

• On August 6, 1995, nine members of the New Orleans Saints football team were questioned by criminal investigators in response to a complaint made by a woman who claimed to have been gang-raped after consenting to sex with one player (see Chapter 4).

As noted in the prosecutor's report on the last incident:

Player 1 . . . and Player 2 did lie down and took their clothes off. . . . He [Player 1] stated that he and Player 2 did perform sexual intercourse with her and that she also had oral sex with him. He stated that at one point when she was having oral sex with Player 2 that he had sexual intercourse with her from behind. . . . When Player 9 entered the room . . . he took his clothes off and then attempted to put a condom on. . . . Player 1 stated that he specifically remembers seeing Player 5 standing in the doorway because he made the comment that he couldn't even get into the room with all the guys in there.

The report went on to point out that when the victim began yelling for one player to stop, Player 1 responded, "Shut up, bitch. Aren't you going to let him do it?"[26]

Setting aside the question of force versus consent, a significant number of today's athletes have clearly engaged in sexual conduct that is at least questionable, and at worst twisted, distasteful, and immoral. Even if players' claims of consensual group sex are taken at face value, their private conduct must be considered pernicious and foul at best by the vast majority of the population.

The sports culture's cavalier approach to gross sexual deviance serves as an incubator for sexually transmitted disease. Infection through assault is the most lethal, yet least traceable, casualty of such attitudes toward women and sex. Given the lurid sexual mores of many athletes, and officials' fainthearted response to them, the incidence of scandal among athletes can only continue to increase. More important, as time passes, a far greater number of women will suffer in solitude the consequences of athletes' depravity.

10

infidelity and domestic violence

Attorney: *In the entire time that you knew Nicole, you never once hit her with your fist? Is that true?*

O.J.:   *Never once did I ever hit her with my fist, ever.*

Attorney: *You never once slapped her with your hand?*

O.J.:   *Never once have I ever slapped Nicole.*

Attorney: *Never once did you strangle her?*

O.J.:   *Never.*

Attorney: *Never once did you beat her?*

O.J.:   *Never.*

Attorney: *Never once did you physically hurt her?*

O.J.:   *Never.*

Attorney: *And if Nicole said you did those things, she would not be telling the truth?*

O.J.:   *Correct.*

Attorney: *She would write notes to herself or journal entries about your beating her when that didn't occur?*

O.J.:   *Yes, that's correct.*

Attorney: *Why would she do such things?*

O.J.:   *Because she wanted me to tear up my prenuptial agreement, and I gather her lawyers and her came up with that as a scheme.*[1]

In filing for divorce in September 1996, Carolyn Sanders, wife of Dallas Cowboys star Deion Sanders, accused her husband of "cruel treatment" in the form of adultery. In times of shifting cultural attitudes toward personal responsibility and self-discipline, such claims of marital infidelity are increasingly common. Moreover, the general population has grown increasingly indifferent to allegations of celebrities' promiscuity. Accordingly, rather than publicly deny the charges, Sanders sought to excuse himself by focusing on the regularity of marital breakdown. "Divorce is a part of life," he said. "The divorce rate right now is about 50 percent."[2]

Sanders's statistic is not supported by data, though it does reflect his perception of the current state of the institution of marriage. From 1960 to 1980, the annual divorce rate in the United States climbed from 10 percent to almost 25 percent, then dropped back to just over 20 percent in 1991.[3] Divorces per one thousand married women climbed from approximately 10 percent in 1960 to approximately 20 percent in 1990.[4] The annual rate at which people get married also fell, from approximately 75 percent in 1960 to below 60 percent in 1991, further reflecting the nationwide decline in the value placed on marriage vows.[5]

But attempts to compare athletes' adulterous ways with national divorce statistics are misleading. While traditional attitudes toward marriage and fidelity have changed in recent decades, they cannot be applied to celebrity athletes, who enjoy limitless opportunity to indulge themselves sexually. National divorce statistics do not even begin to suggest the brazen adultery and callous disregard for family responsibility practiced by many of today's most celebrated athletes. Players' attitudes and actions reflect a complete and utter rejection of traditional standards of marriage and fidelity.

"When I was with other women, I always told them about Cookie [his wife-to-be]," wrote Los Angeles Laker star Earvin "Magic" Johnson in his autobiography. "Most of them already knew about her. I made it clear to everyone that I wasn't looking for a girlfriend. Some women took me at my word. I think that others saw Cookie as a challenge. And a few even told me: 'I'm going to spoil you so much that you're going to forget about her.'

"But nobody ever succeeded. . . . I myself never spent the night with a woman. It just didn't feel right. Often, after we slept together, she'd want to stay. That's why I always explained in advance that I preferred to sleep alone, and that no matter what happened between us, I would be asking her to leave when it was over. That way it was her choice.

"I never let myself get emotionally involved with somebody I met on the road."[6]

Unparalleled opportunities for extramarital affairs have come to be an inherent part of professional athletics. The promiscuous lifestyle available to sports figures is so overt, some players are compelled to abstain from marriage until after retirement. "I had told myself that I would never get married while I was involved in pro basketball," said one NBA player. "Knowing what the lifestyle is, it would be very, very tough to maintain a marital relationship."

Among players who marry, there is an unspoken code that condones infidelity, and in many situations even flaunts it. "There's an old joke in the NBA, and it's probably told in other sports as well," said Johnson. "Question: What's the hardest thing about going on the road? Answer: Trying not to smile when you kiss your wife good-bye.

"But nobody should be shocked by this information. Men on the road have always looked for diversion, whether they're athletes or traveling salesmen. It's natural, and it's been going on forever."[7]

Although infidelity is rife among men of virtually all occupations, indulgence by sports figures is exceptional. A 1994 survey of the general population by the National Opinion Research Center found that 21 percent of married men and 11 percent of married women have engaged in infidelity at least once in their lifetimes.[8] Many of those incidents involved either a single act or a single affair, and the majority of respondents indicated that their infidelities took place after age forty-three. Through comparative data specific to athletes are lacking, it is fair to say that athletes, by virtue of their icon status, have far more opportunity to cheat on their spouses than the average person. Unlike the general population, athletes practice infidelity frequently, and they do so while they are between the ages of twenty-three and thirty-five.[10]

"It's just a different fidelity than most people grow up with," explained one NBA player. "For whatever moral or philosophical reasons, most people believe that once you have a wife, you don't sleep around. But a lot of athletes marry young, and they're in an atmosphere or environment where women are present all the time."

Meanwhile, players expect their wives, fiancées, or live-in girlfriends to tolerate their indiscriminate sexual relations. "I had a job that took a lot out of me, both at home and on the road," said Johnson. "And aside from hanging out with my teammates, one of my favorite ways to relax was being with women. I told all the women I knew that they'd have to take a back seat to basketball. Only one woman really understood that and accepted it. And that was Cookie.

"Some people can't understand how I could love one woman and be with others. But there was a part of me that was always with Cookie. Maybe that was Earvin, and the other part of me was Magic."[11]

Although players' wives seldom publicly display their displeasure with their husbands' indiscriminately sexual lifestyles, athletes' indifference to random sexual liaisons does cause substantial marital strife. Besides trivializing the sanctity of marriage, athletes' sexual habits routinely trigger domestic violence. Between 1990 and 1996, 150 formal complaints (police reports or civil complaints) were lodged against professional and Division 1 college athletes for domestic violence, including assault, battery, stalking, kidnapping, manslaughter, and murder.[12] Largely as a result of increased awareness of domestic violence and increased sensitivity by law enforcement, seventy-seven of those complaints were filed in 1995 and 1996.[13] Of the complaints filed in that period, all but seven involved football or basketball players. Seven of the alleged victims were known to be pregnant at the time of the assault.[14]

Interviews with prosecutors, players, and players' wives, as well as a review of police reports, victims' statements, and other court documents, confirm that sexual deviance is common among athletes who abuse their spouses. In many cases, the player's blatant infidelity sparked a domestic dispute that escalated to violence that resulted in police intervention. "The nature of the game, particularly some of the women who chase after some of the players, creates problems in some of the marriages and relationships," said the wife of one prominent player on the Kansas City Chiefs. "As a result, there is violence both ways, both by the wife and the husband. There have been guns drawn, fights, public fights."

More than one member of the Chiefs was arrested in connection with domestic violence involving a gun. Running back Harvey Williams was arrested twice for abusing women in 1993; one of the incidents involved an assault on his wife with a gun. In 1995, after being traded to the Los Angeles Raiders, Williams was again arrested for battering his wife. Chiefs receiver Tim Barnett was arrested twice for battering his wife, once with a gun, as well as for sexually assaulting another woman.

The Chiefs are by no means an exception; they reflect a dilemma facing virtually all professional sports teams. Recurring abuse by players of their wives and girlfriends is often induced by the athletes' unrestrained sexual relations. The excessive level of infidelity common among athletes devalues women and severely strains their marriages.

Barnett's case offers a typical example of how an athlete's sexual irresponsibility breeds neglect and violence at home. Repeated attempts to address Barnett's violent tendencies toward his wife failed because his appetite for sexual conquest went unchecked.

In June 1993, Tim Barnett was arrested for assault and battery on his wife at their home in Overland Park, Kansas. While fighting with his wife, Barnett had threatened her with a .357-caliber Magnum handgun. In October he pleaded guilty.

Barnett's conviction was his second for domestic abuse in as many years. In March 1992 he had assaulted his wife, and was subsequently sentenced to thirty days in prison. But the judge suspended the jail term on the condition that Barnett undergo counseling and commit no further violations. After his second conviction, this one for the gun-related attack, Barnett's initial jail sentence was supposed to be reinstated. Meanwhile, Barnett, who had fathered five children, had been sued numerous times for failure to pay child support—a lapse indicative of the general disregard for familial responsibility that often accompanies sexual deviance.

On January 4, 1994, four days before the Chiefs' scheduled playoff game against the Pittsburgh Steelers, Barnett appeared in a Johnson County court to be sentenced in connection with the guilty plea he had entered on October 28, 1993. As one of quarterback Joe Montana's primary receivers, Barnett was crucial for the Chiefs' chances of winning the game. Barnett's attorney pleaded with Judge John Anderson III that "Barnett's job with the Chiefs would be in jeopardy if he had to miss the playoffs Saturday."[15] But Anderson was unmoved; he ordered Barnett into custody immediately, sentencing him to ten days in jail.

"I can't really justify treating you a whole lot different than I would treat anybody else just because you're a Kansas City Chiefs player," Anderson insisted. "Now, am I supposed to just cross my fingers and hope this time it's going to stick, and next time we're not going to have you in here for hurting somebody real bad? I don't feel comfortable with that."[16]

Anderson left the courthouse early because of illness, and Barnett's attorney filed a notice of appeal. In Anderson's absence, Judge Robert Morse was assigned to set the appeal bond. Saying he was obligated to set a bond, Morse set it at $1,500, which Barnett's lawyer immediately paid, freeing Barnett on appeal until after Saturday's game. Barnett's attorney agreed the ten-day sentence was fair, but insisted that it created an unusual hardship on Barnett and his family because of his job. After spending just a few hours in jail, Barnett was freed pending his appeal.

That Saturday at Arrowhead Stadium in Kansas City, the Chiefs trailed the Steelers late in the game. But with just more than a minute to play, Barnett scored a spectacular touchdown, sending the game into overtime and the fans into pandemonium. As he scored, ABC Sports commentator Al Michaels made a reference to Barnett's criminal case. His broadcast partner Dan Dierdorf responded, "If it's a jury case, he'll be pardoned."[17]

The Chiefs went on to win in overtime, moving one step closer to the Super Bowl. The following day, the *Kansas City Star* dubbed Barnett "the toast of the town." Barnett declared to reporters that he "had to overcome a lot of adversity . . . with my personal life, but I was able to overcome it. I am happy with my family life now. When I had the problems, that happened over a year ago."[18]

But men who are prone to domestic violence seldom reform without first altering their lifestyle and behavior. Barnett's disrespectful attitude toward women, as evidenced by his sexual practices, went unaltered. As a result, Judge Anderson's apprehension about Barnett "hurting somebody real bad" came to fruition while Barnett was free and awaiting appeal.

On June 24, 1994, less than six months after his ten-day sentence was put on hold, Barnett was staying at the Manchester Suites hotel in Milwaukee when he encountered Tanisha Warren,* a fourteen-year-old housekeeper employed in her first part-time job. At approximately 11 a.m., Warren knocked on the door to Room 215, but received no response. The door was already ajar, so she called out, "Housekeeping." Hearing no response, she repeated, "Housekeeping."

Still getting no response, Warren pushed the door the rest of the way open and entered the room. Inside she discovered three men.

"Do you want any service?" Warren asked.

"Yeah," responded one of the men as he called out to Barnett, who was on one of the beds.

Warren brought in fresh towels and drinking glasses and cleaned

---

*The victim's true identity has been protected.

the bathroom. Preparing to leave the room after completing her duties, Warren was asked by Barnett, "Can I ask you a question?"

"Yeah," responded Warren.

"What is your phone number?" asked Barnett.

Nervous, Warren pulled out a Manchester Suites business card and purposely misspelled her name and wrote down an erroneous phone number. "I didn't want to give him the right one," she later testified in court.

Taking the card from her, Barnett repeated, "Can I ask you a question?"

As Warren responded, "Yes," Barnett took her hands and pulled her down toward the bed.

Barnett then put his hands on Warren's housekeeping dress. "Ain't nobody been in this?" asked Barnett.

Believing that he was asking if she had ever had sex before, Warren nervously responded, "No."

Suddenly, Barnett turned her shoulders down and forced Warren onto her back. "He pulled up my dress . . . and then he started rubbing on my breasts," Warren would later testify. "He was asking me if it felt good. And then he started to rub on my vagina. I kept telling him stop. I had took my leg off the bed to get up and he put my leg back up. Then he put the covers over me. . . . He started licking my ear. He asked me a couple times, 'Did it feel good?' Then he unbuttoned his pants and pulled it down . . . to his knees and started rubbing his penis against my vagina. He said he was going to put it in. Then he started rubbing on my breast again and . . . rubbing his penis against my vagina real fast, and then some of me started hurting. . . ."[19]

Pleading with him to stop, Warren pushed against Barnett's chest. Finally, he climbed off her and scurried into the bathroom. The inside of Warren's thighs were wet, and her panties had semen on them. She hastily pulled down her dress, grabbed her caddie full of hotel supplies, and ran out of the room to find her older sister, who was also a house-keeper at the hotel.

Warren was later transported to the Women's Assessment Center for treatment and the collection of blood samples, pubic and head hair samples, smears and swabs; her clothes were kept for evidence. With the support of her mother and father, Warren reported the sexual assault to Milwaukee police, and an investigation was launched. On June 12, 1995, a Milwaukee jury found Barnett guilty of sexual assault on a child, and on August 21 he was sentenced to three years in prison. Barnett was paroled after serving just over one year of his sentence in a Wisconsin prison. Following his release, he was sentenced to jail in Kansas on January 10, 1997, for violating his probation in the 1993 domestic violence case.

Athletes' sexual encounters with women outside marriage, many of which are consensual, do nothing to teach them restraint. Rather, they reinforce athletes' habitual self-gratification. Like other abusive men who seek to control their spouses through force, athletes can be incited to violence by a wide range of factors. But their sexual license is the dominant source of their domestic strife. Sexual deviance not confined to mere adultery distinguishes players who batter their wives and girl-friends.

Despite the extraordinary public and private humiliation endured by wives of promiscuous athletes, they are extremely reluctant to press charges. Aside from fear, two other deterrents dissuade them: the excessive media scrutiny that follows any celebrity, and the threat of losing their prestigious way of life if the player is convicted.

One of the most prominent examples of a battered wife opting not to press charges against an athlete is Felicia Moon, wife of Minnesota

Vikings star quarterback Warren Moon. On the morning of July 18, 1995, Missouri City police dispatcher Kelly Fantach received a 911 report of an incident of domestic violence in progress in Lake Olympia Estates, an upscale suburb of Houston. The caller was Jeffrey Moon, eight-year-old son of Warren and Felicia:

Dispatcher: *911 Missouri City. What is your emergency?*

Jeffrey: *[Crying]*

Dispatcher: *Hello? What's the problem?*

Jeffrey: *It's my . . . You need to come . . . Hurry . . .*

Dispatcher: *What . . . What's the matter?*

Jeffrey: *It's umm . . . my daddy.*

Dispatcher: *Is he OK?*

Jeffrey: *My daddy gonna hit my mommy. Please hurry.*

Dispatcher: *OK. You need to calm down. We'll get the police there. Just a moment, OK?*

Jeffrey: *They're walking down the street. Please hurry up.*

Dispatcher: *OK.*

Jeffrey: *Please hurry up.*

Dispatcher: *Hold on. Now your daddy hit your mommy, right?*

Jeffrey: *Uh huh.*

Dispatcher: *And they're walking down the street. Does she need an ambulance? Hello. Hello?*[20]

Fort Bend County authorities fielded approximately one thousand reports of assault in 1995, the majority of which were related to domestic violence. There was nothing unusual about this report, other than the celebrity status of the abuser. When police arrived at the Moons' nine-thousand-square-foot, million-dollar mansion, neither husband nor wife was there. After reportedly being hit in the head and choked to the brink of unconsciousness, Moon had fled in one of the family cars, pursued by her husband at high speed. The two were unaware that the family's Spanish-speaking maid had called the police after hearing Moon's cries for help. Unable to communicate the emergency, she had handed the phone to eight-year-old Jeffrey.

Returning after the high-speed chase, Moon entered her home and fell into the arms of a female police officer who was a social acquaintance. "Mary, he beat the shit out of me," she cried. Police attempted to calm her down. "She had blood to the right side of her face and neck," according to the police statement. "She had scratch marks on her face and abrasions on her neck. She appeared to be in pain."[21]

When police asked the cause of the incident, Moon indicated that her husband had come home that morning and attacked her while she was reading her Bible on the grounds of the house. He had not slept at home the previous night and she claimed she was unsure where he had been. "Warren started to slap me on the head by my ears with his open hand," Moon said. "He choked me so that I couldn't talk or breathe. When he choked me I thought he was losing control and that he wouldn't know when to stop choking me. I was afraid for my life."[22]

Moon, a former board member of the Fort Bend County Women's Center, an organization that ran a shelter for battered women, offered an account that mirrored those of countless other victims of domestic violence. While spousal abuse is inherently insidious, the crime takes on added peril when the batterer is a professional athlete, superior in size and strength and trained in physically violent contact.

For example, on September 27, 1993, Rebecca Smith was hospitalized requiring head surgery after her 310-pound husband Doug, a member of the Oilers, choked her, head-butted her in the face, and tried to punch her eyes out following an argument. He later pleaded no contest.[23]

On February 18, 1994, Louisville University basketball player Troy Smith killed his fiancée when an argument got out of hand. Smith was described by his teammates as "a gentle giant" and a "teddy bear."[25] At six feet, eight inches and 240 pounds, he lifted twenty-year-old Kelly Dwyer and slammed her to the floor of their apartment. "She was body-slammed," said officer Robert Disbennett.[24] Dwyer was hooked to a life support system, but failed to regain consciousness and died less than twenty-four hours later. Smith was convicted of voluntary manslaughter.

Though the television-created commercial image of athletes contrasts sharply with popularly held images of wife beaters, abusive players do pose a lethal threat to their spouses. Yet when an athlete becomes violent with his wife, protecting his image often becomes her paramount concern.

As Felicia Moon was escorted to the police station for photographing, her chief preoccupation became whether the press would find out about the incident. Her husband was widely regarded as one of the most genuine role models in all professional sports—a true family man, founder of his own philanthropic organization, the NFL's Man of the Year in 1989, Moon was a favorite of companies seeking a spokesperson. After the police took pictures of her bruises, she asked, "Does that mean this is gonna be on the news tomorrow?"

Under assurance from police that the matter would remain private if she chose not to press charges, Felicia freely divulged the seriousness of the attack to the officers. But when she opted not to charge her husband, she was unaware that prosecutors still had the option to charge him after reviewing the matter.

The day after the incident, her husband told KPRC-TV in Houston that the matter was personal. "My wife and I got into an argument," said Moon. "It was not domestic violence. It was a domestic dispute."[26]

For three days Moon ignored requests by police to report to the station to deliver his version of what had transpired. On July 21 he was ordered to appear at county police headquarters no later than 6 P.M. That afternoon, the Moons opened their home to the local and national media for a press conference. Accompanied by both his sports agent and his attorney, Moon sat with his wife and children by his side on the living room sofa and apologized to family and fans for the embarrassing incident. Insisting that it would be a one-time occurrence, he vowed to seek counseling.

When District Attorney John Healey opted to charge Moon with a class-A misdemeanor first hours after his public apology, the Moons and their attorneys objected. Moon charged her husband was being singled out because of his status, and maintained she would not testify against him at trial.

As a general practice, first-time offenders in misdemeanor domestic violence cases are not brought to trial in Fort Bend County; instead, their cases are settled through plea agreements. "We always maintained a posture that we were willing to allow him to get counseling, pay a nominal fine of $100, perform community service like any other defendant," said Healey. "We were going to let him plead no contest and take a six-month deferred adjudication sentence." Nevertheless, the Moons wanted the case dropped outright. But the state was unwilling to turn a blind eye to the crime.

The media portrayed the trial as one in which the victim was being forced to testify against her husband. Yet defense attorneys welcomed her testimony, for they expected it to win sympathy with the jury. Furthermore, the defense emphasized the Moons' previous marital problems. "We did not bring up the issues of past fights, and there were several," said Healey. "We did not bring up the issue of the divorce petition in which she alleged under oath that he had attacked her on that occasion and at least once in the past. They brought it up. They made sure the jury knew about that. Why? Because their theory of the case was, 'Let's destroy this marriage and we will gain the sympathy of the jury.' That's how far they would go to defend him."

Before getting off the stand, Moon testified that her husband was merely trying to calm her down when he grabbed her by the throat, causing her to cough. He relaxed his grip on her neck, she maintained, but continued to restrain her when he realized she was having difficulty breathing. The jury wasted no time returning a verdict of not guilty. "Their struggle, you don't know who's at fault," said jury foreman James Rogers. "We felt like the Moons needed another chance. It's something they just have to work out and change. I feel like they prosecuted because he is a great celebrity."[27]

The only other male juror, Frank Sparks, agreed that the couple had been unfairly singled out because of Moon's achievements. "It wasn't spousal abuse," he said. "The Warren Moon case was not spousal abuse. It was not. I have seen and heard of spousal abuse, but his was not. That was just little scratches and everything. Something they could have handled themselves at home. He didn't beat her."[28]

Felicia Moon's willingness to protect her husband stunned both advocacy groups for battered women and neighbors close to the Moon household. "I was surprised that she let him off the hook," said one of the Moons' neighbors. "There had been previous domestic disputes that led to Warren moving out for periods of time. Felicia was a down-to-earth person who cared for the children and was a terrific neighbor. I think her decision not to prosecute was mainly due to the publicity."

A week after the trial, the Moons appeared together on "Larry King Live," where they applauded the verdict. "If I wasn't a popular athlete, I would have never went to trial," said Warren Moon. "I think the fact that I was a celebrity football player with the same type of circumstances as [O. J. Simpson], this was a thing where the DA . . . talked about want[ing] to send a message."[29]

King informed the Moons that Simpson had reportedly said that "battering and wife spousal abuse is a two-way street." King then asked Moon if Simpson had a point. "I think he does," said Moon. "There is a statistic out there that 35 percent of domestic violence out there is caused by the woman or provoked by the woman. Only 2 percent of those are ever talked about by men. That's not something a man is really going to admit to much. But it does happen.

"I am sure there are cases where guys either are under the influence of alcohol or drugs or whatever, and take it out on their wives. Or whether they are depressed about something and take it out on their wives. But there are other cases where people just aren't getting along and it becomes violent sometimes. And we've had a couple of instances in our marriage, but it's nothing like what people think it is."[30]

Felicia Moon verified her husband's assertion that his aggression was in self-defense. "On July the eighteenth I just completely lost control," she said, indicating that she had triggered his anger.[31] But while the Moons successfully characterized the assault as an overblown domestic spat, they scarcely addressed Warren's rampant infidelity and its link to their fights.

"We had begun to experience some recurring problems," Felicia Moon admitted to King's audience. Warren Moon explained, "We started to live separate lives." He described his extramarital affairs as "a weakness." "It was something that probably shouldn't have happened, but because of the attention that I didn't think I was getting [it] led me other places," said Warren. "I felt like this is what I needed. And it became a problem. I have not been a saint, there is no question about it."[32]

Moon's assessment of the situation grossly downplayed the extent of his involvement in adulterous behavior, as well as its effect on his marriage and his subsequent domestic violence. A series of seamy encounters and relationships, not uncommon among athletes of his status, had preceded his arrest for assaulting his wife. In 1990, Moon began an affair with Kymberly Coleman, a Houston-area model described as "an outgoing, athletic beauty . . . who might laughingly flip up her blouse above surgically enhanced breasts just to get a rise from pals."[33] Reportedly, Moon and Coleman belonged to a group of celebrity athletes and former topless dancers who frequented nightclubs. In September 1993 Coleman died along with five other passengers on a privately owned Lear jet when it crashed into a ridge outside Santa Fe, New Mexico.

Although Coleman had traveled with Moon and accompanied him to Houston nightclubs and functions, their involvement received no real scrutiny until after her death. The *Houston Press* reported that Coleman's participation in numerous nude photo sessions for *Playboy* magazine in 1992 and 1993 had angered Moon, precipitating their break-up.

Months before her death, Coleman had claimed to be pregnant

with Moon's child. Despite receiving monthly cash payments and other gifts from Moon throughout their three-year affair, she demanded a more substantial settlement when they formally severed their ties, just before the plane crash. After the crash, Moon's performance with the Oilers suffered. He was benched for the first time in his career and was traded to the Vikings in 1994.

When Moon moved to Minnesota, his wife and children remained in Texas. Soon, Moon became involved with another model, twenty-four-year-old Michelle Eaves, a former Ms. Hawaiian Tropic with experience as an exotic dancer. Moon met Eaves after she was hired as a cheerleader for the Vikings in 1994. On April 28, 1995, just two months before Moon was charged with beating his wife, Eaves filed a lawsuit alleging a pattern of sexual harassment that had culminated in a sexual assault.

Married with one child when the Vikings hired her, Eaves charged that Moon had begun making sexual overtures from the start of her employment with the team. According to her suit, following repeated attempts to initiate a sexual relationship with Eaves, Moon telephoned her hotel room while the team was away on the road. When Moon asked her to come to his room, Eaves was suspicious, and asked fellow cheerleader Amy Kellogg to go with her.

According to the complaint, Moon dismissed Kellogg from the room, and "insisted on having oral sex with [Eaves]. Without consenting, [Eaves] finally relented to Moon's insistence on oral sex. Defendant Moon then attempted to coerce [Eaves] into sexual intercourse, but [Eaves] refused and finally succeeded in leaving his room."[34]

Both Moon and the Vikings vehemently denied Eaves's charges, and Moon's lawyers succeeded in persuading a Minnesota judge to seal the complaint. Meanwhile, Eaves, who had been fired by the Vikings prior to filing her suit, was accused of targeting Moon out of revenge.

The team said she had been dismissed for fraternizing with an opposing team's player during a road trip; yet Eaves maintained that her dismissal was linked to Moon.

Because of past problems with player misconduct during road trips, Vikings management instituted a set of team rules for hotel stays. Vikings president Roger Headrick claimed that strict policies governed both cheerleader and player conduct when the team traveled. "We put security people on the floor of every hotel where we travel," said Headrick. "There is a curfew at 11:00. Once they are in that room, they can't leave without somebody noticing. If they leave, they are subject to termination. They understand that going in, and it has happened.

"The big question everybody asks is, 'If Warren Moon did that, would it [termination] happen?' I can't tell you because I do hear about these things, but I don't know."

As the team's premier player, Moon had a status and salary that distinguished him from his teammates. Like any star player, he received special treatment. His privileges, Eaves insisted, carried over to his personal behavior with the cheerleaders. "It sounds like sour grapes that she was fired and went after somebody," said a member of the Vikings' security team, "but there's more smoke to that fire."

Based on their experience with Moon and the exceptions made for him regarding routine bed checks, numerous Vikings security personnel believed Eaves's claims. "We make a quick knock, don't wait for an acknowledgment, open up the door, step in the room, and take a quick look," said one security officer. "We make sure that both players who are assigned to a room are in the room and that no women are in the room. After checking every player's room, I sit in the hallway until six in the morning making sure none of them try to leave and that no women are invited up."

While these guidelines were aimed at preventing after-hours

involvement between players and women, they did not apply to Moon. "It was an unofficial policy that if you worked the hotel, the players were to stay in their rooms after 11 o'clock bed check, nobody on the floor, nobody off the floor—except for one player, Warren Moon. And he had a room to himself," said the officer.

A regular patron at strip bars, Moon dropped substantial amounts of money to watch nude women entertain.[35] His time away from the field was increasingly filled with sexual activity. Like an addictive drug, habitual self-gratification through sexual promiscuity fosters an out-of-control lifestyle that does not mix well with marriage. Frequently, the lifestyle of the sexually indulgent athlete sparks marital discord that leads, among other things, to domestic violence.

On May 24 Moon reached an undisclosed settlement with Eaves, which included a confidentiality agreement that barred Eaves from further discussion of the allegations or the manner in which they were settled.

On July 17 Moon was preparing to leave Texas to return to Minnesota for the start of the 1995 training season. He spent that evening in a Houston-area strip club before returning home and entering into a violent dispute that led to his son Jeffrey's 911 call. Prosecutors later chose not to introduce Moon's whereabouts the night of the assault. Even when a celebrated athlete's conduct is excessively deviant, prosecutors are usually reluctant to bring it up, fearing that the public and the jury will see it as an unfair attempt to discredit a hero.

"We had done an investigation and knew that he had a girlfriend and that he had been out at a topless club the night before," said District Attorney John Healey. "We did not want to degenerate the trial by bringing that out. We thought that the jury would be alienated from our case if we sought to smear Moon. And then we would get a backlash. It would look like we couldn't try the case on the merits of the case, so we had to go into a smear to try and make the jury feel bad about him and not like him so they would vote our way."

There is little doubt that Moon's repeated infidelity hurt and angered his wife. Dealing continually with the rumors and innuendo about his promiscuity must have created tension and an atmosphere in which arguments could easily turn violent. Healey, who had handled close to five hundred cases of domestic violence in his career, pointed to the extent of Moon's infidelity as an obvious cause of violence. "It wouldn't shock me if infidelity is behind the scenes of many domestic abuse situations," he said.

Infidelity, in and of itself, is not recognized as a cause of domestic violence. Furthermore, attending topless bars and engaging in extramarital relations are not illegal acts (laws against the latter are on the books in some states but are only rarely invoked). None of those factors, viewed individually, explains spousal abuse. But viewed in the aggregate—and considering the degree to which athletes indulge in this kind of behavior—such a pattern lays the groundwork for broken marital relationships and subsequent violence.

Of the 150 domestic violence complaints made against athletes between 1990 and 1996, only twenty-eight brought convictions, most of them through plea bargains. The overwhelming majority of the cases went unprosecuted, following the victims' wishes. Only ten of the complaints were resolved by a criminal trial, six of which resulted in a guilty verdict. Four of the six guilty verdicts involved a case in which the victim was either killed or threatened with death.[36]

11

stopping the bleeding

WITH ATHLETES' DIMINISHING SENSE OF SHAME OVER THEIR SOCIALLY degenerate behavior has come a corresponding rise in the frequency of their arrest, particularly for crimes involving women. The link between athletes' unbridled sexual appetites and their crimes is most poignantly illustrated among the upper echelons of revenue-producing sports, both college and professional, which have recently experienced escalating rates of violence against women. The increasing severity of the crimes mandates that policies be put in place to reduce the frequency of so-called role models running afoul of the law. Violent assaults, rape, kidnapping, and crimes involving seamy sex, drugs, and weapons have become all too common in the ranks of celebrity athletes.

But as the association between athletics and lawlessness has been coming into sharper focus, the voice of denial from some coaches and other sports apologists has reached a crescendo. "We frequently read about athletes and coaches who are in trouble with the law," said Richard Lapchick, columnist for the *Sporting News* and director of the Center for the Study of Sport in Society at Northeastern University. "There are few denials of that image. Many seem ready to believe the worst. . . . The cases of a notable—but not extraordinary—number of football and basketball players who have assaulted women [are a] . . . misconception. . . . I have not seen anything that convinces me there is something about playing or coaching sports that made them [players accused of crimes] bad and evil."[1]

Merely "playing sports" does not, of course, cause people to commit violent crimes—an obvious conclusion that can be reached simply by considering the millions of individuals, young and old, who participate in amateur athletics. Athletics per se has no known relation to the perpetuation of criminal behavior. When famous athletes violate the law, their behavior is more a function of their fame and background than their athletic training. "Why do we put our kids in athletics?" asked Greg Garrison, who prosecuted the rape case against Mike Tyson. "To teach them teamwork, discipline, practice, sacrifice of the individual for the benefit of the whole, sportsmanship, and goal setting. If you want to get rich so you can have lots of broads, which is right where athletics goes nowadays, then we've missed the boat completely.

"I'll think we've come around the corner when I drive around through the projects and I see the photograph of the local black neurosurgeon on the front of the kids' T-shirts supplanting Magic Johnson, whose greatest contribution is to be the spokesperson for AIDS. 'There's nothing wrong with it if he can get it.' Yet his own conduct and his own dirty behavior is what caught him and nobody wants to say that because it's Magic Johnson. That's where sports has come off the tracks as a vehicle to a greater good."

Repeated denials that lawlessness among revenue-producing athletes is on the rise only perpetuate the potential for further, more serious crimes. Consider that during 1995 and 1996, no fewer than nine college and professional athletes landed in court for homicide-related crimes, which resulted in the deaths of seven people, five of whom were women.[2] In all nine cases, the accused denied responsibility for their actions. In all but three the athletes went free.

Stardom, by nature, dulls adherence to social norms, luring athletes to overindulge in illicit temptations. The enticements available to rich, famous athletes can prove particularly irresistible to the growing number of players who come from socially and economically deprived environments. In 1996, an unprecedented forty-two underclassmen declared themselves eligible for the NBA draft, including three high school players who opted to skip college altogether.[3] Two of the most commonly cited reasons for the mass exodus of these teenagers and twenty-year-olds to professional sports, without finishing—or even starting—college, were financial hardship and a desire to remove their single mothers from unsafe neighborhoods.

The roots of dysfunctional families, crime-overrun neighborhoods, and family violence are many. Underneath the glamorous image of professional sports lies a growing number of young men exposed to all three of these conditions. "That happens to be, more often than not, the world from which they [professional athletes] come," said Roger Headrick.

Nonetheless, sports leagues and corporate advertisers rely more and more on popular athletes to attract consumer dollars. Ironically, the tacit expectation that athletes serve as model citizens is being thrust on vulnerable young men whose backgrounds offer little or no preparation for exceptional public scrutiny. Headrick offered the following composite sketch of the current professional athlete.

"My description of a typical professional athlete is that at twelve years of age they are either bigger, faster, or stronger than the rest of their male classmates. The other males in the school really admire them, and they get a certain amount of prestige and recognition out of that. By ninth or tenth grade, they have all the girls because the girls get attracted to star athletes in the school. By their senior year in high school, they start traveling for Friday night games. They take off Friday and there is usually a test on Friday and they miss it. But on Monday, some girlfriend gives them the test. So they pass it on Monday afternoon or Tuesday. And they get through high school that way, with a lot of help.

"They get into college, they get tutors—paid for—because they have a scholarship. So the tutors get them through. And they get summer jobs from alumni. By the time they are juniors or seniors, they have agents running around, who will advance them money against a future contract so they can get cars and stereo equipment and anything they want. Assuming they are drafted pretty high, and even if they aren't drafted pretty high, the minimum salary in the NFL this year [1996] is $129,000. How many twenty-three-year-olds or twenty-two-year-olds get $129,000? All of a sudden, for the first time in their life, they're out there on their own. They've never had to negotiate, write checks for themselves, negotiate a lease on an apartment, buy furniture . . . and they think, 'Why don't you just give it to me? I'm part of [team name deleted]. Give me the furniture. Give me the apartment. Give me this. Give me that.'

"It's always been given to them for the first twenty-two years. Boy, that's a real change of environment. Some adjust, some never do. They are immature, not terribly well educated, may not be the smartest people in the world, but they are out there in the public eye and they say things and do things that [most people] wouldn't condone, because they are just not equipped."

Of course, this generalization is not applicable to all college and professional athletes, but it describes a growing number of the nation's most popular role models well enough. At a time when society is searching for legitimate heroes, the traditional credentials of heroism—courage, honesty, bravery, self-sacrifice—are being replaced by visibility, wealth, and fame. "Athletes are more visible in society today, and they make a lot of money," said one NFL executive. "They are the way to a better life for a large segment of our population—at least, they are perceived to be. You go into ninth grade in the city of Los Angeles and ask all the kids that are playing basketball, you'd probably get 75 to 90 percent who believe that they can make it into the NBA. Yet there probably aren't going to be more than one or two. But when you have 75 percent who *think* that they can make it to the NBA, that's the life you want, that's the hope and dream out of whatever reality is at that point in time. Athletes have to accept some responsibility as being different. They accept the money, I guarantee you that. So coming with the money comes some sense of responsibility."

Celebrity is a poor substitute for legitimate leadership, however. The fact is, athletes' primary function is to entertain—a priority that often comes at the expense of responsible citizenship and perpetuates a kind of ethical relativism. "Professional athletics has become such a megagod that it is sometimes unresponsive to the morals of a community," said Garrison. "Sometimes it just doesn't matter what a superstar does, it's okay."

By virtue of their fame, athletes are not held to the same standard of conduct expected of the public at large. Americans display an unusual willingness to overlook deviance when it involves beloved athletes. Seldom do spectators display sufficient moral resolve to resist the urge to patronize cultural idols, even when their behavior descends below that of common criminals. One social policy expert warned,

"Once society loses its capacity to declare that some things are wrong per se, it finds itself forever building temporary defenses, drawing new lines but forever falling back and losing its nerve."[4]

With little or no resistance from paying customers, the sports industry continues to condone lawlessness by offering scholarships and million-dollar contracts to criminally convicted athletes. The case of Nebraska's troubled running back Lawrence Phillips, a wonderfully talented but deeply troubled young man, illustrates the problem. The following remarks, collected during the predraft analysis period, were made by owners, general managers, and coaches who were considering drafting Phillips.

"When you get someone as respected as Tom Osborne vouching for a player's character, you have to put a lot of stock in that," said John Butler, general manager of the Buffalo Bills.[5] (Following Phillips's much publicized conviction for brutally attacking his ex-girlfriend, Osborne had personally written every NFL team to compliment the character of his star running back.)

"I don't think he's an angel, but I think he's OK," said one team official, who wishes to remain anonymous. "I can't believe that anybody in their right mind that knows anything about personnel would pass this guy up."

Said Baltimore Ravens owner Art Modell, "I was impressed with the young man. He's quiet, has a good sense of humor, a sculptured body, enormously strong looks, big shoulders. There's a resemblance to Mike Tyson."[6]

One team scout candidly stated that Phillips's best attributes as a running back were that "he's angry and hungry."

Ultimately, Phillips was drafted by the St. Louis Rams, who awarded him a $5-million contract. "Everybody deserves a second chance, sometimes a third and a fourth," said Rams assistant coach

Johnny Roland. "What Lawrence did had nothing to do with drugs. It was harassment. He didn't kill anyone. He didn't stab anyone."[7]

Unfortunately, the Phillips case was not an isolated one, but rather part of a pattern. Consider that prior to drafting Phillips, the Rams had elected to retain the services of defensive back Darryl Henley, despite the fact that he was free on bond, awaiting trial on federal drug trafficking charges. Henley's legal problems had caused him to miss most of the prior season. The Rams' 1994 media guide noted, "[Henley] missed most of season with team-granted leave of absence for personal reasons."

Badly in need of defensive help, the Rams wasted no time in returning Henley to the playing field while he awaited trial. Thanks in part to the testimony of Rams cheerleader Tracy Ann Donoho, whom Henley had recruited to carry twenty-five pounds of cocaine from Los Angeles to Atlanta, he was convicted in March 1995. While in prison, Henley orchestrated a murder-for-hire plot to kill both Donoho and U.S. District Judge Gary Taylor, who sentenced him. To finance the murders, he attempted to set up a $1-million cross-country drug deal. In July 1996 Henley was accused of plotting the killings in a thirteen-count indictment. On October 16, 1996, he was convicted. On March 10, 1997, U.S. District Judge James Ideman sentenced Henley to forty-one years in prison. "If there is a guy who needs to be locked down 24 hours a day, it's Henley," said Ideman. "The defendant obviously is a complete and hardened criminal."[8]

The day after Henley was convicted, a jury in San Antonio, Texas, convicted NBA player Alvin Robertson of a crime against his ex-girlfriend Sharon Raeford. Robertson was accused of kicking Raeford's door, taking her wallet, destroying property, slashing furniture, and attempting to torch her home. Months before the incident, when Robertson was offered a contract by the Toronto Raptors, the team's management had defended its decision to stand by him despite his prior convictions for violence against women. Soon after they signed Robertson, he was arrested for assaulting a woman in a Toronto hotel room. Later that year he was convicted of assaulting women in two separate incidents in Texas.

The practice of embracing skilled athletes who are criminals is not unique to professional sports. In the month prior to Henley's and Robertson's convictions, a slew of college athletes appeared in courts around the nation to answer charges for second and third offenses. On September 13, 1996, Texas Christian University football player Ryan Tucker was preparing for a court hearing on his involvement, along with three other teammates, in the beating of another student. The victim, Bryan Boyd, had been jumped from behind by the four players, who rammed his head into a brick wall, then severely beat and kicked him in the head. Boyd was left with a swollen brain, a fractured skull, and facial paralysis.

Prior to Boyd's beating, Tucker had been charged with two other assaults, and had been arrested the previous year for public intoxication. But Tucker remained on the football team and on scholarship at Texas Christian while awaiting trial for Boyd's beating.

Also on September 13, Mississippi State University basketball star Marcus Bullard appeared in a Guilford, Mississippi, court, where he was sentenced to three years in prison for violating his probation on drug charges. Five months earlier Bullard had led his team to the NCAA Final Four. An exceptional athlete on a team that was competing for a national championship, Bullard was allowed to retain his scholarship, despite a prior conviction for possession of cocaine with intent to distribute. Then in August 1996, Bullard was arrested on campus for pistol-whipping another student. "The court, whatever they do decide, please take it easy on me," Bullard said at his sentencing. But Judge

Robert Walker did not extend the lenient treatment afforded Bullard by his basketball coaches. "I don't feel sorry for you, Mr. Bullard," said Walker, "because I feel you've received more breaks than one person is entitled to."[9]

Coaches' willingness to employ criminals perpetuates players' off-the-field problems, virtually assuring that trouble-prone players will become repeat offenders. Coaches defend such practices by insisting they are trying to do what is best for troubled players. In reality, ruthless, self-serving greed motivates them to legitimize the criminal actions of deviant players.

Three proposals

In fairness to the sports industry, it must be pointed out that the problem of crime among athletes did not arise overnight, but is rather a product of years of social breakdown. Violence against women pervades our society and is far too complex a social problem for the entertainment industry to solve. Nonetheless, the employers of athletes are not powerless to address the problem within their own ranks. The following proposals are designed, first, to reduce the occurrence of violence among athletes and, second, to send a message of nontolerance for such crimes. In other words, these proposals are not designed to treat the deep-seated symptoms associated with abuse; at best, they are short-term initiatives intended only to stop the bleeding.

First, there should be a code of conduct for men who are privileged to earn a living playing sports. It should explicitly forbid all criminal behavior—particularly crimes of violence involving women. Athletes, by virtue of their standing in American culture, are symbols of manhood and heroism. A bad message is sent when these cultural icons are regularly arrested for rape and battery yet continue to reap the benefits associated with their participation in revenue-generating sports.

Employees in many professions are duty-bound to uphold certain standards of ethics and conduct. The basis for such ethical canons is the public trust those professions enjoy. While playing sports is not nearly as important as practicing medicine or law or holding public office, none of those professions brings the public visibility professional athletes enjoy. Furthermore, there is an inherent relationship between players' salaries and their public visibility.

At present, both the NCAA and professional sports leagues prohibit certain conduct, including drug use, gambling, and the use of performance-enhancing drugs. Those provisions need to be expanded to include criminal violence.

For college athletes, behavioral standards are typically set by individual institutions. In the NBA and NFL, such provisions fall under the leagues' collective-bargaining agreements between players' associations and owners. Today, at both the college and professional levels, whenever a crime like rape is reported, matters are usually left up to the courts. Colleges may institute their own disciplinary procedures, but suspensions of star student-athletes are rare.

If the NCAA and professional leagues can dictate behavior with relation to drug and alcohol use and gambling, they can certainly make rules that govern other off-the-field behavior, such as rape, assault, and similar crimes. Yet officials hesitate to interfere in such matters, as the following remarks by one NFL source indicate. "A provision exists in the collective bargaining agreement for penalties for actions which are considered 'not in the best interest of the National Football League,' " he said. "The problem is that it is left somewhat open. We don't have a specific code of conduct or a very prescribed set of guidelines as to what is acceptable and what is not acceptable behavior.

"When you get into things like behavior that is not on the field or doesn't affect performance, then you get into somewhat of a more gray area. It is almost like society in general has to take over. What will society accept in terms of off-field behavior, whether it involves physical abuse or anything else that may be breaking the law?"

Conduct requirements and penalties are supported by most players, whose good names are repeatedly soiled by the actions of a few. "The league has a right to step in at some point, especially now that we are in a collectively bargained situation where the players have the union to advocate some sort of reasonableness in the punishment," said one NFL veteran, whose team has seen a rash of player arrests. "Every corporation or company has the right, when employees are out there doing these kind of things, to [impose] consequences within the organization."

Consider also the following comments by another NFL player:

"We are in the public eye, so the things that we do off the field directly impact the public's perception of the team. [Off-the-field incidents] translate into fans out there who don't buy the same gear they would buy, who don't buy the tickets, so that impacts the business. Off the top of your head, you'd say, 'Well, look, when you walk out the door, your job is done. You can do whatever you want.' In reality, because we do exist in a fishbowl, we have to be conscious of what we are doing all the time, because it is going to reflect on our jobs and our ability to perform the job and bring revenue into the organization."

Second, penalties should be imposed on athletes who transgress the code of conduct. Rather than fines, penalties associated with criminal behavior should bring a loss of playing time, the length based on the seriousness of the crime. As one NFL player said, "I don't think fines have all that much impact on very many players, even the lower-paid players. The real impact on players comes when it affects their playing time. You work so hard to get on the field and you become proud of what you do. When the league suspends players and takes away their playing time, it has more of an impact than taking the money away. You can always make more money, and money is kind of an abstract thing to some guys because at our age, some of us have made so much we don't even know what that money means. There are guys who are fined $10,000, and it is only a tenth of what they are making that week. When the league affects play time is really when they have an impact."

The following criteria are simple and can be broadly applied.

College Athletes   Prior to determining the merits of a complaint against a student-athlete, schools should immediately suspend the scholarship of any athlete arrested or otherwise formally charged with committing a crime against another student. After suspending a criminally accused athlete's scholarship, school officials can determine whether to merely suspend the scholarship pending the outcome of criminal proceedings or revoke it altogether. Short of concluding— independent of criminal proceedings—that the alleged incident indeed occurred, school authorities are warranted in revoking a formally charged athlete's scholarship if either of the following circumstances can be established: (1) additional student conduct code violations that are not in fact criminal conduct but are nonetheless associated with the more serious pending criminal charge, or (2) a record of previous, albeit unrelated, criminal misbehavior by the athlete that has led to arrest, indictment, or conviction.

A recent case at Brigham Young University offers an illustration of the first circumstance. After five scholarship football players were reported to Provo police for allegedly raping a woman in 1995, both civil and university officials conducted investigations into the matter. The incident involved alcohol consumption, and the players insisted that the sexual contact was consensual. Ultimately, law enforcement authorities declined to file formal charges, citing insufficient evidence. But BYU officials nonetheless expelled all five athletes, although they never determined the validity of the rape allegation. Once the school's internal investigation found that all five players had clearly violated other aspects of the student honor code, the athletic department was notified that the five were no longer eligible to attend the university on an athletic scholarship.

Incidents of alleged rape and other serious criminal charges are invariably accompanied by a host of less serious student conduct code violations. When campus authorities are determining whether to suspend or revoke a criminally accused athlete's scholarship, such violations provide ample grounds for removing a scholarship and in no way offend due process.

Schools are also justified in revoking a criminally accused athlete's scholarship if it is discovered that the athlete has had prior involvement in criminal behavior. Only an extremely small percentage of student-athletes is reported for criminal acts, and, the few who are accused of crimes more often than not have had previous trouble with the law, often going back to their high school years. While evidence of prior arrests and convictions is generally not admissible in a criminal proceeding, it is certainly appropriate for institutions to consider prior incidents when assessing whether a criminally accused athlete is worthy of retaining scholarship privileges.

School officials should conduct their investigations and form their conclusions independent of the athletic department. By and large, coaches have demonstrated an inability to appropriately discipline scholarship players who run afoul of the law. This policy would eliminate the delay tactics described in Chapter 8.

Professional Athletes   Response to a player's arrest should be left to the discretion of the team. But in cases in which a player is convicted in a court of law, the league should impose consequences. Conviction for a felony of any kind should result in an automatic suspension of one year at minimum. If a player is convicted of a felony as a repeat offender, he should be suspended indefinitely. If a conviction involves a misdemeanor crime, the player should be suspended from play for 25 percent of the regulation games in a given year. More than one conviction for misdemeanors involving violence should be treated the same as a felony. Why? Because incidents of serious violence are often watered down in the plea-bargaining process: a two-count rape charge can be reduced to a misdemeanor, for example.

A silent majority of players supports stricter disciplinary measures. One NFL player said, "Ultimately, image is the product in sports, especially in the football business. People don't pay money to go watch rapists and child molesters and wife beaters run around on the field. They want to see people that they can relate to, that they have some sort of connection to. They don't want their children going to games, paying money buying shirts for people, and looking up to those people and their bad examples. It is appropriate for football teams to step forward and do things. It is almost a moral obligation, like it or not. There are a great number of children who think that the things that we do make us role models. That is not necessarily true. That's not necessarily good judgment. But because it is a fact that kids look at us as role models and they act like us, we have a responsibility to at least make the effort or to act in ways that are worthy of being emulated. The team has a right and an obligation to encourage that."

Third, a screening process should be instituted to minimize the presence of players who exhibit criminal behavior. The need to impose suspensions for off-the-field criminal conduct would be reduced by establishing guidelines that prohibit the drafting of college players who have more than one felony on their records. Furthermore, college players who have been convicted of one felony or misdemeanor should be labeled "probationary" on draft day. Under this designation, players who are convicted of a crime after being drafted will automatically lose their eligibility to play for an indefinite period.

Professional teams already possess the ability to thoroughly investigate virtually every aspect of a prospective draftee. "We talk to all the players we are most interested in, at least the first three, four, five rounds, as much as we can," said one NFL executive. "You can't cover 330 players, but we talk to all the principal ones, particularly in the early rounds, whom we may have an interest in. We try to get some indication what kind of individual he is. We do that through our whole scouting process. You get as much eyeball-to-eyeball interface with them as you can. The league does a lot of background reference checking. We can go back to age twelve if we want to . . . where they have gone to school and get their criminal record. And occasionally you'll be able to get some records of things like substance abuse or marijuana or whatever the case. That is transmitted through the medical side to the individual teams. And it gets made known to the chief executive, such as myself. So we know who is a drug-related risk. We do our own checking as well through the league and other sources—if we're really interested in the top couple of rounds—with the local authorities in the state or the city where these kids grew up. We also try to find out if they are related to any gang background."

With such resources at their disposal, the leagues are well aware of which players have criminal records. Implementing the screening of draftees for violent crimes requires no financial costs or procedures that are not already in place. It requires only a commitment to make the removal of criminals from the playing field a priority.

Not all owners and coaches will like taking such steps, but in time they will improve the quality of on-field performance. As one player pointed out, "You can't restrain guys all the time, but the big thing is that players can be brought in who are, one, good athletes, and, two, who are decent people that fit into an atmosphere that is not conducive to off-the-field problems. My team has worked very hard to find those kind of players and to eliminate the other kind of players that were on the squad. When you take a look around the locker room now, we're all pretty decent people. This year [1995] was the best locker room I've ever been around in my career as far as not having any bad seeds in there."

This three-step proposal does not attack the cause of athletes' abuse of women, but it does place some boundaries on such behavior. It is intended to eliminate the cancer of lawlessness that plagues high-profile sports today. While not without flaws, it offers a simple, clear set of guidelines that are easily understood by all sides, particularly the players.

Sources and notes

Before I wrote this book, I was involved in three sociological studies of athletes and crimes against women. The findings of those studies formed a small part of this book, and I also drew on them for background material. My two primary coresearchers in those projects were Dr. Todd Crosset of the University of Massachusetts at Amherst and Dr. Alan Klein of Northeastern University. Details of the studies can be found in the following sources: "Male Student-Athletes Reported for Sexual Assault: A Survey of Campus Police Departments and Judicial Affairs Offices," *Journal of Sport & Social Issues* 19, no. 2 (May 1995): 126; "Athletes and Rape: How Sports Culture Complicates the Establishment of Consent," Northeastern University archives (June 1995); "Male Student-Athletes and Violence against Women: A Survey of Campus Judicial Affairs Offices," *Violence against Women* 2, no. 2 (June 1996): 163; and "Arrest and Conviction Rates for Athletes Accused of Sexual Assault," *Sociology of Sport* 14, no. 1 (1997): 86–94.

The primary source material for this book was my interviews with the individuals involved in the cases described in this book. In all, I conducted well over three hundred interviews, many of which I recorded and transcribed. Because most of the quotations in the book were derived from these personal interviews, they are not footnoted. I also relied on correspondence in the form of letters and memoranda from participants in the cases, as well as some previously published reports, all of which I have cited. Finally, I consulted criminal and civil case files, all of which I have referenced.

Abbreviations and Short Titles Employed in Notes

AP	Associated Press		USA	USA Today
SI	Sports Illustrated		NYT	New York Times

Author's note

1   For all the cases predating 1993, I made an extensive search of the popular press through Lexis Nexis and the newspaper databases. After identifying cases, I followed up with phone calls to the prosecuting attorneys who presided over them. For cases that took place in 1993 and thereafter, I monitored the major daily newspapers, as well as the Associated Press wire service.

2   Ibid.

3   Todd W. Crosset, Jeffrey R. Benedict, and Mark A. McDonald, "Male Student-Athletes Reported for Sexual Assault: A Survey of Campus Police Departments and Judicial Affairs Offices," *Journal of Sport & Social Issues* 19, no. 2 (May 1995): 126.

4   Tom Osborne, *On Solid Ground* (Lincoln: University of Nebraska Press, 1996), p. 195.

Introduction

1   For a more thorough treatment of O. J. Simpson's rise from the streets to sports icon, see Teresa Carpenter, "The Man behind the Mask," *Esquire* 122, no. 5 (November 1994): 84.

2   Sanders to Tagliabue, January 24, 1996.

3   Brown to Sanders, April 19, 1996.

4   Richard E. Lapchick, 1995 Racial Report Card, Center for the Study of Sport in Society, Northeastern University.

weak men in wide bodies

In addition to conducting extensive interviews for this chapter, I also relied on the reporting of the *Seattle Times, Cincinnati Post, Cincinnati Enquirer,* and *Dayton Daily News.*

1   Christopher Kilbourne, "Like 'Feeding a Tank of Piranhas,' " *The Record,* October 22, 1992, p. 1.

2   See note 3 under Author's Note.

3   See defendant's trial brief, filed under seal June 5, 1992, case no. C92-658M.

4   For more information on the Lisa Olson incident, see "New Issues Emerge in Olson-Patriots Case," *Boston Globe,* June 28, 1992, p. 54; and "Trouble in the Locker Rooms," *Time,* October 15, 1990, p. 97.

5   Peter King, "Curtain Call," *SI,* October 15, 1990, p. 38.

6   *Boston Herald,* "Bengals May Suspend Players," April 16, 1992.

7   Telephone recording, May 11, 1992, verbatim transcript, case no. C92-658M, p. 830.

8   ABC News, *20/20* transcript no. 1348, p. 3.

9   Court's jury instructions, case no. C92-658M.

10   *USA,* April 12, 1993, p. 13C.

11   Tom Farrey, "Jury Rules in Favor of Bengals," *Seattle Times,* April 10, 1993, p. B1.

when women are the opponent

In addition to the interviews I conducted for this chapter, I relied on reporting by ESPN and Greg Garrison and Randy Roberts, *Heavy Justice: The State of Indiana v. Michael G. Tyson* (Reading, Mass.: Addison-Wesley, 1994).

1   For arguments suggesting that the sexist sports environment and the violent nature of sports contribute to athletes' violence against women, see Mariah Burton Nelson, *The Stronger Women Get, the More Men Love Football* (New York: Harcourt Brace & Jovanovich, 1994); Michael A. Messner and Donald F. Sabo, *Sex, Violence & Power in Sports* (Freedom, Calif.: Crossing Press, 1994); and Michael A. Messner, *Power at Play: Sports and the Problem of Masculinity* (Boston: Beacon Press, 1992).

2   For a summary of the characteristics of male perpetrators of sexual assault, see Alan Berkowitz, "College Men as Perpetrators of Acquaintance Rape and Sexual Assault: A Review of Recent Research," *College Health* 40 (January 1992): 175. See also Mary P. Koss and John A. Gaines, "The Prediction of Sexual Aggression by Alcohol Use, Athletic Participation, and Fraternity Affiliation," *Journal of Interpersonal Violence* 8, no. 1 (March 1993): 94–108.

3   Jerry Greene and Luz Villarreal, "Billups, 30, Dies in the Fast Lane," *Orlando Sentinel,* April 10, 1994, p. C1.

4   See transcript of ESPN *Sports Weekly,* September 1–8, 1994.

5   Ibid.

6   Ibid.

7   Ibid.

8   Ibid.

9   Ibid.

10   The text of the letter was published in the *Orlando Sentinel* on April 10, 1994, p. C1.

11   Continuation of arrest narrative, case no. E92-4510CKA, p. 3.

12   Robert Perez, "More Women Say Billups Raped Them," *Orlando Sentinel,* December 18, 1992, p. A1.

13   Ibid.

14   Ibid.

15   Ibid.

16   See Robin Warshaw, *I Never Called It Rape* (New York: HarperCollins, 1994); Linda A. Fairstein, *Sexual Violence: Our War against Rape* (New York: William Morrow, 1993): Alice Vachss, *Sex Crimes: Ten Years on the Front Lines Prosecuting Rapists and Confronting Their Collaborators* (New York: Random House, 1993); Andrea Parrot and Laurie Bechhofer, *Acquaintance Rape: The Hidden Crime* (New York: John Wiley, 1991).

17   Garrison and Roberts, *Heavy Justice,* p. 162.

18   Ibid., p. 163.

19   Ibid.

20   Ibid., p. 222.

easy prey

1   "Cocaine Connections," *SI,* December 12, 1988, p. 15; "Cocaine Connections II," *SI,* February 6, 1989, p. 7.

2   Manny Garcia, "Jury: Duper Was Entrapped," *Miami Herald,* March 16, 1995, p. 1A.

3   Ibid.

4   County of La Crosse, Office of the District Attorney, investigation summary.

5   Ibid.

6   County of La Crosse, Office of the District Attorney, declination report, case no. 95-29998.

out of bounds

1   E. M. Swift, "Dangerous Games," *SI,* November 18, 1991, p. 40.

2   AP, "Dancer: Irvin Used Drugs at Motel Where Later Bust Occurred," July 12, 1996. See also Kelly Carter, "Topless Dancer to Continue Irvin Testimony," *USA,* July 13, 1996; and Christine Biederman, "In Testimony, Irvin Accused of Drug Use," *NYT,* July 13, 1996.

3   Will McDonough, "Latest Brush with Law Shows Pattern in Dallas," *Boston Globe,* April 2, 1996, p. 69.

4   See note 3 under Author's Note.

unreasonable doubt

1   Janet Kornblum, "No Charges vs. Barry Bonds in Domestic Spat," *San Francisco Examiner,* September 22, 1993, p. A2.

2   Ibid.

3   Joan Ryan, "Why Sports Heroes Abuse Their Wives," *Redbook,* September 1995, p. 83.

4   Jeffrey Benedict and Alan Klein, "Arrest and Conviction Rates for Athletes Accused of Sexual Assault," *Sociology of Sport* 14, no. 1 (1997): 86–94.

5   Ibid.

6   Ibid.

7   Lynda Gorov, "Ex-Celtic Ponders Future as Legal Troubles Unfold," *Boston Globe,* March 28, 1993.

8   Lynda Gorov, "Webb's Past Offers Glimpse of Man Part Brat, Teddy Bear," *Boston Globe,* March 28, 1993, p. 17.

9   Steve Fainaru, "Webb Incident Probed," *Boston Globe,* January 13, 1993.

10   Mark Murphy, "De Mum on Wellesley Police Problem," *Boston Herald,* May 1, 1992, p. 81.

11   Steve Fainaru and Sean P. Murphy, "Webb Case Still Murky," *Boston Globe,* January 14, 1993, p. 35.

12   Ericka Gail Gomes to Judge Robert A. Barton, July 20, 1993.

13   *Commonwealth of Massachusetts v. Marcus Webb,* case no. CR 93-533, July 20, 1993, p. 7.

14   Ibid., p. 10.

15   Ibid., p. 19.

16   Paul Langner, "4 Found Guilty of Rape in Lowell," *Boston Globe,* September 29, 1993, p. 33.

17   *Commonwealth of Massachusetts v. Derek Larson et al.,* case no. 92-1280-1-3, October 20, 1993, p. 57.

it takes Miss America to convict an All-American

1   Terry J. Wood, "Assault Case Dropped," *Arkansas Traveler,* March 11, 1991, p. 1.

2   Debbie Becker, "Players' Penalties Reduced in Arkansas Assault Case," *USA,* April 18, 1991.

3   Ibid.

4   Candace Meierdiercks, "Hall Charged, Faces Jan. 9 Date in Court," *Arkansas Traveler,* December 12, 1994, p. 1.

5   Lincoln Police Department, supplementary investigation report, June 11, 1993, p. 4.

6   Lincoln Police Department, incident report, October 25, 1993.

7   Ibid.

the appearance of respectability

1   "O.J.'s Lawyer Tells How to Use Media," *USA,* August 1, 1994, p. 11A.

2   *SI,* January 23, 1995, p. 14.

3   Phil Mushnick, "Tom Foolery: Nebraska's Good-guy Image Is Just a Sham," *New York Post,* January 6, 1994.

4   Tom Weir, "Significance of Phillips Call Lost on Nebraska," *USA,* November 2, 1995, p. 12C. See also Filip Bondy, "The Other Side of Husker Glory," *New York Daily News,* January 8, 1995.

5   The following sources describe the litany of arrests of Nebraska players, and Coach Osborne's subsequent actions and statements. George Vescey, "Why Can't Champions Stay Clean?" *NYT,* September 12, 1995; Malcolm Moran, "Nebraska Is Reeling after Arrest of Running Backs," *NYT,* September 12, 1995; Malcolm Moran, "Nebraska Allows Phillips to Return," *NYT,* October 25, 1995, p. B14; Ira Berkow, "Huskers Hardly Shun the Easy Way Out," *NYT,* October 26,

1995; and Malcolm Moran, "Osborne Says Decision on Phillips Was Simple," *NYT,* October 27, 1995, p. B18.

6   Lee Barfknecht and James Allen Flanery, "NU Football Endures Off-field Scrutiny," *Omaha World-Herald,* February 4, 1995, p. 39.

7   Moran, "Osborne Says Decision Was Simple."

8   Moran, "Nebraska Allows Phillips."

9   In addition to compiling an exhaustive collection of writing both by and about Tom Osborne, I interviewed him on July 11, 1995. Furthermore, I received written correspondence from him on June 14, 1995, and August 8, 1995. It should be noted that all our correspondence was conducted before the extensive media scrutiny of the Nebraska program following Phillips's arrest on September 10, 1995. In his book, *On Solid Ground,* Osborne wrote that I interviewed him in November 1996, and that he abruptly ended the interview when he suspected I was a reporter. Neither of those claims is accurate.

10   Michael Farber, "Coach and Jury," *SI,* September 18, 1995, p. 32.

11   Chuck Green, "Coach Says State Won't Pay Legal Fees," *Daily Nebraskan* 91, no. 115: 1.

12   Chuck Green, "Police Officer Protests Baldwin Case Funding," *Daily Nebraskan* 91, no. 144: 1.

13   Ibid.

14   Paul Hammel, "N.U. Game to Become a Benefit," *Omaha World-Herald,* April 14, 1992, p. 1.

15   *Boston Herald,* August 29, 1995, p. 60.

16   Moran, "Nebraska Allows Phillips."

17   Ibid.

18   Steve Wieberg and Jack Carey, "Reinstatement of 'Huskers Star Renews Debate," *USA,* October 26, 1995, p. 2C.

19   Moran, "Nebraska Allows Phillips."

20   Steve Wieberg, "Osborne Taking Heat for Phillips Move," *USA,* October 25, 1995, p. 8C.

21   Moran, "Nebraska Allows Phillips."

22   AP, October 29, 1995.

23   Ibid.

24   Osborne, *On Solid Ground,* p. 98.

25   Tom Junod, "What If Tom Was One of Us?" *Gentlemen's Quarterly,* October 1996, p. 224.

26   Joe Lambe, "Phillips Sued for Assault," *Kansas City Star,* September 4, 1996, p. D1.

27   Tom Jackman, "Phillips and Ex-girlfriend Settle Lawsuit," *Kansas City Star,* September 26, 1996, p. D1.

28   AP, September 26, 1996.

29   Paul H. Robinson, "Moral Credibility and Crime," *Atlantic Monthly* 275, no. 3 (March 1995): 72.

30   Shannon Querry, "Rams' Phillips Faces Lawsuits," AP, February 19, 1997.

31   "Rams Running Back Faces New Problems with Traffic Accident," AP, February 21, 1997.

the price of justice

1   Garrison and Roberts, *Heavy Justice,* pp. 36, 53–54, 103, 133, 179, 223–34.

2   Ibid., p. 76.

3   Ibid., p. 223.

4   Ibid., p. 224.

5   E. R. Shipp, "Tyson Accuser Tells of Offer to Drop Charges," *NYT,* February 21, 1992.

6   Brief of appellant Michael G. Tyson, case no. 49A02-9203-CR-129, September 18, 1992, p. 1.

7   Garrison and Roberts, *Heavy Justice,* p. 250.

8   Alan M. Dershowitz, "The Rape of Mike Tyson," *Penthouse,* May 1993, p. 58.

9   Thomas P. Wyman, "Indiana's High Court Refuses Tyson Appeal," AP, September 22, 1993.

10   *Emerge,* December–January 1994.

11   Ron Borges, "Civil Suit Filed against Tyson in Rape Case," *Boston Globe,* June 23, 1992.

12   Ibid.

13   "Tyson Accuser Says Publicity Not Goal," *USA,* April 17, 1996, p. C3.

sexually transmitted disease

1   In Swift, "Dangerous Games," p. 40.

2   "Morrison Overwhelmed by Temptation," AP, February 14, 1996.

3   Gerald Eskenazi, "Morrison Speaks and Proves Full of Remorse," *NYT,* February 16, 1996, p. B7; Steve Wieberg, "Morrison Sends Message," *USA,* February 16, 1996.

4   "Excerpts from the Opinions on Random Drug Testing for Student Athletes," *NYT,* June 27, 1995.

5   Ibid.

6   Michael Hobbs, "Athletes in the Age of AIDS," AP, February 7, 1992.

7   Accounts of professional athletes who have died from AIDS are scarce. Chad Kinch, ex-basketball star and first-round draft choice of the Cleveland Cavaliers, died in April 1994; see "Chad Kinch, 35, Ex-basketball Star," AP, April 8, 1994. Former lightweight boxing champion Esteban de Jesus died from AIDS in 1989, at age 37.

8   Arlene Schulman, "Boxing's Brutal Intimacies Require a Careful Look at AIDS," *NYT*, May 9, 1993.

9   Lawrence K. Altman, "AIDS Cases from Sex on Rise for Women," *NYT*, July 23, 1993.

10   Felicity Barringer, "1 in 5 in U.S. Have Sexually Caused Viral Disease," *NYT*, April 1, 1994, p. 1. See also Lawrence O. Gostin et al., "HIV Testing, Counseling, and Prophylaxis after Sexual Assault," *Journal of American Medical Association* 271, no. 18 (May 11, 1994): 1436.

11   Ken Rodriguez, " 'Seed of Death' Sown," *Miami Herald,* March 31, 1996, p. 1.

12   Earvin "Magic" Johnson, *My Life* (New York: Ballantine, 1992), p. 246.

13   Anita Clark, "Minnesota Players Will Stand Trial," *Wisconsin State Journal,* February 7, 1986, sec. 2, p. 2.

14   Ibid.

15   Ibid.

16   Doug Grow, "Madison Jurors: Too Many Doubts," *Minneapolis Star and Tribune,* July 26, 1986, p. 1A.

17   Jim Souhan, "Anniversary to Forget," *Minneapolis Star and Tribune,* January 2, 1986, p. 1.

18   Ibid.

19   Ibid.

20   Dennis Brackin and Kevin Diaz, "Aftermath: Incident Last Year in Madison Has Changed Many Lives," *Minneapolis Star and Tribune,* January 25, 1987, p. 1A.

21   Grow, "Madison Jurors."

22   Brackin and Diaz, "Aftermath."

23   See note 3 under Author's Note.

24   Ibid.

25   AP, "Former Prep Star Pleads Guilty to Sexual Abuse," September 16, 1996.

26   Paul Hammel, "N.V. Game to Become a Benefit," p. 1.

infidelity and domestic violence

1   Deposition of O. J. Simpson, *USA,* January 23, 1996.

2   *USA,* September 19, 1996, p. 1C.

3   William J. Bennett, *The Index of Leading Cultural Indicators* (New York: Simon & Schuster, 1994), pp. 56–59.

4   Ibid.

5   Ibid. See also David Blankenhorn, *Fatherless America: Confronting Our Most Urgent Social Problem* (New York: HarperCollins, 1995).

6   Johnson, *My Life,* p. 250.

7   Ibid., p. 251.

8   Jerry Adler, "Adultery: A New Furor over an Old Sin," *Newsweek,* September 30, 1996, p. 54.

9   Ibid.

10   Ibid.

11   Johnson, *My Life,* p. 249.

12   These figures were arrived at by monitoring the Associated Press wire service, major daily newspapers from around the nation, and student newspapers on campuses with Division 1 sports, as well as through telephone solicitation of district attorneys' offices in the jurisdictions where cases against athletes had been reported.

13   These figures were arrived at by daily monitoring of the Associated Press wire service from January 1, 1995, through December 31, 1996. Telephone calls were made to district attorneys' offices to verify the status of the cases.

14   Ibid.

15   Tony Rizzo, "Barnett Gets Jail Sentence but Is Freed on an Appeal,"
      Kansas City Star, January 5, 1994, p. D3.

16   Ibid.

17   Transcribed from an ABC broadcast on January 8, 1994.

18   Kent Pulliam, "Barnett Makes Most of Second Chance," *Kansas City
      Star,* January 9, 1994, p. C10.

19   Transcript of the preliminary hearing in *State of Wisconsin v. Timothy
      A. Barnett,* case no. F-942749, August 8, 1994.

20   Transcribed from an audio recording of a 911 tape in the Moon case
      file.

21   "Moon Family Coping with Media Scrutiny," AP, October 22, 1995.

22   "Moon's Wife Reveals Details of Attack," AP, October 4, 1995.

23   *Houston Chronicle,* June 11, 1994.

24   "Ex-Card Troy Smith Is Charged with Girlfriend's Death," AP, Feb-
      ruary 19, 1994.

25   Russ Brown, "Smith Had Troubles, but Teammates Stunned," *Cou-
      rier-Journal,* February 20, 1994, p. 2C.

26   "Moon's Marital Dispute Investigated," AP, July 21, 1995.

27   Terri Langford, "Moon Jurors Say Some Violence in All Marriages,"
      AP, February 22, 1996.

28   Ibid.

29   *Larry King Live,* February 28, 1996, transcript no. 1682.

30   Ibid.

31   Ibid.

32   Ibid.

33   Tim Fleck and Bonnie Gangelhoff, "Bad Moon Rising," *Houston
      Press,* August 10–15, 1995, p. 9.

34   *Michelle Eaves v. Warren Moon and the Minnesota Vikings Football
      Club, Inc.,* April 28, 1995.

35   Ed Fowler, "Moon's Dull Side Missing the Point," *Houston Chronicle,* August 4, 1995, p. 1. See also Fleck and Gangelhoff, "Bad Moon Rising."

36   Fleck and Gangelhoff, "Bad Moon Rising."

stopping the bleeding

1   Richard Lapchick, "Justice Always Deserves a Second Look," *Sporting News,* February 19, 1996, p. 8.

2   In 1995, O. J. Simpson was acquitted on charges of murdering his wife and another man; former University of Connecticut football player George Franklin Booth was convicted of murdering his ex-girlfriend; Louisville basketball player Troy Smith was convicted of killing his fiancée; Fresno State basketball player Derrick Riley was convicted of murdering his wife; and University of San Francisco football player Jonathen Beauregard was charged with attempting to murder his girlfriend. In 1996, Seattle Seahawks wide receiver Brian Blades was acquitted of manslaughter; former New York Mets pitcher Julio Machado was convicted of murdering a woman; Los Angeles Rams defensive back Daryl Henley was convicted of soliciting the murder of his ex-girlfriend; and University of Nebraska wide receiver Riley Washington was awaiting trial for attempted murder.

3   "NBA Early-entry List Totals 42," AP, May 17, 1996.

4   Neal A. Maxwell, *If Thou Endure It Well* (Salt Lake City: Bookcraft, 1996), p. 17.

5   Fred Mitchell, "Phillips' Potential Far Outweighs Past," *Chicago Tribune,* April 18, 1996, sec. 4, p. 2.

6   Don Pierson, "Phillips' Stock Falls among Wary Teams," *Chicago Tribune,* April 20, 1996, sec. 3, p. 1.

7   S. L. Price, "The Face of Uncertainty," *SI,* October 7, 1996, p. 51.

8   AP, March 10, 1997.

9   "Basketball Star Gets Three Years in Prison," AP, September 13, 1996.

Appendix

Male Student-athletes Reported for Sexual Assault

A Survey of Campus Police Departments and
Judicial Affairs Offices

This study examined the relationship between collegiate athletic participation and reported sexual assaults at Division 1 institutions. The research was based on the internal judicial affairs records of ten institutions covering a three-year period from 1991 through 1993.

We purposely solicited Division 1 institutions with highly ranked popular sports, presuming that those institutions were more likely to support insulated athletic programs. Well aware that schools would be reluctant to participate in a study of this nature, we spent months cultivating the trust of officials at the schools we approached. Even when they were guaranteed anonymity, many schools declined to participate.

We viewed data on judicial affairs as more important than campus police data, for a number of reasons. First, more sexual assault complaints are filed with judicial affairs personnel than with campus police. And second, judicial affairs offices are not required by the Campus Security Act to reveal statistics regarding student violations of codes of conduct.

We asked the ten participating institutions to provide statistics on the total number of male students on campus; the total number of male athletes on campus (broken down by sport); the total number of assault complaints against

Appendix

nonathletes; and the total number of assault complaints against athletes. In total, sixty-nine sexual assaults were reported to the schools' judicial affairs offices between 1991 and 1993, of which thirteen (19 percent) involved athletes. Yet athletes represented just 3 percent of the male student population at these schools.

I. Summary of Data Collected from Two Sample Sets

	Campus police questionnaire[a]	Judicial affairs questionnaire (1991–93)[b]
Men not on intercollegiate sport teams		
Student population	182,091	252,630
Perpetrators	36	56
Men on intercollegiate sport teams		
Athlete population	6,975	8,739
Perpetrators	2	13

a. Institutions reporting = 20.
b. Institutions reporting = 10; annual reports = 27 (1991 = 8, 1992 = 10, 1993 = 9).

II. Results of *t* Test for Campus Police Questionnaire (CPQ) and Judicial Affairs Questionnaire (JAQ)

Survey	Number of male nonvarsity athlete perpetrators	Men/ 1,000 incident rate	Number of male student-athlete perpetrators	Men/1,000 incident rate	*t* Statistic
CPQ (1992)	36	0.19	2	0.33	−0.70
JAQ (1991)	16	0.20	5	2.21	−2.45*
JAC (1992)	19	0.21	6	1.72	−1.29
JAQ (1993)	23	0.25	2	0.67	−0.57
JAQ (1991–93)	56	0.22	13	1.49	−2.47*

*$p < .05$.

Index

An asterisk following a name indicates that it is fictitious.

Code of silence, 16

Coleman, Kymberly, 207–8

Collective bargaining agreements, 222–23

Confidentiality agreements, 18–19, 22, 210

Congress, xiv

Consensual sex, 54, 169; as leading to rape, 41–43, 57. *See also* "Groupies"

Consent: age of, 106; and date rape, 160–61; Dershowitz on, 160–61; and "groupies," 41, 42–43; perceptions of, 41, 75–76, 160; scope of, 99–100; and sexual history of victim, 82–83, 92–93; stereotypes of, 80–81; trivialization of, 59

Continental Basketball Association (CBA), 66, 76

Convictions, 16–17; and athlete's view of women, 155; avoidance of, 34–35; difficulty in obtaining, 80, 134, 155

Cooper, Howard, 85–86, 91–92, 93, 94, 98, 100

Court TV, 83

Criminality: increase in among athletes, 20–21, 187–88, 213–15; linkage with race, xvi; predictors for, xvii; prior history of, 16, 225

Curtright, Cindi, 22–23

Daily Nebraskan, 136–37

Dallas Cowboys, 63–64

D'Amato, Cus, 36

Dancing, exotic, 4, 53, 58–59, 61, 207, 208, 210; assaults on dancers, 63

Dartmouth College, 86

Date rape, 114, 149; and consent, 160–61; jury's view of, 152; lack of knowledge about, 153, 186–87

Day, Todd, 103, 105

DeMuth, Melissa, 117–20, 132

DePaul University, 187–88

Dershowitz, Alan, 41; on consent, 160–61; *Penthouse* article, 162–63; on Desiree Washington, 156–57, 158, 160

Deterrence, 146–47

Dierdorf, Dan, 198

Disbennett, Robert, 203

Divorce rate, 192–93

Dixon, David, 14

Domestic violence, 79–80, 143; as caused by woman, 206; charges, decision not to press, 203–5; increase in reports of, 195; and infidelity, 191–93, 195–96, 200, 207, 210–11; link with sexual deviance, 200, 210–11; and pregnancy, 195; and protection of athlete's image, 203–4; victim as being forced to testify, 204–5

Donoho, Tracy Ann, 219

Doubletree Suites (Seattle), 8

Douglas, Sherman, 85

Drug dealing, 45–46, 52, 219. *See also* Substance abuse

Duper, Mark, 45–47, 52

Durkin, Brendan, 82

Dutcher, Jim, 184–85

Dwyer, Kelly, 203

Eaves, Michelle, 208–10

Ego: immature, 11, 71, 72, 216; threats to, 31–32, 36–37, 76

Eligibility requirements, 110–11, 181

Emerson College, 83, 88

Equal access rule, 7–8

Esiason, Boomer, 8

ESPN, 159

Evidence tampering, 133

Eymann, Dick, 11